SafeCyberHome

Billy VanCannon

DEDICATION

This book is dedicated to my wife and two daughters who always inspire me to be better.

Table of Contents

Preface

Most of us handle identity theft and cybersecurity the same way we handle world peace. We see the headlines and feel upset, anxious, frustrated, and insecure. But then we think to ourselves, "What can I do?" and we go on living our lives. When it comes to world peace, we may have to do this to keep our sanity. But when it comes to protecting our identity and being secure online, there is plenty we can and should do. The problem is that most of us do not know what that is or even where to start.

The bad news is if a smart hacker with time and resources is specifically targeting you, then you better have an equally good team protecting you. The good news is it usually does not work this way. Attackers are generally doing a "spray and pray" approach where they hit thousands or millions of people and hope for success a small percentage of the time. By educating ourselves and taking some basic precautions, we can make it hard enough that we are not worth the effort and attackers move to the next victim.

A good way to think about this is comparing a bank with millions in the vault versus your home. There are a lot of people constantly thinking about how to rob that bank, and since the payoff is so big, they can really put time and resources into plotting a heist. When it comes to individuals, however, the hacker approach is more like running down the street trying the front door to see if it is locked. If you just lock the front door, chances are the hackers will move on until they find a neighbor who did not.

I have been in cybersecurity for more than a decade helping the US Federal Government and corporations of all sizes defend against cyber threats. When I had kids, things like setting up a trust, will, life insurance, and college funds became priorities. I wanted to protect my children and set them up for the future. One day it occurred to me that I had not taken steps to protect my family against the same forces I was fighting all day at work. When I started looking, it became clear that the best resources were directed at technology experts. There were few decent resources telling me the exact steps I needed to take in plain English. This is the purpose of this book.

Preface

There are many things about cybersecurity that are counter-intuitive, and most people have it completely wrong. Antivirus software is a good example. Experts believe that antivirus software has been a net negative for cybersecurity because, though important, people tend to believe that once it is installed, they can be careless with security. Car insurance companies know this phenomenon very well. When people get car insurance, they tend to drive less cautiously because, hey, they are insured.

Google did a survey[1] of both security experts and nonexperts on the most important security measures. Among nonexperts, the number one response was to use an antivirus program. However, here was the experts' top-ten list:

1. Install software updates (35%).
2. Use unique passwords (25%).
3. Use two-factor authentication (20%).
4. Use strong passwords (19%).
5. Use a password manager (12%).
6. Check if HTTPS (10%).
7. Do not share info (10%).
8. Use antivirus software (8%).
9. Use Linux (7%).
10. Use verified software (6%).

(>100% because they chose the top three)

Experts have antivirus software at number eight. We will discuss antivirus software in this book, but for now, know that antivirus software is far from comprehensive, and you should rarely, if ever, pay for it. The reason experts list keeping your software updated first and foremost is that they are the ones teaching the bad guys how to break into your computer. This is mind-blowing, but this is how the preview goes: Experts find a security vulnerability and then tell the software companies to fix it. The software companies issue patches (updates to fix the vulnerability) and publish what the patches fix. The problem is, people do not update immediately (or at all), so the bad guys read about the fixes and exploit the vulnerabilities before people update their software. This is a race most of us did not even know we were in.

Beyond software updates, experts seem to focus in on something far more basic: passwords. Your passwords are unbelievably bad, and I know because I have seen them. And, yes, "password" and "123456" are used by an astonishing number of people. Hackers know this. Using unique passwords (#2), strong passwords (#4), and a password manager (#5) are all practically the same thing, so we are going to start there in the first chapter.

There are many aspects beyond what the Google experts list that need to be addressed because it is directed toward protecting against technical attacks and not fraud in general. It might seem odd to have *Cyber* in the name of this book and cover things like credit reports, payment types, and even why you should have a shredder. However, due to technology, you can be a victim of fraud in ways far beyond your computer. The most important nontechnical aspect we need to cover is protecting our credit, so that will be the focus of chapter 4. If you are paying for credit monitoring, I have more good news. You will be able to ditch it and be more secure for free.

This book is divided into three parts – The Basics, Technical, and Advanced. The Basics section everybody should read, understand, and implement in everyday practice. Doing the basics will massively reduce the risk of cybercrime and financial fraud to you and your family. The Technical section is where we dive into setting up your computers, phones, and network for protection against cyberattacks. However, don't let the "technical" part scare you. I offer step-by-step guidance, and if you are a professional working from home, then none of it is more difficult than what you do every day. The Advanced section is for people who want extra layers of protection and have the technical capabilities to implement them.

What This Book Does Not Cover

Nobody is an expert on everything, and I do not claim to be even close. There are some things this book does not cover.

Evading Law Enforcement

I say this a few times in the book, but if you are trying to evade the NSA, good luck to you. They have a $1.7 billion facility in Utah[2] where they record and monitor all our phone calls, texts, emails, and probably all the rest of our internet communications. In theory, they are only supposed to monitor international communications, which is bad enough. But it is too hard to bother differentiating when you can just monitor all of it.

I probably know enough to evade local authorities digitally, but even that would be exhausting, and eventually everybody messes up something. The only tip I will give here is on "burner phones." A burner phone is a prepaid phone you only use for nefarious activities and then throw away when done. The tip is if you carry your regular phone around with you, then both phones are constantly pinging the same cell towers, so law enforcement can just correlate the two phones as you move around. Also, if you buy the burner at Wal-Mart and pay with a credit card, they might be able to track it that way. Even if you pay with cash, there is probably a camera on you at the point of sale. To avoid that, you must bribe a homeless person or kid to go buy it for you. Fun stuff.

Preface

I mention this because there are many articles out there that are well intended but convolute personal security with government surveillance. I am sure many people then tune out because (1) this massively complicates things, and (2) they think since they are not doing anything wrong, there is nothing to worry about.

Well, there is plenty to worry about. As freedom-loving Americans, we should hold our politicians responsible for what the feds can do, but that is beyond the scope of this book. If you are interested in this aspect of cybersecurity, check out the book *Data and Goliath* by Bruce Schneier about government and corporate surveillance. After I read that book, I curled up into the fetal position and sucked my thumb for about two weeks. I am not sure that was Mr. Schneier's intent, but he does suggest some ways to "fight the man," and this book picks up on some of those suggestions as far as corporate surveillance.

Evading Corporate Surveillance

You might think Google and Facebook are free, but they are above or approaching trillion-dollar valuations on the stock market. I assure you that there is no such thing as free software of any kind. Instead of paying by credit card, you are paying with your data so they can advertise to you. They are so good at it that most of us have seen ads that creep us out a bit because it feels like they are watching our every move. Well, they are.

Most books like this will tell you this is 100 percent bad. The hardest part of writing this book was trying to sort out the most egregious things they do and blocking them, while taking advantage of the good things. A great example is Gmail. Yes, they have machines read your email so they can serve up ads. On the flipside, they need to read your email anyway to sort out spam. In several places in this book, I dig something out of my Gmail spam box to illustrate a scam. If you have any doubt about the value Google is providing here, open your Gmail spam folder (do not click or download *anything*) and check out all the girls that want to send you pictures, girls that are upset at you, companies that need you to contact them, just all kinds of nonsense. Here is a small sample of mine:

Adult.DatingPro Your Subscription To Our AdultDatingPRO List Has Been Confirmed. - Your subscription to our Adult Da

Jessicaa   We have received a request from you to be removed from our "Adult" list - Hi b   To stop rece

Congratu., ❄C ❄Walmart® 🖥 We Have An Important Message 🎁 for you {b   - Walmart® (

b   SUSPICIOUS CONNECTION TO b   - G o o g l e Dear ! login attempt blocked RES

camelia   Are You [b   ?? - Hey b   I wanna talk To you ... Answer me ASAP!

Hi   Client #b   -8982510 To STOP Receiving These Emails From Us Hit Reply And Let Us Know

I can even tell you that an old friend of mine was once breached, and his contacts stolen. I know this because I get emails supposedly from him that, if I am not paying attention, I could click bad links on or reply to. Most of them end up in spam, but not all.

Even if you say, well, I can sort the spam myself, email would be exceedingly difficult to navigate if you could not sort or search it. The machines must read it to do those simple things. The real question is what do the email providers do with this data and how well do they protect it?

The bottom line is if you do not trust Apple, Microsoft, and Google to at least some extent, then you are going to have to go to great lengths to avoid them. I believe that you could very well avoid Facebook. I assume, however, that most of you will keep your account, so I will show you how to cut off their most egregious surveillance. Technically, you can use Linux on your computers and convert your Android phones to non-Google versions, but this requires a technical capability beyond most of us. Even then, who are you going to email, when all your friends are using Gmail?

As hard as I can, I try to walk the line in this book between privacy and valuable services. There is no doubt that other security experts will say I do not go far enough in some places and maybe go too far in others. If in the end you do not like the settings I suggest, or one of them breaks your favorite website, at least I am providing you with the information to determine for yourself if the risk is worth the reward.

Child Monitoring

Microsoft, Apple, and Google all provide ways to monitor your children's websites, screen time, applications, location, and probably other things. There is a plethora of devices you can connect to your network to block bad websites and monitor screen time. Even your internet provider offers tools to do much of this. These are helpful tools, but also limited. They work well for little kids in blocking the bad websites but do nothing to prevent cyberbullying or predators from calls, texts, or social media. Little kids on the internet must have near-continuous parental monitoring to be safe. Bigger kids, on the other hand, need to be taught the things in this book with an emphasis on cyberbullying (as both bullies and victims) and predators because they will find a way onto the unfiltered internet no matter what their parents do. All they have to do is go to a friend's house or find a public Wi-Fi connection.

In any case, this book does not go into depth on child (or girlfriend or spouse or employer for that matter) monitoring.

Credit Restoration and Retrieving Stolen Funds

A huge part of this book is geared toward protecting your credit and avoiding financial scams in the first place. However, once they happen, I turn it over to others with better insight on how to fix it. See the chapter on freezing your credit for some examples.

References:

[1] https://security.googleblog.com/2015/07/new-research-comparing-how-security.html

[2] https://www.foxnews.com/tech/in-pictures-the-nsas-enormous-utah-spy-data-warehouse

Basics for Everybody

This section of the book is for everybody from teens to retirees. We start out with how to set up online and real-world protections. Then we discuss how to identify scams.

PASSWORDS
Your Passwords Suck!

Every year, Verizon (the phone company) does one of the most-read cybersecurity reports in the industry. Year after year they find 80+% of all cybersecurity attacks start with stolen or cracked credentials.[1] By credentials, they mostly mean passwords. If you get nothing else out of this book, this chapter will pay for itself in security dividends.

Can't I Replace Passwords with My Face?

Many smart people have thought long and hard about eliminating passwords, yet the end is nowhere in sight. The truth is there is no good alternative to passwords and PINs (personal identification numbers.)

The newest phones and computers enable you to log in using your face. Fingerprint, facial, iris, and voice recognition are called *biometric recognition*. There are two things to understand about why biometric recognition, or biometrics, will not replace passwords. First, biometrics can never be changed. If that file containing a face scan is ever compromised by hackers, then they have it forever. Biometrics do not even have to be stolen, because we give them away. We leave our fingerprints everywhere, and all our pictures are on Facebook with our names tagged to them. On the other hand, if a password is compromised, then it can be changed. Obviously, this is not something Apple mentions when they brag about Touch ID. The other reason biometrics will not replace passwords has to do with who will store the reference files (files that are used to store biometric information so they can be compared). If employers, banks, or tech companies like Google and Facebook wanted to implement biometrics, they would have to store copies of the reference files. The vast amount of information these corporations maintain on people already is frightening. Adding our biometrics to this list is downright terrifying.

That said, it is okay to use face or fingerprint recognition as a convenient way to log into your devices. The reference file is stored locally (on the device itself), That is usually on a chip called a *trusted platform module* (TPM) that is specifically designed to protect its contents. The key thing in this use case is that biometrics are an alternative, but not a replacement. The devices can still be accessed with a PIN or password, so they must be strong and well-protected.

How about Logging in with Google or Facebook?

There are many websites that offer the choice of using Facebook, Google, or other social media (Twitter, LinkedIn, etc.) accounts for logging in. Take this login banner from Quora:

This is called *federation*, and Google or Facebook is acting as an identity provider. It works by logging into Google, say, and then Google provides the relying service (Quora in this case) a token (a text file that is digitally secured). This indicates that Google has verified the user's identity. I highly recommend ignoring that and creating a separate account using an email address and a unique, strong password. In one sense, using a federation service is more secure because that token is only good for the one login. If Quora is hacked, there is no password for the attackers to steal. On the other hand, you must trust Google and/or Facebook. Both have failed to protect their users' passwords in the past.[2,3,4] Besides not protecting their own users'

passwords, both companies make their money advertising and violating people's privacy in a myriad of ways. There is an entire chapter on the evils of social media later, but be aware that using federation is telling these companies what other websites you are visiting, providing them an even larger trove of data about your personal web-surfing habits that they can sell to advertisers later. You have absolutely no control over who buys this data or what they do with it.

How Hackers Attack Passwords

The term for outright guessing every possible password is *brute-force attack*. A hacker with a powerful computer, yet something an individual could afford, can try billions of passwords per second. Therefore, experts consider passwords to be *strong* if they contain letters, capitalized letters, numbers, and symbols, and are at least thirteen characters long.[5] All those characters must be completely selected at random.

Nerd Alert! Password Strength

The strength of a password depends on the number of possible characters (N) and its length (L). Using those characteristics, the number of possible combinations is N^L. The math nerds among us can see by the formula that increasing the password length generally has far more impact than increasing the number of possible characters.

Another way of looking at these large numbers is to calculate something called *information entropy* (H). It is calculated as follows:

$H = L*(\log N/\log 2)$, where log can be to any base. If we start with a password 10 characters long and only allow lower case letters, then L = 10 and N = 26. The entropy is about 47. If we double N by also allowing upper case letters, then entropy is about 57. However, if we go back to only lowercase letters, but double the length, then the entropy is 94. So doubling length has a far larger effect than doubling the number of possible characters.

Generally, experts recommend an entropy over 80. If you use any combination of lower case, upper case, numbers, and the nine symbols (!@#$%^&*?), then N is 71, so using an L of 13 gets to an entropy of 80.

There is a hitch to this if the password is required to contain at least one of each of the different character types, because then combinations are eliminated. All passwords consisting of only lowercase letter must be eliminated to start, then only lowercase and uppercase letters, but no symbols. It gets complicated, so I will just listen to the experts on the above recommendation.

The other thing about the minimum password complexity is if the attack can be offline or online. If the password hash and algorithm are discovered by a hacker, then he can take it offline and do the billions of guesses. However, if he is trying to log in to a website and there is any kind of delay between allowed guesses, then a much less complicated password would be needed. The problem is that as a user, we have no control over the website's security and therefore must assume that the offline attack is possible.

The "completely random" part is beyond most humans. At work, the IT admin can force the use of all types of characters and set minimum password length. But they cannot make people choose those characters randomly. Hackers have figured this out, so before they try the brute-force attack, they take a more structured approach.

First is the *dictionary attack*. The reason word processors can instantly indicate misspellings is because computers are so fast now, they can literally run through an entire dictionary in milliseconds. A hacker can also try every word in a dictionary; so "banana" and "football" are instantly cracked. People think they are one step ahead by replacing letters with homoglyph numbers, like 0 = O, 3 = E, 1 = !, S = $, etc., so "password" becomes "Pa$$w0rd!" (This is called *leetspeak* in the computer world.) They should think again. Hackers figured this out and just include these substitutions in their dictionary attacks and create specialized cracking dictionaries.

It also turns out that we all use the same terrible passwords! Analysis of passwords found in past data breaches has shown that the most common passwords people use are "password" (and variants like "password1" and "passw0rd"), "1234" (variants include "abc123" and "123456"), and "qwerty," the top left row of the keyboard. People also use common names such as "ashley" and "Michael." And do not forget their favorite NFL team, "cowboys1."[6] Passwords like this are worthless and are part of any decent cracking dictionary.

If attackers are going for a specific person, they can use any other information they know about the victim. That includes birthdays, child names, pet names, phone numbers, Social Security numbers, and anything else you post on Facebook. In response, there are free programs for attackers that will take information like this and run millions of permutations for the sole purpose of cracking a specific password. So "Pa$$word1984," where 1984 is the user's date of birth, is also no good.

One last attack to cover is called *credential stuffing*. In this move, attackers are taking advantage of two phenomena. The first is that humans cannot remember a lot of passwords, so they find one they like and reuse it on all (or many) of their accounts. The other phenomenon is that so many companies and websites have already been hacked. It is quite staggering how many huge corporations and governmental agencies have been hacked and had usernames and passwords dumped onto the internet. Attackers can find these data dumps on something called the *dark web*. The dark web is kind of an alternative internet where everything is secretive and encrypted.

This website, https://haveibeenpwned.com/, is a database of hacked sites that includes LinkedIn, Yahoo, Adobe, and countless others. The owner of this website, Troy Hunt, made it his mission to search the dark web for us and compile all his findings. You can go to his website and type in your email, and if it is in the haveibeenpwned database, you will be emailed the account information.

Back to credential stuffing. Attackers find all these username/password combinations and just start trying them everywhere: banks, email clients, social media sites, you name it. Even if you use a strong password but reuse it in several places, you could be a victim of credential stuffing. Passwords must be unique to each account.

The Dilemma: Passwords Are Hard

We all know the problem with strong passwords. They are hard to make up and impossible to remember. Strong passwords generally look like this: r$h6!dvze^Rjw. It is almost impossible to remember one password like this, let alone a unique password for every account.

Many authorities have tried to help people remember passwords by suggesting passphrases and (sort of) making an acronym. For example, "I love to ride my motorcycle!" becomes "Iluv2rmm!" Note Love = luv, to = 2, etc. I find this is just as hard to remember across accounts. There is the passphrase itself, what substitutions were used, what letters are capitalized, and if that exclamation point is stuck on the end.

Another expert suggestion is to use four or more dictionary words, as this *xkcd* cartoon shows:

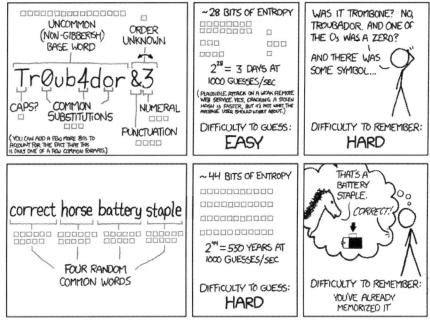

THROUGH 20 YEARS OF EFFORT, WE'VE SUCCESSFULLY TRAINED
EVERYONE TO USE PASSWORDS THAT ARE HARD FOR HUMANS
TO REMEMBER, BUT EASY FOR COMPUTERS TO GUESS.

These are strong despite not having upper case letters, numbers, or symbols simply due to how long they are. In any case, this approach is much better but ultimately has the same memory problems. It is too hard to memorize four-word combinations across many accounts. Plus, many websites will not let you use that many characters.

The Solution: Get a Password Manager

Password managers generate passwords that are far more random than humans can create, can be as many characters as the site allows, and can easily be different for every site, and rotating passwords with them is easy.

It takes a little effort to install them and get all your websites set up. Once this is done, however, you will wish you had known about password managers long ago. No more trying to dream up new passwords, finding the right sticky note, or outright forgetting passwords.

The most common password managers are LastPass, 1Password, and Dashlane. However, I recommend Bitwarden (https://bitwarden.com/) because it has all the necessary features, works on all your devices, and is free. Even the first paid tier is only $10 a year, which is a fraction of the price of the others. However, the user interface is not as polished as the rest and it turns out that it has two trackers in it.[7]

My second recommendation is 1Password because it is the best one as far as the interface, security, and features. There are no known trackers, but it is a bit pricey at $36 a year.

All password managers have versions for your phones, both iPhone and Android. For your computer, they often have native applications, but I recommend something called a *browser extension*. A browser extension is a program that works in your browser (Google Chrome, Mozilla Firefox, Apple Safari, and Microsoft Edge are the most common) and will sense when you go to a website and need a login. It will then fill in the credentials if you have them, or prompt you to create them.

Now, the logical question is how is a password manager different from creating one good password and using it everywhere? After all, now every password to every account is in one place. Well, it is different because if hackers can breach any one of the accounts and get access to the password, then they have access to all accounts. I previously mentioned credential stuffing. However, in the case of using a password manager, there is only one account that can be hacked. This comes down to statistics. (See the Nerd Alert! for details.) And logically, password manager companies are going to be more diligent than the average website because their reputation depends on it more than the average site. They are marketing based on security, so a hack is bad for business.

Nerd Alert! Odds On

Let us say one person goes with one strong password across ten different accounts and there is a 10% chance the average account could be hacked. That means there is an overall $\{1-(0.9)^{10}\} = 65\%$ chance of that password being compromised. To go further, say this person has fifty accounts where they use the same password. The math is now $\{1-(0.9)^{50}\} = 99.5\%$ that one of the accounts will be hacked and the credentials available on the internet.

Alright, so the odds are better with a password manager, but that is not the warm-and-fuzzy feeling we want. More importantly, password managers store passwords in encrypted form and do not even keep the encryption key. They put the encryption key on the user's computer or phone in something called a *trusted platform module* (TPM) where there are many additional safeguards. Actually, LastPass was once hacked[8] and had many/all the encrypted passwords stolen. However, because they do not keep the encryption keys, those passwords remained secure. If there is anything we have learned from all the hacking by China, Russia, and the NSA, and Edward Snowden's revelations, it is that these modern encryption methods have not been broken.

That password managers are also more secure comes down to how you implement them. First, they allow an exceptionally long master password like the example I will show in a few paragraphs, whereas many sites may limit the number of characters allowed. The other reason is they allow two-factor authentication for access. There is another entire chapter on two/multifactor authentication in this book, but enabling this feature is absolutely required when setting up a password manager. The short version of *two/multifactor authentication* is, something in addition to your password is required to log in, like a PIN that is texted to your phone.

Finally, password managers can protect against phishing. I will discuss this in detail later, but say a bad guy sends you an email that looks like it came from your bank, Bank of America. The real web address is www.bankofamerica.com, but this guy created a website that looks exactly like it and called it www.bankofamerica-info.com. Well, you may not see that, but if you use your password manager to autofill your logins, it will not recognize this site and will not fill your login.

As noted previously, password managers do need a password themselves. They all call this the *master password*, and, yes, it needs to be strong, but it is the only password to remember. I recommend the four-word combination suggested in the *xkcd* cartoon shown earlier, but with an additional twist. A Google search of "random words" will find websites that do this for free. Doing this as I write, I got ancestor-coerce-possible-facade. It can be made even more difficult by using numbers or symbols in between each word and capitalizing the same letter in each word, i.e.: ancestOr^coerCe^possibLe^facaDe. The idea is that you memorize the four words and then come up with a couple of rules so you do not have to memorize the specifics. If one of your rules is purposely misspelling one of the words, then you have a very secure password indeed.

Memorize the master password (your own, of course, not this one), put it on paper, and then store it in a physical vault or maybe even a bank safe-deposit box along with your will. This way if the master password is ever forgotten, it can still be accessed. Also, if appropriate, notify family that if anything happens, they can get the master password along with the will and use the password manager to access all accounts.

For every other password, use the password manager's password generator. Here is the one in the Bitwarden browser extension with proper settings.

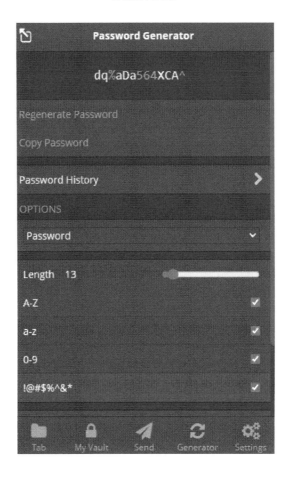

Security Questions

Use the password manager for security questions too. They are often questions related to where you got married, your first car, your first pet, etc. Many websites use security questions in addition to a password, supposedly for more security. This is not true two-factor authentication, as we will discuss later, but it is better than nothing . . . although barely. Yet other websites use security questions in case you forget your password.

Google did a study[8] and found that many people lie about the challenge questions. Most people know things like this are easy to find out. Ironically, according to that Google study, the lies are somehow easier for hackers to guess but harder for the rightful owner to remember! I am amazed at how often I forget exactly what I put as an answer. My first concert was Van Halen, but when I had to recall it, I could not remember if I capitalized the V and H, or if I put a space in there. On the other hand, a guy in Russia could find that out by reading my Facebook account.

The best way to handle these is to have your password manager generate fake answers by using the password generator. In every account entry, your password manager obviously has a place for the username and the actual site password. But they also have a notes section. In that notes section, copy the questions and password-manager-generated answers. Here is a Bitwarden entry with the security questions in the notes that you can refer to when needed. Nobody is guessing these!

Notes

Middle name of my mother !9Aw@Tjv%#DUp1Bi
City of where maternal grandfather was born yp4R6EB#uhD!!xUH
Dream Car 9!%9%wjUJ9UhPge3

Password Manager Tip

All of the password managers I mention enable you to export and import your passwords using a .csv file. If you ever want to switch to a different manager, or even the same manager but a different account, it is easy to do so. Once you do this, make sure you delete the old account.

Password Rotation

At work, most people have been forced to change (rotate) their computer passwords periodically, usually ninety days. The idea, of course, is that if the wrong person gets the password, then changing it every so often will minimize the damage. Password rotation used to be considered a top priority, but experts are rethinking that because of the trouble people have coming up with strong passwords.[10] It usually means people try to rotate through a preset list or they make miniscule changes ("password1" becomes "password2"); in either case defeating the purpose. The other thing is an attacker with malicious intent can really do the damage they need to do in ninety days, or even thirty days. Since a password manager makes generating strong, unique passwords easy and keeps them secure, the need to rotate passwords is minimal. I recommend only rotating passwords if you suspect something or get a notification that an account has been breached and even then, only on that specific account. Another reason would be if you shared the password with somebody for some reason. Of course, you should never share passwords, but when reality steps in and for whatever reason you must, then the password manager makes it easy to generate a new one and be secure again.

Some password managers can rotate passwords automatically on a schedule. I do not recommend using this feature because it means the password manager server (computer that the employees could access) then gets access to the passwords unencrypted, though just for a short time. This somewhat negates a primary security feature of the major password managers: that they do not know your master password and therefore your encryption key.

Passwords at Work

You might have a lot of passwords to remember at work. You can use your work email to sign up for a free Bitwarden (or other password manager) account and keep your work passwords in a totally separate account.

Your IT admin will be thrilled that you are now using strong, unique passwords for every account and stopped calling the help desk because you forgot them. Many will not agree with me on password rotation, so you will continue to have to do that, but with the password manager it will be a snap for you to come up with and remember new ones. Finally, when you leave that company, delete that account.

References:

[1] https://enterprise.verizon.com/resources/reports/2020-data-breach-investigations-report.pdf

[2] https://fortune.com/2019/03/21/facebook-unencrypted-passwords-privacy/

[3] Facebook data leak: Half a billion users' information posted on hacking website, cyber experts say (msn.com)

[4] https://www.bankinfosecurity.com/5-million-google-passwords-leaked-a-7299

[5] http://bugcharmer.blogspot.com/2012/06/how-long-should-passwords-be.html

[6] https://www.cnn.com/2019/04/22/uk/most-common-passwords-scli-gbr-intl/index.html

[7] https://www.theregister.com/2021/02/25/lastpass_android_trackers_found/

[8] https://www.hackread.com/password-security-company-lastpass-hacked/

[9] https://elie.net/publication/secrets-lies-and-account-recovery-lessons-from-the-use-of-personal-knowledge-questions-at-google/

[10] https://duo.com/decipher/microsoft-will-no-longer-recommend-forcing-periodic-password-changes

2

MULTIFACTOR AUTHENTICATION

Your Passwords Still Suck.

When you log in to an account with your username and password, the password is something you know. Security experts call that an *authentication factor*. They classify three types of factors, and they are something you know (password, PIN, answers to security questions), something you have (email, phone, card), and something you are (biometrics like fingerprint, face, iris, voice recognition).

Because cybersecurity experts are generally nerds, there are several overlapping terms. *Two-factor authentication* (2FA) requires exactly two different types of factors. *Strong authentication* and *multifactor authentication* mean two or more different types of factors.

In all three of those terms, notice I said, "different types of factors." If you first enter your username and password and then must answer a security question, then that is not two-factor; rather it is two-step authentication because you entered two things you know. The theory is that two-step is only a little more secure, but 2FA is far more secure. You might write down all your passwords and security answers in one place and have them discovered, but if you have two-factor authentication enabled, then the hacker also needs to get your phone or somehow spoof your fingerprint.

Email, Text, Calls

Online accounts usually use a password for the first factor. The most popular second factors are text (also known as *short messaging service* or SMS), email, and phone calls. After entering your password, one of these methods sends you a one-time code to enter the website.

Email is not a great second factor because if somebody is able to hack your email, they can usually reset your account passwords that way. If they can do that, then it is just another step for them to get the 2FA code.

Texting and calls are better because at least you need your phone in addition to the hacked email. However, bad actors can sometimes take over your phone number by a method called a *SIM swap*. Here the bad actor calls up your phone company and convinces them to move your phone number to a phone (more specifically to a SIM card that goes into a phone) that they have. To counter a SIM swap, you can go to your phone company account and have them provide you a PIN that will be required to move your phone number to a different SIM card or make any other changes to your account in the future. This makes it more difficult (though still possible) for somebody to take over your phone. Store the PIN in your password manager. There are a couple other ways hackers can intercept your texts without you knowing. One is to take advantage of an insecure protocol telephone companies use called *SS7*,[1] and another way is to simply pay a service to do it for you.[2]

Because email, text, and calls as a second factor have the issues I list, some experts consider them worthless. Though I understand their frustration, I completely disagree. For many websites, these are the only options, and forcing the bad guys to up their game over just breaking passwords is good security. At a minimum, they buy time and send signals to you that something could be up. When you are under attack, these two things can be all the difference.

Software Authenticator – TOTP

Another alternative is something called a *time-based one-time password* (TOTP). The most common apps are Google Authenticator, Authy, and Microsoft Authenticator. These apps can be installed on your smartphone and/or computer. When you first set up a TOTP with your online account, they give you a huge code to type in or a QR code (those square barcodes) to scan. Then the TOTP app creates codes that change about every minute. Because this app on your phone does not use the cellular system, it is immune to the SIM swap and SS7 attacks. Since the code is generated on your phone, it will even work if your phone does not have an internet connection. The biggest downside is that most websites do not offer TOTP yet, but if they do, this is a great option.

Google Authenticator (TOTP)

Software Authenticator – Push

Like the TOTP, this method requires an app on your phone, but once set up, it is more convenient. To log into a given account, you enter your password as usual. Then the website will connect to the phone app and send you a notification that you need to confirm that it is truly you logging in. All you must do then is click the Approve button. Here is a common one, called DUO:

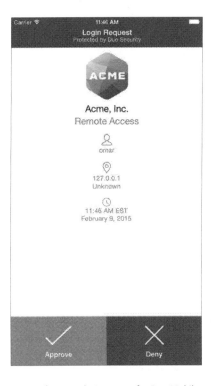

Image from Apple App store for Duo Mobile

This method is technically secure because like the TOTP, it is not vulnerable to a SIM swap or SS7 attacks, although it does need a data connection.

One downside is the human factor, because it is so easy to just hit Approve that somebody could do that without thinking. Unfortunately, the biggest problem with the Push method is that I have never seen this method implemented on consumer accounts. However, you might see this method at work because it is quite popular for business applications.

Hardware Authenticators – FIDO

The strongest two-factor authentication is based on the FIDO (fast identity online) standard. It uses a small piece of hardware that plugs into your computer. After you enter your password into a website, you must then touch or push a button to activate the FIDO device. The website sends a challenge that only the device can answer using something called public-key cryptography (PKI). The device also works with the browser to ensure that you are on the right website in the first place rather than an imposter (often phishing for credentials, which we discuss later). YubiKey is the most popular U2F (universal 2nd factor) hardware provider right now. U2F is not supported on many sites yet, but it is hoped it will gain popularity. Google implemented this on all their internal business applications and claims to have virtually eliminated breaches related to logging in.

Image from YubiKey website.

Biometrics

One might think that biometrics would be popular. But only recently have scanners been cheap and reliable enough to be integrated into all our smartphones. It is yet to be determined if they gain as much acceptance in computers. However, there are some pretty major issues with biometrics that I discuss in the chapter on passwords, so I will not rehash those here. Biometrics can be decent second factors if used in the right circumstances, say at work where they require a password or ID card and then a fingerprint. But biometrics for home users is not readily available or useful.

It is important here to note that the fingerprint (or face) reader on your phone is a biometric and could have been a second factor, but that is not how they are implemented. At any time, the PIN can be used to access your phone. Fingerprint or face recognition on your phone is only an alternative, not a second factor. If your phone required you to enter your PIN *and* do the fingerprint scan, then it would be 2FA. Given this, make sure you have a strong PIN even if you use the biometrics.

Just in Case – Break Glass

This really happened to me. I have 2FA on my password manager and my Google account. Then I lost my phone. When we talk about smartphones later, you will see that one thing you can do is log in to your Apple or Google (for Android) account and try to locate your phone. Normally, my computer automatically logs me into my

Google account because it is set as "trusted," but I had just deleted all my cookies for some reason. Now, I could not get into my password manager because I did not have my phone. And I could not get into my Google account because I did not have my password or phone. I was freaking out for a while, but fortunately found my phone in the couch cushions.

My point is you need to have a way to get into at least your password manager and email account if you lose your phone. This will help you get your phone back, and if not, at least having access to these accounts will make it easier to get access to all your other accounts.

Set up 2FA, and make sure there is a backup method. If using text or email, then set up a backup phone number (your spouse's perhaps). If using a TOTP, when you get the initial code, either put the same code into two phones or in both your phone and your computer.

Another option is one-time codes that you can generate in your password manager. As the name implies, these are super-long random passwords that are only good once but can be used in lieu of a password and 2FA. Generate a couple of these, print them out, and then put them in the vault I will tell you to purchase later.

In your Google and Apple accounts, you can set up multiple 2FA options. In Apple, all your devices are sent notices if you need 2FA.

They Are Not Asking for 2FA?

This is something that might be confusing if you set up 2FA but for some reason you are only asked for it once. As an example, Google's Gmail allows you to set up 2FA. (I highly recommend that you do so.) However, most of the time you do not have to enter it. Heck, you do not even have to enter your password. The first time you use a computer or phone to access your Gmail account, you will need to enter your password and 2FA. Once logged in, Google will put a cookie (a small text file) on your computer that has an access token (a cryptographically signed password) and check the information it can on your computer and browser. If nothing changes, then you can log in. This is secure unless you lose your computer or phone (and we discuss securing them later). If that cookie is deleted, then Google will require the password and maybe 2FA. If you log in for the first time from another device, then Google requires a password and 2FA, and they send an email indicating that somebody has logged in from a new device. If that was not you, then investigate immediately.

I Did Not Ask for 2FA?

Let us say one day while watching TV (or doing anything except logging into your bank account), you get a text (or email or call) on your phone along the lines of:

MyBank: Your security code is 345246.

(or if you get a push notification out of the blue). This is a warning that something is not right. The first thing you should do is log in and change your password because it might mean that somebody else has figured out your password.

The next thing that could happen is somebody might call you pretending to be the bank and ask for that code. Your bank should never have a reason to do this, so it is far more likely that a hacker figured out your password and is now trying to get you to tell them your 2FA code.

The other thing to pay attention to is if your phone disconnects. By this I mean the famous signal bars disappear and are replaced by "No Signal" or "No Connection" or . It could be that your cell service is down or out of range, or it could be that somebody did a SIM swap and took over your phone so that they can defeat your 2FA. Look into this quickly!

Final Say on 2FA

I strongly recommend that you make sure that 2FA is enabled on your email, password manager, banking, financial, healthcare, and government accounts at a minimum. Think about any accounts that have any data about your work, health, payments, or other personal data. Also determine which sites do not need it. You probably do not need it on news sites or Reddit unless you have some embarrassing comments on there. If you think you need to protect an account and the website or app does not have a way to do 2FA, then think about if you want to do business with that organization.

References:

[1] https://www.theguardian.com/technology/2016/apr/19/ss7-hack-explained-mobile-phone-vulnerability-snooping-texts-calls

[2] https://www.theverge.com/2021/3/15/22332315/sms-redirect-flaw-exploit-text-message-hijacking-hacking

3

DUMPSTER DIVING AND A VAULT

Crooks Have No Shame

You might think dumpster diving is only for the less fortunate, but it can be a literal treasure trove for identity thieves. Your trash, both in paper form and on old computer equipment, has all the information that any hacker could ever want: Social Security numbers, utility bills, financial accounts, health records, workplace check stubs, and more. There are also no laws against dumpster diving because when you throw something out, you have given up rights to it.[1] However, trespassing is still illegal, so you can call the police if someone is dumpster diving on your property.

Get a Shredder

Any documents that have any kind of personal or financial information on them should be shredded before going into the trash or recycling bin. Think about anything with Social Security numbers, email addresses, phone numbers, health records, and financial statements. Check stubs from work, utility bills, tax forms, credit card statements, and even preapproved credit card junk mail should all be shredded. You might consider making all these you can electronic for the environment.

If you are getting junk mail from legitimate businesses, you might be able to request that they stop. The preapproved credit cards can be stopped, and I write about that in the chapter on freezing your credit.

Amazon has shredders from $30 up. Get one that crosscuts: shreds paper into tiny squares that would make reassembly incredibly time-consuming. Most also claim to be able to shred credit cards, which is also a good idea. The more expensive ones claim to shred CDs and DVDs. I hardly ever use CDs or DVDs anymore, but if you do and there is sensitive information on them, then maybe invest in a shredder that can handle those also.

Get a Vault

You should also consider getting a vault for your most critical papers: your password manager master password, will, trust, kids' birth certificates, car titles, house deed, those kinds of things.

Put your families' Social Security cards in this vault. Do not carry them around in your wallet or purse. Losing them is a great way to have your identity stolen.

Vaults are not only for protection from thieves and keeping the kids out, but they can protect against things like flood and fire damage. I got a SentrySafe SFW123GDC which is supposed to be fireproof for up to an hour at 1,700 degrees and waterproof in eight inches of water for up to twenty-four hours.

References:

[1] https://www.legalmatch.com/law-library/article/is-dumpster-diving-illegal.html

4

FREEZE YOUR CREDIT

Credit Bureaus Are Not Helping the Situation

This critical advice does not even have to do with computers or the internet. Get a security freeze on your credit report (a.k.a. credit freeze). Do not get your credit monitored, protected, locked, or fraud alerted. It is a little inconvenient, but the only method aimed at preventing fraud.

A credit report is your entire history of loans (mortgage, car, student, etc.), credit cards (from banks and retail stores), utilities (water, gas, electric, phone, etc.), and sometimes rental history. This history forms the basis for your FICO score and determines if third parties will provide you credit, and if so, how much and at what rates.

How Identity Theft and Credit Reports Are Connected

Most banks, credit unions, and other financial institutions will not open an account or give you a loan until they see your credit history. Many employers today also consider good credit a sign of a good employee, landlords decide if they will rent to you or not, and even government agencies use credit history as an indicator for security clearance. In other words, your credit report is crazy valuable.

Attackers can easily get your Social Security number and address (I will back this claim up later) and then apply for loans or credit cards, or even get an apartment as you. When the bills come, they are nowhere to be found. This is identity theft.

If you get a credit freeze, then these third parties cannot see your report and subsequently will not open an account, provide a loan, rent you an apartment, or give you a job. This is good in that it can stop an attacker from getting anything good from stealing your identity. Of course, it is a hassle because when you legitimately need any of these things, you will have to temporarily lift the freeze.

Even if you freeze your credit, your credit activity is still reported. What I mean by that is existing accounts like loans and credit cards will still report your payments (or nonpayments), so make sure those reports are correct. If you are making payments and your bank is reporting that you are not, there is a serious issue.

What Are These Other Options – Fraud Alerts, Monitoring, Lock?

Fraud Alerts

Fraud alerts are free, but temporary, and all they do is tell whoever is checking your credit that they should take extra measures to ensure your identity. There are no laws, however, defining what these verification measures should be, and certainly none enforcing that. Do not bother with this waste of time.

Monitoring

Monitoring is exactly what it says. You get notified if anything happens on your credit report, including somebody checking your report, or a new account being created. Monitoring your credit is a good idea even if it is frozen, but there is no reason to pay these goofballs under normal circumstances. The federal government forced each of the credit bureaus to provide one free credit report per year, and you can get yours at annualcreditreport.com. Since there are three major bureaus, you can set a calendar notice to check one every four months for year-round monitoring. The main thing is to watch for any new accounts that you did not open and see who requested credit checks. Now, in theory, if your credit is frozen, there should be no way for credit checks or new accounts to be opened. But check for that anyway, because there have been reports of hackers being able to get the freezes lifted.

I should say that if you are (or suspect you are) a victim of identity theft and did not freeze your credit until recently, paying for credit monitoring can help. The thieves may have applied for a loan or account before you froze your credit, and the bank or company has already approved them, but you are not aware of it. So if this is the case, get monitoring for six months or a year so you get immediate notices of any changes. After the dust settles, then cancel the monitoring.

There are so many data breaches now that you have most likely received free credit monitoring from some company or organization that lost your data. This is more of a public relations initiative and/or liability mitigation than something of any value. I would like to say sign up just to make them at least have to pay for that. However, be careful that they do not have fine print that says if you get this monitoring you cannot sue them later.

Locks

Some of the bureaus offer to "lock" your credit for a fee, which gives you an easy way to freeze and unfreeze your credit with a phone app or through their website. Once you freeze your credit initially, however, it is not difficult to unfreeze, and there are very few times in life when you need to open it. Get this only if you want to pay for the convenience, but in my opinion, it is a con.

Why Credit Bureaus Try to Stop You

Fraud alerts, monitoring, and locking were all created to deflect people from getting a credit freeze. The companies that offer these are apparently run by former used car salesmen who thought they could come up with even sleazier ways to fleece people.

Later I guide you through the process of freezing your credit. During my research for that section, I found many links that were dead ends, had completely unintuitive instructions, and required that you use regular mail rather than sign up easily online. Therefore, in my instructions, I provide as many direct links as I could to the correct forms.

It is important to know why credit bureaus make it so hard to freeze your credit: you are not their customer. Credit bureaus make money selling your credit information to third parties. The last thing credit bureaus want is people to freeze their credit, because that cuts off their primary way of making money. If they can prevent you from freezing your credit and instead sell you credit monitoring, then they get to make money off you twice. Most credit monitoring starts at something like $20 a month ($240 a year).

Experian and Equifax Breaches

Since I am railing on the credit bureaus, we should cover the Experian and Equifax breaches. There is something fundamentally obnoxious about a company collecting data on people without their permission, making money on it, and then making it difficult for people to block abuse (also talking to you, social media!). When I said at the beginning of this chapter that it is easy for identity thieves to get your information, a big part of it is because of these clowns.

Experian had a breach in 2015 in which they lost Social Security numbers, birth dates, addresses, and driver's license numbers and military IDs for 16 million T-Mobile customers. They lost a $22 million settlement providing credit monitoring and some compensation for victims.[1]

In July 2017, Equifax was hacked, and the credit history of 145.5 million US customers was released. This includes Social Security numbers, birth dates, addresses, and often driver's license numbers. Consider that the US population is about 330 million, that most people under eighteen do not have credit reports, and that the labor participation rate (i.e., working-aged people with jobs) is not quite 70%. That means virtually every person with a credit history was breached.

Equifax was breached because they did not bother to update their web server software that had a known security vulnerability and patch. Beyond their security incompetence, their reaction to the breach was truly duplicitous:[2]

A. They did not tell anybody about the breach for a month, so nobody could take measures to protect themselves.

B. Three executives sold $2 million in company stock before announcing it. (Insider trading, anybody?)

C. When Equifax finally announced the breach, they set up a website for people to see if they were victims of the breach. The results were nonsense. I have no idea if this was incompetence or fraud, but leaning toward the latter due to the next one.

D. If you used this website, they offered credit monitoring (of course not a freeze) for "free." *Free* is in quotes because it was not free. You had to agree to waive any rights to sue for damage due to the breach.

Equifax was sued and lost and had to create a website for people to sign up for free credit monitoring. Or it was $125 if you signed up for credit monitoring yourself and claimed for losses due to having to protect yourself or actual losses due to identity theft. Unfortunately, by the time I get this book out, the deadline (January 22, 2020)[3] to sign up will have passed.

LifeLock

LifeLock (now NortonLifeLock) is one of the most well-known credit monitoring services outside the credit bureaus. The bottom line on any credit monitoring is that when you get an alert, it is too late, because the theft has already been done. Freezing your credit prevents the banks from giving the loan or credit in the first place. However, LifeLock is especially suspect. They started out running infomercials, and their CEO was so confident in the service that he put his Social Security number in the commercials (and on billboards.) While I can admire the willingness to put his money where his mouth is, so to speak, it is reported that he subsequently had his identity stolen at least thirteen times, and that is just the known times.[4] No matter how secure you think you are, it is quite foolish to make yourself a target. This lack of judgment comes through in their business practices because they had to pay the FTC (Federal Trade Commission) $100 million for not keeping customer data safe and making false claims to consumers.[5] So this company that is supposed to be protecting you doesn't even try to protect the data you give them and flat-out lies about being able to prevent fraud. Do not waste your money.

Doesn't Freezing My Credit Hurt My Credit Score?

Absolutely not. If anything, it will protect your score. Not only from identity theft, but part of your score includes how many times your credit report is checked by entities of which you are not even aware. Freezing your credit report will block that nonsense.

What if My Credit Score Is Bad?

There are many resources out there on how your credit score is determined and how to raise it if needed. This is not one of those resources. This book is only geared to blocking others from using your credit history for themselves.

What if I Am a Victim of Identity Theft?

Go to the Federal Trade Commission's website, www.identitytheft.gov, where they provide step-by-step plans for reporting and recovering from identity theft.

Another option is the Identity Theft Resource Center (ITRC) at www.idtehftcenter.org or 1-888-400-5530. The IRTC is a nonprofit organization created specifically to help identity theft victims. They even provide actual humans to guide you through the recovery process free of charge. The only catch may be that they try to sell you credit monitoring or insurance. I have not used them, so I cannot be sure, but remember what I have said about credit monitoring if they do.

Can I Get Identity Theft Insurance?

Amazingly, yes. The same companies that insure your car and/or house offer various forms of identity fraud insurance. These policies seem to vary substantially in services offered and prices. It is impossible for me to advise how much coverage is appropriate, but the key things are as follows:

1. If they offer credit monitoring . . . meh.

2. The losses they cover are generally not the money you lose from the actual theft, rather the expenses you accrue from fixing your identity, with lawyer fees being the largest potential piece. You can get a million dollars in coverage here, but that seems excessive; $25k is probably more realistic.

3. For the direct losses, there are extensions you can buy for damage to data and

equipment or extortion due to cyberattacks. If you are a victim of various fraud schemes, your homeowner's policy may cover some of it, but there are extensions for that too. Bank funds may be covered by FDIC and brokerages covered by SPIC. But those are most likely to only kick in if the bank or brokerage is attacked directly as opposed to you being defrauded.

4. In my opinion, the most valuable part that most of them offer is human case managers to help you through the identity restoration process. However, I cannot vouch for how good this is in absolute terms or even compared to the ITRC I mention above, which is free.

State Farm: https://www.statefarm.com/insurance/identity-restoration

Allstate: https://www.allstate.com/identity-protection.aspx

Farmers: https://www.farmers.com/home/identity-shield/

Liberty Mutual: https://www.libertymutual.com/identity-theft-insurance

Get to It

There are three major credit bureaus, Transunion, Experian, and Equifax. Additionally, Innovis is a lesser-known credit agency. ChexSystems is used by many banks and credit unions to determine if they should give you a checking or savings account. The National Consumer Telecom & Utilities Exchange (NCTUE) is where phone companies and utilities go to determine if they will provide you an account. Freeze them all.

It used to cost up to $10 (depending on your state) to freeze and unfreeze your credit. Fortunately, in 2018, Congress and the president signed the Economic Growth, Regulatory Relief, and Consumer Protection Act that forced the credit bureaus to offer this service for free.

Here is the latest information on contacting the bureaus to get your credit frozen.

Equifax:

Phone: 1-800-685-1111

I have never tried to do this by phone at any of the bureaus, and it might be difficult to get a human. If you do, it is likely they will try diverting you to monitoring or fraud alerts. Don't let them.

<u>Online</u>: You must create an account called myEquifax here: https://my.equifax.com/consumer-registration/UCSC/#/personal-info. They request a bunch of personal information to set up the account.

Use your password manager to generate and store a strong password. Once you have an account and log in, they display a dashboard:

Welcome, Billy

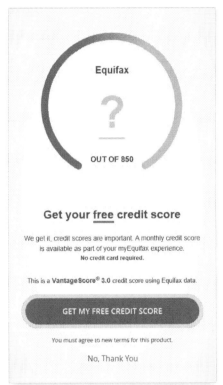

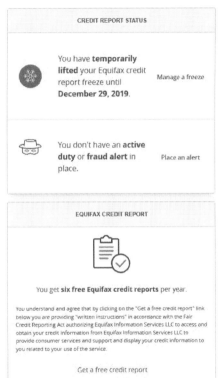

You can see on the right your current "freeze" status. In this case, I lifted my freeze for one day, but this is where you will start the process to freeze your credit.

When I first did a freeze, Equifax gave me a PIN instead of an account. If you have an old PIN, it appears it is no longer needed.

Experian:

<u>Phone</u>: 1-888-397-3742

<u>Online</u>: Main page is: https://www.experian.com/freeze/center.html.

To freeze, fill out this form https://www.experian.com/ncaconline/freeze.

Add a security freeze 🔒

*=required

A security freeze is designed to prevent credit, loans and services from being approved in your name without your consent. In addition, adding a security freeze to your credit report may also delay or interfere with or prohibit the timely approval of any subsequent requests or application you make regarding new credit, loans or services. When you add a security freeze, you will be provided with a Personal Identification Number (PIN) which will be required in order to remove the freeze from your credit report, either temporarily or permanently.

First name*   Middle   Last name*   Generation

Address*   City*   State*   ZIP Code™*

Social Security number*   Date of birth*

☐ Display Social Security number

Provide your e-mail address for faster delivery of your results.

Email address ⑦   Confirm email address

Have you lived at your current address longer than two years? ⦿ Yes ○ No

Would you like to select your own PIN? If not, you will be provided with a PIN. ⑦ ⦿ Yes ○ No

Please enter your PIN below

Enter 5 to 10 digits for your personal identification number. As a security precaution, you may not use your Social Security number as your PIN.

You get the choice of creating your own PIN or having them create one. If you create your own, go with ten random digits. Either way, store your PIN in your password manager.

Experian does not set up an account like the other two. To unfreeze, you get a form that looks like the freeze form: https://www.experian.com/ncaconline/removefreeze. Fill it out, use your PIN, and set the date range for temporarily removing the freeze.

TransUnion:

Phone: 1-888-909-8872

Online: Here is the main page: https://www.transunion.com/credit-freeze. From here, you can navigate around.

Like with Equifax, you will have to create an online account starting here: https://service.transunion.com/dss/orderStep1_form.page.

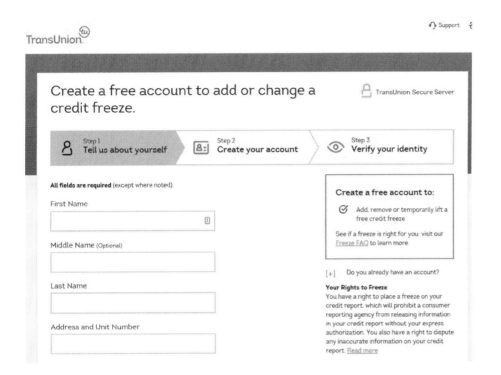

You must fill out the information in three steps. Step 1 is the basics. When creating your account in Step 2, use your password manager to create and store a strong password. They also ask for a security question. As mentioned in the "Passwords" chapter, security questions are an oxymoron. Instead use your password manager to generate a fake answer (password) and then in the notes for your Transunion entry, put both the security question you select and this additional password as the answer. Your password manager notes for the TransUnion entry will be something like, "What city were you born in?: tLr^8%%fVIgk!". Step 3 is a few questions based on your credit history.

Once you have an account and log in, you get a screen like this:

Freeze Your Credit

Your Report is:

FROZEN

REMOVE FREEZE   TEMPORARILY LIFT FREEZE

ⓘ What's this?   ⓘ What's this?

Need to Change your PIN?

ⓘ What's this?

When I first did a freeze, TransUnion gave me a PIN instead of an account. If you have an old PIN, it appears it is no longer needed for online transactions. However, if you click What's This? under Need to Change your PIN?, then it mentions that a PIN is needed for freezing/unfreezing by phone.

Innovis:

Phone: 1-800-540-2505

Online: https://www.innovis.com/securityFreeze/index has a form:

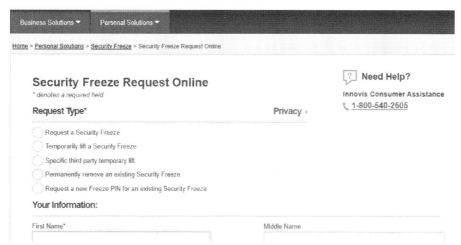

You can see this form is the one for all actions relating to freezing/unfreezing your credit. When completed, Innovis does the request and sends a confirmation in the mail. When freezing for the first time, they include a PIN in that mail. I suggest putting that PIN in your password manager. You will need it to unfreeze in the future as shown here:

ChexSystems:

Phone: 1-800-887-7652

Online:
https://www.chexsystems.com/web/chexsystems/consumerdebit/page/securityfreeze/placefreeze/

This is form looks like the one at Experian. You also get a PIN for when you need to unfreeze. Here is the link to the unfreeze page:
https://www.chexsystems.com/web/chexsystems/consumerdebit/page/securityfreeze/liftfreeze/.

NCTUE:

Phone: 1-866-343-2821

Online: https://www.exchangeservicecenter.com/freeze/#/

This is a form that also looks like the one at Experian. You also get a PIN for when you need to unfreeze. It is the same link and form to unfreeze.

Not Done Yet – Pre-Approved Credit Cards

Freezing your credit should mean exactly that. But maddeningly, it still does not prevent credit card companies from being able to look at your credit report and mail preapproved credit card applications to you. If a bad guy gets one of these mailers, they can use them to open accounts in your name. So there is yet another step you must take to block this, again, because you are cutting off a major revenue stream for credit bureaus.

Go to https://www.optoutprescreen.com and fill out the form or call 888-567-8668. If you only want to opt out of credit offers for five years, you can select that option and do it all online. However, if you want it done permanently, then you must fill out the online form, print it, and then mail it to them. They purposely make it a pain, but the good news is one form handles all four credit bureaus.

Have all the adults in your household go through these steps of freezing their credit at all the bureaus and opting out of the credit cards. Consider helping your parents do this, too, especially given they are excellent targets if they have good credit, and are much less likely to be checking their credit very often. If you have children, you have yet more work to do.

Still Not Done – Freeze Your Children's Credit

It is a big problem if identity thieves get your child's Social Security number. They might use your children's credit to do all the things you will want your kids to be able to do one day: open bank accounts, get credit cards, rent an apartment, access utilities, and even apply for government benefits. It is an ideal situation for thieves because kids have a clean slate, and they do not check their credit for years. When your kids do come of age, then they might start out with ruined credit.

When it comes to credit reports, your children should not have one because they do not get created until credit activity is detected. This is somewhat mind-blowing, but all this means is somebody (like a bank) tries to check the credit of somebody with your kid's name and Social Security number at a credit bureau. They do not bother to verify that it is really you or your kid. This leaves the possibility for fraudsters to create a credit account in your child's name. If you check and your kid already has a credit report, then order a copy immediately. If the only thing that the report shows is that somebody checked it, then you might have found it in time. Call that entity immediately and tell them that you did not make that request, so you can shut down whatever they planned on doing (like giving somebody a loan or credit card in your kid's name). If there is already an open account, then you have a mess to clean up. See the resources in the "What if I Am a Victim of Identity Fraud?" section.

Warning signs that your child's identity has already been stolen are really limited to two things: (1) You apply for something on their behalf and are turned down because of bad credit or benefits already being paid out. (2) You get notices from debt collectors (or the IRS or utilities or businesses) in your child's name for products or services you never signed up for. Given that, it is key to be proactive on this.

Of course, try to protect your kid's Social Security numbers in the first place. Only give them out when required and really push on if it is necessary. Many school forms require Social Security numbers, so ask them why they need the number, how they store it, policies on who has access to it, and how they dispose of them.

SafeCyberHome

The FTC used to have this horrible advice on their website:

> It is a good idea to check whether your child has a credit report close to the child's sixteenth birthday. If there is one—and it has errors due to fraud or misuse—you will have time to correct it...

Why wait until you are already a victim and go through all the pain of fixing it? This is a great example of corporations influencing the government agencies that monitor them.

Credit bureaus make it as confusing as they can to freeze your credit, and they make it more difficult to freeze your child's credit. First, it cannot be done online or by phone. Rather, it must be requested via mail along with other documentation such as copies of birth certificates and Social Security cards. Of course, all bureaus have slightly different requirements. Here are the direct links to the forms:

Equifax: https://assets.equifax.com/assets/personal/Minor_Freeze_Request_Form.pdf

Experian: https://www.experian.com/freeze/form-minor-freeze.html

TransUnion: https://www.transunion.com/credit-freeze/credit-freeze-faq#freeze-other (not a form, but scroll down and they provide instructions)

Innovis:https://www.innovis.com/personal/lc_minorsProtected

ChexSystems:https://www.chexsystems.com/web/chexsystems/consumerdebit/page/securityfreeze/placefreeze/ (not a form, but instructions are provided under the "Age Verification" section)

NCTUE: Their website doesn't indicate any method of freezing a minor's account, but when I entered my kid's information in the regular freeze form (https://www.exchangeservicecenter.com/freeze/#/U), they could not find an account and then provided their phone number. So I ended up calling for this one. 1-866-343-2821.

References:

[1] https://www.expdatabreachsettlement.com/

[2] https://qz.com/1079253/the-complete-guide-to-the-equifax-breach/

[3] https://www.ftc.gov/enforcement/cases-proceedings/refunds/equifax-data-breach-settlement

[4] https://www.wired.com/2010/05/lifelock-identity-theft/

[5] https://www.ftc.gov/news-events/press-releases/2015/12/lifelock-pay-100-million-consumers-settle-ftc-charges-it-violated

5

OPEN ACCOUNTS TO PROTECT THEM
The Best Defense Is an Existing Defense

True or false?: If I do not open a banking account online, then there is no way an attacker can get to my bank account.

Unfortunately, this is false. An attacker can gather information on you and then call the bank and request that an online account be opened, and then they have free reign to ruin your life. This is another form of identity theft.

I will note that this entire chapter is inspired by a Brian Krebs blog called "Plant Your Flag, Mark Your Territory," and it was one of his most popular.[1] Brian is a renowned cybersecurity journalist that has been so good at his job that hackers around the world have openly attacked and threatened him for identifying them and uncovering their methods.

We need to back up a bit and define some things. First, there is having a bank account, where the bank has some of your money and your name is attached to it. You can physically walk into the bank, show your driver's license, and withdraw, deposit, and whatever else you do with a bank account. Separately, that account can be enabled to work online. This is what enables you to access your bank account over the internet and make deposits or withdrawals or do whatever else you do with a bank account. Obviously, you need the actual bank account first. This can get even more confusing given you can go online and open an account, transfer money from somewhere else, and enable it for online use and create the credentials (username and password) all at once.

Open Accounts to Protect Them

Let us say you have a bank account but never enable online access to it. You assume your money is safe from attacks from the internet. The problem is that banks are eager for your business, so they might not verify a person as well as they should online or by phone. The attacker then calls them up, pretends to be you, and then enables online access and sets up their own credentials. You have no idea this is happening until your next statement or your check bounces.

How is this possible? I mentioned the Experian and Equifax breaches, so the attackers can get most of the information they need from those credit reports like Social Security and driver's license numbers. The credit reports themselves will indicate what banks you have loans with and what credit cards you own. Any checks you write have your bank and account numbers written on them, so they are out there. You might have even thrown away old checks, statements, or other bank correspondence without shredding it. (See the chapter on dumpster diving.) Best of all, your Facebook (see the chapter on social media) profile is wide open, with information on where you lived in the past, where you live now, where you work, where and when you go on vacation, and your favorite color. There are simply many, many ways for the bad guys to get your information.

I believe many banks are finally getting wise to this. They are setting up more security around remotely enabling online accounts and may even now require that you physically come in with identification. But this same problem goes for online accounts of every kind.

Let us follow the hacker's attack methodology to understand why setting up online accounts and securing with multiple layers is better than not having online accounts at all. When we talked in chapter 4 about freezing our credit reports, we noted that all the bureaus have credit reports on you. However, when we wanted to freeze them online, we had to create online accounts and create passwords or PINs. You might not have thought about it at the time, but it was incredibly easy to do this. Yes, they all make it hard to find the right place to do it. And, yes, it is a lot of work because we had to open different online accounts for every bureau for each adult plus our children. But once we got past that, the information needed to open each account was minimal. That is what I mean by "easy."

Now that you have followed my advice, however, and opened that online account and put an incredibly strong password on it, it is much more secure. If an attacker tries to open an account at this point, they will get a notice that you already opened an account. Now, instead of just needing your Social Security number, that they can get anywhere, they must hack your unbreakable password. Since they cannot get through that password, they will have to try to get it reset. So now they might have to answer the security questions. The real answers to the security questions are posted on Facebook, because it is important that everybody on earth know your first pet was a dog named Fru-fru. However, you did not put "Fru-fru" as the answer. You put something that looks like "K%Jnjd&2r5" in there. There is no way they are guessing that. The next attacker move is to request a reset to your email address. If the attacker can break into your email, then they can reset your password and delete that email, so you do not see it. However, your email is also protected by an unbreakable password and has 2fA on it. The attacker is defeated.

Going further on this idea. When we ask the credit bureaus to freeze our children's accounts in an earlier chapter, we are asking them to open an account and then freeze it. Your child should not have a credit report yet, so the attackers get one created themselves. This is better than breaking into an existing account because nobody is going to check on it or get notifications of changes.

So even if an attacker is successful at breaking into an online account that you opened, your final defense is that you will be notified. If the attacker opens the account first, they will be notified, and you may never know. If you open the account, you will get emails of any changes to it, and you at least have a chance to investigate before damage is done. Many times, banks and government agencies will send letters in regular mail indicating that a change was made in the account. If you did not do it, call them immediately!

Ironically, if you are alerted by email, BE CAREFUL! The email itself may be a fraud. We will cover email scams later, but this should be noted here too. Say you get an email from your bank that you made a change to your account, or they need to verify something. It might look very official, or it might look like a child created it. Either way, DO NOT call the number, download any files, or click any links. Rather, go to their website separately and log in to your account and see if any of the changes did indeed happen. Then call them using the phone number you find from their webpage, not any that might be in the email, and tell them about the email and any account changes you notice. Change your account password regardless of if any changes were made or not and monitor for unauthorized activity.

Okay, let us hope this has convinced you to open online accounts for access to the credit bureaus, your banks, credit unions, brokerages, and any other accounts for your money. Use your password manager to create and store rock-solid passwords and fake but rock-solid security questions and finally, set up 2FA. You do not ever have to use them online, but do watch your mail or email for any notifications of changes.

It turns out there are other accounts you need to open before attackers do.

Social Security Online – Retirement Surprise!

Go to the Social Security Administration page at this address

Open Accounts to Protect Them

https://www.ssa.gov/myaccount/ and set up a My Social Security account. The purpose of this account is to be able to monitor your Social Security retirement benefits both before and after retirement. Most people just wait until retirement. Hackers figured out that if they open the account before you do, they can have your benefits routed to them. Thank you, Social Security Administration! By opening the account first, you protect against that, even if you are a long way from retiring.

Note that when you try to open this account, the SSA will ask a series of questions based on your Equifax credit report.[2] If you took my earlier advice, you may have to unfreeze Equifax (only them) for it to work. However, when I did it, the answers to all the questions were "none of the above," most likely because I had frozen my Equifax credit. This was terribly distressing, knowing that being more secure in one area made me vulnerable in another area. It has been a few years, so I hope those jackasses fixed that. This is yet another reason to open your SSA account before the bad guys do. When I try now, I get a big banner that says, "An account has already been created with the information you entered." Good.

I noticed when I did this that you can also use a state-issued ID (driver's license) to prove your identity. This is fine for the SSA account, but now if you lose your driver's license, you have another thing to worry about unless you already created a SSA account.

Just as with all accounts, use your password manager to create and store a strong password. The Social Security Administration will also require several security questions for the purpose of resetting your password or additional verification later. You know what to do; answer them with bogus password-manager-generated passwords and store both the question and answers in the password manager notes.

They also require two-factor authentication (2FA), allowing you to choose either text or email to get a code sent to you. After you enter your username and password, you then enter this additional code into the website. This means the account has an extra layer of security.

They also added the ability to request "extra security." You must answer a financial question to verify your identity, and then they mail you an "upgrade code." When you enter it, future logins require an additional verification question. This is a third step, though not an additional factor. I will leave it up to you on whether to enable this one.

Repeat this action for all adults in your household and consider your elderly parents. As for children, you are not supposed to be able to create an account until they are eighteen. I tried to do this, and the website stopped me when I both lied and told the truth about their ages, so that is good. Put this on the calendar for when they turn eighteen.

Once you have this account set up, it is up to you whether you will ever visit it again until you do finally retire and want to draw your benefits.

Post Office Account – Uninformed Delivery

The US Postal Service had a somewhat cool idea, but only fraudsters seem to know about it. You can get an online account and do a bunch of things you would expect, like buy stamps or figure out how to send a package. But there are two services we need to cover.

The first is a change of address. If a bad actor can get this account, then they can just have your mail rerouted to them or to an abandoned property where they can pick it up later. Now, this is a bit of a crapshoot because you are eventually going to figure out that your mail is not getting to your house, and the bad actor may get something of value in the meantime. Still, if your mail stops one day, it would be good to have this account to check to see if your mail was forwarded.

However, there is another service called Informed Delivery that offers a much better chance of success for the bad guys. With Informed Delivery, the USPS takes scans of your regular mail and emails them to you before the mail is physically delivered.

Ironically, the USPS probably thought this was a good security measure against people stealing mail out of your mailbox. But say I am a bad actor and want to know what mail you are getting. Say I want to do an IRS scam (see next section) and want to catch your W2s. I could sign up as you and check every morning for the telltale ADP envelope. When I see it is coming, I can run to your house, watch for the mailman to drop it off, and then go yank it out of the mailbox. There is a good chance you will be at work, but even if you are home, there is a good chance I can beat you to the mailbox and not be seen. If not W2s, I could look for cards from Grandma (often with cash in them), paychecks, preapproved credit card applications, health records, the list is practically infinite. Thank you, United States Postal Service!

Go to https://www.usps.com/. In the very top right, click "Register/Sign In." The option to create a new account is on the right. As always, use your password manager to create a strong, unique password and to make up and store fake answers to the "security" questions. Signing up for Informed Delivery is up to you, but the important thing is to have an account at your address. To enable 2FA, go into your name in the top right, click "My Profile", then "Preferences" and it is under the security section.

IRS – Please Scam Me

In recent years, tax scams have become all the rage. The IRS has barely needed more than a valid Social Security number to allow people to submit their taxes. Consequently, fraudsters can either steal or make up their own W2s and submit them for a nice big fake return. Either way, the IRS just assumes that the first one to file in your name is the right one. If the fraudsters get there first, then they get a refund and then the IRS assumes that you submitted the fraudulent 1040. Thank you, Internal Revenue Service!

The first response the IRS had was to issue PINs to people who had already been scammed, which is just a tad reactive and behind the curve. They did not seem to think about protecting others. However, they are finally waking up and issuing a PIN to anybody who asks.

Go to https://www.irs.gov/identity-theft-fraud-scams/get-an-identity-protection-pin. From this page, click Get an IP PIN and sign up for an account. They will assign you a PIN to use for the current year that you must include on your taxes (online or mail). They set you up with text-based 2FA by default.

Now that you have a PIN, the IRS does not rely on the first to submit a 1040; it is the first to submit with the correct PIN on their tax form.

Get an account and a PIN for your spouse too. Next year, both of you will have to log in before the April 15 deadline to get a new PIN.

Just like with the other pre-emptive accounts, watch your email for notifications that something changed. I purposely changed my account password so I would see what a change-of-account email would look like. Here it is:

IRS.online.services@irs.gov   12:53 PM (48 minutes ago)

to me ▾

A user registration identity verification update has been performed on IRS online services per your request.

If you did not perform this user registration identity verification update, please contact us at 888-841-4648.

This is an automated email. Please do not reply.

The IRS will never initiate contact through email asking taxpayers for personal or financial information.

Since I just made a change, I knew this email was legit. But as I have warned multiple times, bad actors know that people will open and respond to emails that say they are from the IRS. If you get any emails supposedly from the IRS, do not click any link, do not download anything, and do not even call the number. First, go to the account yourself and change the password. That should lock out the attacker if they got access. Go through your profile to see if anything changed. If you cannot get in, that might mean they changed the password to keep you out! If there are any changes you did not make or you cannot get into your account, call that number (888-841-4648) and tell them you got an email that there was a change, but you did not make it.

State Unemployment Office

In response to the COVID-19 pandemic, the federal government passed the CARES Act. It was a multipronged effort to flood the world with money and blunt the economic effects of the pandemic. The part we care about here is that many people were unemployed during this time and the federal government added $600 a week on top of the standard unemployment benefits. Fraudsters saw a massive opportunity. You can Google "unemployment fraud" and see thousands of articles on how various states have been defrauded. That is bad enough in that it will cost all of us in tax dollars. And because states did not respond with more restrictions, it will mean a lot of people who need unemployment will be denied.[3] But the biggest threat to the rest of us as individuals is that a bad actor will steal our identity to get unemployment benefits, and then when the state figures it out, they will request the money back from the real you.

Here is the email my wife got from her employer (yep, spouse of Mr. Security man):

> We received notice from the company who handles our unemployment claims. They received a claim in your name. This is a fraudulent claim since you are currently employed by us. But you need to respond to them that it is a fraudulent claim and that you did not file for unemployment by 12/17/2020. Please write a letter stating that you did not apply (To Whom it May Concern) and have it notarized as soon as you can, then scan and email it to me or see me after they notarize it for you.
>
> I have attached a letter about steps you can take.
> You need to try to get ahold of the State Dept. of Employment to let them know that you did not apply. Check your credit reports. Check your bank accounts. File a police report.
> Keep an eye out on your mail for a debit card from them. Do not use it.

When we went to the state employment website and tried to create an account, sure enough, there was already one created. Again, the best thing to do is set up an online account for your respective state or territory, enter your email, set up a strong password, and enable 2FA if they have it. Then if you need benefits, that part is done. If you do not need benefits, then it is that much more difficult for a fraudster to do it on your behalf.

Open Accounts to Protect Them

References:

[1] https://krebsonsecurity.com/2018/06/plant-your-flag-mark-your-territory/

[2] https://www.ssa.gov/hlp/mySSA/df-idverification.html

[3] https://www.npr.org/2020/10/14/921857968/so-hard-to-prove-you-exist-flawed-fraud-protections-deny-unemployment-to-million

6

PROBLEMS WITH PLASTIC AND OTHER PAYMENTS

Security vs. Temptation

Credit and Debit Card Fraud

There are three primary ways thieves get your payment card information.

1. Card lost or stolen
2. Skimmers
3. Data breach

Losing your card or having it stolen obviously means the information on it could be stolen. One way the information could be stolen without your knowledge is through bad employees that handle your credit card (usually at restaurants and bars) that either run it by a skimmer or write the information down.

Skimmers are pieces of equipment that can be installed over payment terminals or ATMs. Here is a YouTube video of a couple guys installing a skimmer in a convenience store in plain sight https://www.youtube.com/watch?v=5b1axnNK-wI. Gas station pumps are favorites because they are outside and can be shielded from the attendant's view. ATMs are great targets because they do not have attendants by definition, and the payoff is cash rather than having to buy something. To also get the PIN, thieves often put cameras over the keyboard. When using any payment machine or ATM, be sure to look for loose or suspicious additional hardware, and when typing your PIN, use your other hand to shield what you are entering from view.

Data breaches happen almost constantly these days. They are not supposed to, but stores, online merchants, utilities, or governments may keep your card data. You might also provide it voluntarily on file for automatic payments or just so you do not have to re-enter the information the next time you shop or pay bills. I am not even going to bother listing big credit card hacks here, but it is almost certain that your credit card information has been compromised at some point. The information flows freely on something called the dark web where hackers buy and sell credit card numbers for a few bucks.

It might be surprising, but my response here is that there is practically nothing you can do about data breaches, so we must deal with it. Maybe more surprising, despite this, I will explain later why credit cards are still the best option for payments. For in-person transactions EMV credit cards eliminate a lot of the issues.

Demand EMV Credit Cards

Credit cards in the US have been slowly moving to EMV (Europay, MasterCard, and Visa) or chip cards. These cards have a small metallic square that must be inserted into the payment terminal rather than swiping the black magnetic strip.

EMV chip

The magnetic strips are not encrypted, and therefore it is easy to steal the information (your name, card number, expiration date) on them. Not only that, but the information never changes, so it can be used by others. The EMV cards are far more secure because they are difficult to copy and the information is encrypted. Additionally, that little chip creates a code (also known as a *token*) that is only good for one transaction. So even if a thief could somehow unencrypt the information, that code will not work for any future transactions. Since EMV came out, Mastercard reported an 81% drop in fraud between 2015 and 2018 for card-present (as opposed to online) transactions.[1]

The biggest barrier to complete EMV acceptance is merchants converting to payment equipment that accepts the cards. We cannot get rid of the magnetic strip until enough merchants switch over to EMV. A big holdout was gas stations, so the credit card companies had an October 2020 deadline for gas stations to convert to EMV.[2] Then the coronavirus hit, so they got an extension. Let us hope the magnetic strips go away someday.

Debit vs. Credit

A credit card or a charge card allows you to get a very short-term loan from the bank to purchase something right now regardless of whether you have the money to pay for it. A credit card allows a revolving line of credit; i.e., you do not have to pay it all back at the end of the month but pay interest if you do not. A charge card, however, must be paid in full at the end of the month. I do not know anybody that owns charge cards today, but American Express apparently still offers them.

A debit card has access to money you have in an existing bank account and often comes free when opening said bank account. Debit cards started out as ATM cards, and even today some only allow ATM usage. However, most now also allow direct purchases of goods and services. We are not talking about prepaid debit cards here but will return to that later.

Nerd Alert! Debit and Credit Card Networks

The first thing to understand about credit cards is that there are the card companies (American Express, Discover, MasterCard, Visa) and then there are the issuing banks. Your credit card has the logo of both your bank and the card company on it. (There also might be a third and far more prominent logo of an airline, NFL team, whatever, but they are only advertising or running a rewards program and are irrelevant to this conversation.) The card companies built and run the credit card payment system, but the bank is the one giving you the loan.

Debit cards got their start as ATM cards. An entirely separate system was set up to support ATM transactions. Some big players here are the Star Network, Allpoint, Pulse, Co-op (for credit unions), and Money Pass. Debit cards generally show the logos of these networks on the back of the card. Whenever these networks are being used, you must also supply a PIN.

Then people had the idea to allow the ATM cards to be used to purchase goods directly. Naturally, these debit networks started the process of getting into retailers, but it is a massive undertaking to get the millions of retailers to update all their point-of-sale systems. The credit card companies saw this competition coming, so they jumped in and said, "Hey we already have this massive network installed. Just

---

put our logo on the front of the card and use the credit card networks." Thus the dual-network card was born, and this is the dominant type today.

In the past when you used a dual-network debit card, the first question on the card reader was, "Debit or credit?" This was very confusing to users because it refers to the payment system, not debit versus credit in the accounting sense. If you chose credit, then the PIN was not needed, and the payment was processed on the credit card system but still came out of your bank account (i.e., not a loan). If you chose debit, then you needed the PIN, and the payment was processed on a debit network. Today, they do not ask, "Credit or debit?" Instead, when you get to the PIN entry, if you enter a PIN, it is processed on the debit network, but if you do not enter a PIN, it is processed on the credit network.

On the surface, using the debit payment system gives the appearance of being more secure than a credit card because a PIN is required at the time of purchase. This is 2FA—something you have (the card) and something you know (PIN). However, US liability laws and these different systems tip the balance in favor of credit cards, which I talk about in the main section.

If fraudulent charges appear on your credit (or charge) card, you have a $50 maximum liability. This is federal law. Call your credit card bank and tell them your card (or card information) was stolen, and they will start the process of reversing the charges and issuing you a new card. You need to be as prompt about reporting this as possible, but relatively speaking, this is an easy process. Not only that, but also most of the time the $50 liability is even waived.

If somebody steals your debit card and PIN and withdraws money it is removed directly from your bank account. Once that happens, if you do not move quickly, it is on you to prove that the money was stolen. Even then, there is a good chance you will not get that money back. There is a federal law called Regulation E or the Electronic Funds Transfer Act on debit cards that has the following rules on what "moving quickly" means:

If lost or stolen:

You have two days to notify the bank to keep your liability limited to $50.

If you miss two days but up to sixty days, the liability is $500 max.

After sixty days your liability is almost unlimited.

If the card is not stolen:

You have sixty days from when the statement is sent to report it with only a $50 liability.

After that the liability is unlimited.

Not only can they drain the bank account that the debit card is attached to, but if you have any overdraft protection, they also can take money that your bank covers. Often overdraft fees are on the order of $35 an instance.

Not only is this convoluted, but when they say the liability is unlimited, that means it is on you to prove to the bank that the money was stolen to get it back. Even then, it is up to them to determine if they will refund the money.

That last paragraph is the real difference when it comes to getting your money back from fraudulent transactions. On credit cards when you make a dispute, the banks can just reverse the charge to the merchant. The merchants eat it because the card issuers and banks have all the power. On the other hand, in the debit situation, the money comes out of your bank account and your bank might have to be the one that eats the loss if they cannot reverse the transaction. Why can't they just reverse the transaction? you may ask. I am not going to pretend to know the exact reasons, but it comes down to the fact that there are two different payment systems involved. Those two- and sixty-day milestones in the liability laws are related to how easy it is for the bank to reverse the charges.

The credit card companies like to advertise "zero liability" on fraudulent transactions regardless of whether it is a credit or debit card.[3,4] Do not be deceived here because they can enforce this on the credit cards, but not on debit cards because again, that is up to the banks.

Nerd Alert! Credit Card Caveat

Credit card versus debit card liability is not the case outside of the US. In most of Europe, credit card companies are not allowed to simply reverse charges to the merchants without dispute resolution. Since consumers have more liability with fraudulent charges, they tend to be more careful. I talked about EMV chips earlier. The EU mandated that credit cards use EMVs and PINs years before the US.

In the US, the credit card companies and banks have paid off every politician in Washington, DC. Believe that no Democrat or Republican swamp draining will happen anytime soon with all the cash coming their way. Hence, the card companies get to write their own laws, and the number one concern they have is making people use credit cards as much as possible. Limiting the liability and not requiring a PIN maximizes the number of credit card transactions.

Credit card companies get to push the losses onto merchants, which ultimately are pushed to consumers in the form of higher prices. On the other hand, the cost to merchants to use credit cards is around 2.5–3% of the purchase prices plus transaction fees. Think of this: banks and credit card companies are skimming 3% off the top of virtually every transaction in the US (and probably the world). Merchants have been fighting some of these fees in lawsuits for years, but the credit card companies and banks are able to fight this forever.[5] Case in point: Visa alone made over $12 billion in profits in 2019.[6] Walmart is the biggest company on earth in terms of revenue but that year made $6.6 billion in profits. You get things of value from Walmart.

Even more hideous is that there are state laws that do not allow merchants to charge different prices for cash versus credit cards.[7] Regardless of the state laws, Visa and Mastercard include this in their contracts for accepting credit cards. What all this adds up to is the merchants cannot pass the costs only to the customers that use credit cards. Instead, the higher prices are paid even by the customers using cash. This hurts everybody but hurts the poor even more because they often cannot get credit cards. And, in effect, it subsidizes rich people's credit card rewards like frequent flier miles and cash back.

Bottom Line on Debit Cards

This book is about security, so I recommend credit cards over debit cards for daily use based solely on the potential liability. There is a high probability that your card will be abused in some way, and credit cards make it far easier to get that money back.

Debit cards are more attractive in ways beyond security, such as you cannot spend money that you do not have. They also lack the absurd interest and fees credit cards often charge. However, most of those can be avoided if you can completely pay off the balance every month. I realize some people trying to get their spending under control might have eliminated all their credit cards in favor of debit cards. I am only looking at the security perspective with my recommendation.

I do have a debit card because I prefer to have access to cash from an ATM in case of emergencies. However, I do not use it for anything else, and the account it is tied to would not be too damaging to me if I lost the card. Additionally, most ATMs have a withdrawal limit, usually in the $200–$500 range, so a thief would have to hit several to get any substantial amount. Then on top of that, your bank usually has a 24-hour maximum ATM transaction limit, usually around $500 or less. If you cannot afford to lose this range of money, then do not use a debit card at all. Get cash from old-fashioned human tellers during business hours. Banks used to offer ATM-only cards. These are identifiable because they do not have a Visa or Mastercard logo on them and are ideal if you can find one because they cannot be used for purchases.

As a bonus, I noticed that my bank allowed me to set alerts on my account based on activity. Pretty nifty. I set mine up such that any transaction over $0.99 will send me a text message. I will know within minutes if somebody is using my ATM card other than me, and I can call the bank immediately.

Do Not Connect Anything to Your (Important) Bank Account

Beyond the liability laws, the key problem with debit cards is the direct access to your bank account. It follows that you should connect as few things to your bank account as possible. If you are living paycheck to paycheck, and many of us do, then having that account attacked could mean not paying rent that month. In this case, use a credit card account to provide the isolation between your bank account and all the external places that could get hacked. Big items like a mortgage or car payments will generally be to another account in your bank or another bank, so you can auto-pay to them safely. See this diagram:

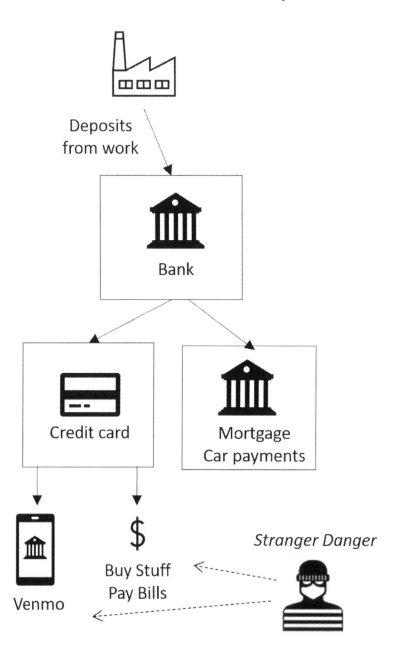

Deposits
from work

Bank

Credit card

Mortgage
Car payments

Venmo

$
Buy Stuff
Pay Bills

Stranger Danger

For those of us who can put more aside and need the services that the bank provides, I recommend separate bank accounts. One, a savings account that must be highly isolated, and two, a checking account that is used for daily life.

Most banks will let you open multiple accounts, but unfortunately, they allow access to them through the same online account. (See the discussion in the chapter on setting up online accounts versus physical bank accounts.) They just assume people want this convenience, and most people do, but it is not the best setup for security purposes. You can ask your bank if you can have accounts under different online accounts, but it is probably better to simply use two different banks.

The bank with the savings account should be protected at all costs. Never have checks made for it (or it would be a checking account), debit cards, automatic bill paying, none of that.

The checking account should have a smaller balance that you can afford to lose and is the one connected to everything. It could have checks, debit cards, Venmo, auto-pay utility bills, and whatever else attached. The idea is that the amount of money in this account is small enough that you will be okay if it is stolen. It would completely suck, mind you, but you would continue to eat and live in your house.

Problems With Plastic and Other Payments

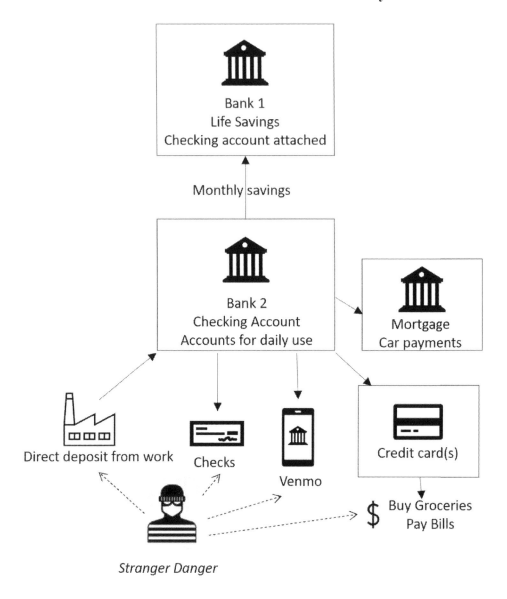

I would still avoid checks (we will discuss them in a minute) because of all the information potentially on them, but sometimes you have no other choice. I would also still use the credit cards for additional isolation because it is so easy to dispute fraud that way.

Notice that I have direct deposits from work going to the checking account. You had no option but to do this in the single account setup, but here, you do not even have to trust your employer. If you do this, and I recommend it, then the logical question that follows is, "How do I get money into the savings account?"

From the savings account, you can attach an external account (the checking account) to it and set up ACH payments. You can manually do one-time ACH transfers when your checking account balance starts getting higher than comfortable. Or you can set up automated monthly transfers to automate your savings. This would also help with budgeting.

Most commonly, to set up the external account, the bank will send two small transfers under $1.00. You have to log in to the other account to see them and then come back and enter them to prove you have access. Then, you can transfer funds in either direction. It is critical that you set this up in the savings account because that is the one you are isolating. If you set this all up in the checking account and it is hacked, the hacker could initiate transfers from your savings account.

Now, let's say your savings has grown to the point where you want to invest and you go set up a brokerage account. You can set up the brokerage account as an external account for ACH transfers the same way you did for the checking account. However, in this case, as soon as the money is transferred, I would go back into the savings account and delete the brokerage account connection. The idea is that both accounts will be valuable, but if one gets hacked, you do not want the hackers to have access to both accounts. My assumption is that transfers like this will not be common.

Pay with My Phone

Apple, Android (Google), and Samsung all have ways to pay with your phone. All of them start by entering your credit, debit, or prepaid cards. Given this, you might think the only thing that makes it better is that it is cool to just wave your phone over the terminal rather than swiping or inserting the card. However, it turns out this is similar in security to the EMV method mentioned above because it uses encryption and tokens. Both EMV and these phone methods are far superior to the magnetic stripe. However, neither works for online purchases.

The same rules apply if you go this route. Only use a credit card (or debit card connected to a daily-use checking account) and make sure you follow the security measures I lay out in the chapter on securing your phone.

PayPal

PayPal was invented for regular people trying to sell something occasionally, like on eBay or Craigslist. Today, PayPal is accepted by millions of merchants as well. If you sell something and the buyer pays with PayPal, then the key thing to look out for is the buyer sending you an email or message claiming, "The money is there, send the item." Do not take their word for it; check your PayPal account. The money is considered yours the moment you accept it, and it says "Completed" in your Activity. The only way the buyer can get the money back is by asking you for a refund or taking it up in the Resolution Center.[8]

Of course, the Resolution Center may find that a legitimate account holder was hacked, and the payment will be reversed, in which case you are out of luck. This is simply a risk you take selling online, but PayPal has been successful because it does a good job of minimizing this issue versus the alternatives. There are scams around PayPal, and we will cover them in the chapter on scams.

PayPal.me is an additional service where you can set up a unique link and webpage. This page is public and allows others to see some of your information and initiate transactions. It is meant to allow easy payments between trusted friends and family. If you are only an occasional PayPal user and keep a low balance, then you can treat it like Venmo or Square Cash, which we discuss next.

It is connected to your business PayPal account however, I would avoid PayPal.me. Many scammers trying to buy will try to get you to provide this link instead of the usual PayPal route. Do not do it.

Venmo and Square Cash App

Venmo is owned by PayPal but is not even close to the same business model. Where PayPal was meant specifically to enable goods and services purchases online, Venmo's terms of service explicitly forbids the use of Venmo for purchasing or selling goods and services. Cash App is run by Square, the company that makes the device that a merchant can attach to a phone and take credit cards. Cash App is a copy of Venmo, and the same warnings apply here.

As a buyer, once you send money, it is gone. Venmo sees fraud two ways, which is odd, but important to understand. The first is if you are tricked into sending the payment, Venmo will do virtually nothing to help you. On their Help page, when you click on what to do if you are a victim of a scam, it does not even bother to say, "Sorry you lost some money." Rather it takes you to the Terms section where they literally tell you that you should not have sent the money to someone you do not trust. The other type of fraud Venmo sees is if your account is hacked. If you can prove this is the case, they will reverse the charges. However, proving this will require time and effort on your part.

This might sound good as a seller. The payment is instant and irreversible. Well, as mentioned, it is reversible if the buyer can prove fraud either because a hacker took over their account or the buyer used stolen credit cards to fund a fake account. Either way, Venmo is not going to eat those charges, so they take the payment back from the seller.[9]

Without a doubt, use PayPal or a credit card when buying from a merchant or person you do not know.

Fund Venmo with credit cards and not your bank account (unless it is a daily use checking account) as previously mentioned. In theory, once you get some starter money into your account, you will be both sending and receiving payments and should not have to refill often.

Venmo made payments into a social activity by allowing comments to be attached and then showing the world the feed. Knock that idiocy off! In the app, go to:

> **Settings > Privacy > Private** and make sure this is checked.

We will come back to Venmo and Cash App in the chapter on scams.

Zelle

Zelle is like Venmo and Cash App in that it is meant for payment between trusted friends and family. However, the only way to fund it is a direct connection to your bank account. If your Zelle account is hacked, so is your bank account.

Zelle also is a system that several banks use, but the security they put around it depends on the individual bank. Amazingly, some banks are not taking security on this thing seriously. There are even reports of people who do not even use Zelle being defrauded with it.[10]

Do not use Zelle.

Prepaid Debit Cards, Gift Cards, Merchant Cards

There is a massive array of other cards out there that allow you to add money to them and then spend the money just like a credit or regular debit card. Virtually every retailer offers gift cards where you prepay. These generally cannot be reloaded and can only be used at the retailer that issued it (closed loop). On the other hand, there are prepaid cards that can be reloaded and used anywhere credit cards are taken (open loop). Some common ones are Money Pack, Vanilla Reload, and Reloaded.

The biggest difference is that you hand the money over to whomever is running the card first. They then create a temporary account for you to track your balance. The only thing needed to get money from these cards are the numbers on them. There is no tracking where the money goes, let alone the ability to reverse charges. Once the money is gone from these accounts, it is gone.

Fraud around these cards has skyrocketed for those specific reasons. In the early days of gift cards, scammers would go to stores and write the numbers down. Then, on a regular basis, they would check the balance to see if anybody bought and added money to them. That is why now you must scratch the numbers off to see them, or at least peel a sticker off. When we talk about scams in another chapter, often the payoff for the scammers is to get somebody to send them the numbers of a prepaid card.

The prepaid cards can be ideal for people who cannot otherwise have a bank account for whatever reason, or for parents to give their college kids some spending money. The two things I recommend on any of these cards is (1) do not ever have more money on them than you can afford to lose, and (2) no legitimate creditor is going to demand that you use prepaid or gift cards to pay them back. A legitimate creditor will take money in just about any form other than gift cards. If the "IRS" calls and threatens to throw you in tax jail if you do not run to Home Depot and buy $2,000 worth of gift cards to pay them, know that this is a guaranteed scam.

Western Union, Wire Transfers, and ACH

A common way to send money is to use Western Union or MoneyGram. These companies have offices throughout the world so you can transfer money between them for a somewhat hefty fee. I suggest only sending money this way to people you know, because once money is transferred, it is irreversible.[11] And if the bad guys are overseas (part of many scams demanding Western Union as payment is convincing the victim that the scammers are local when they are not), it is almost impossible for law enforcement to prosecute.

Wire transfers are from bank to bank, but otherwise like a Western Union transfer in that it is fast, irreversible, and a fee is charged. It is great for the person receiving the money, but a bit risky for the sender. When buying something big, like a house, the bank of the seller often requires a wire transfer of the deposit because they want to be guaranteed they have the money. This is a source of a horrible potential scam we will talk about in the chapter on scams, so be 100% sure you are sending the payment to the right account.

ACH is also bank to bank, but takes a couple of days, is cheap or even free, and is trusty for both the sender and receiver. However, if the sender contests the ACH and can show fraud was involved, then it can be reversed. There usually is not much fraud involving ACH.[12]

Personal Checks, Cashier Checks, and Money Orders

Do not use personal checks as payment anymore. They already have your name and address printed on them as well as your bank routing number (ABA [American Bankers Association]) and account number printed on them. Places that accept checks often also request to see your driver's license and/or Social Security number and/or birthday and then write that information right on it. Then the check is passed through many people's hands before it makes it back to your bank, exposing all that extremely sensitive data all over the place. Use credit cards instead and pay online. For larger amounts, have your bank provide a cashier's check or wire transfer. They charge a fee of course, but your information is not all over them. The biggest thing from a payer's perspective on these methods, as mentioned before, is that once the money is cleared, it usually cannot be reversed.

When accepting payments, we all know that personal checks can be fake or can bounce (the buyer has no money in his account). However, it might be surprising to hear that fake cashier's checks and money orders are often used in scams, until you stop and think about it. Would you be able to tell if one is real?

Real cashier's checks and money orders are guaranteed to have the funds by whoever issues them. But the only way to know for sure if they are real is to go with the person into the issuing bank or store and get confirmation.

The key for any check or money order is to understand that the money takes several days to two weeks to clear. In the meantime, your bank will add it to your account balance and let you spend it. However, if the check or money order bounces, your bank will hold you liable for it. Unless you can verify the checks are real, do not accept these, or wait at least two weeks after depositing them to send the goods off to the buyer.

If you saw the movie *Catch Me if You Can*, then you know that Frank Abagnale Jr,. the conman and main character, walked into banks with fake checks and was paid repeatedly. He relied on this system to take several weeks for the checks to clear because he would spend the money in the meantime and then switch banks or leave town by the time the jig was up. It is amazing that the same issue from the 1960s is alive and well today. We will revisit this in the chapter on scams.

Bitcoin

Bitcoin is the most famous digital currency, meaning it only exists in computer memory and is not backed by any government. It can be used to buy goods directly in some cases. But mostly you must convert it to some currency issued by a government (like dollars) to buy something. I will not spend much time on this except to say that no legitimate organizations will demand payment in Bitcoin or any of the other digital currencies (Ethereum, Ripple, Litecoin, etc.) Scammers like it because it is irreversible and difficult or impossible to trace.

Problems With Plastic and Other Payments

References:

[1] https://creditcards.usnews.com/articles/how-do-emv-chip-cards-work

[2] https://www.scmagazine.com/home/security-news/network-security/mastercard-and-visa-push-emv-liability-deadline-to-2020-for-automated-fuel-pumps/

[3] https://usa.visa.com/pay-with-visa/visa-chip-technology-consumers/zero-liability-policy.html

[4] https://www.mastercard.us/en-us/personal/get-support/zero-liability-terms-conditions.html

[5] https://www.paymentcardsettlement.com/en

[6] https://www.macrotrends.net/stocks/charts/V/visa/gross-profit#:~:text=%20%20%201%20Visa%20gross%20profit%20for,%2420.609B%2C%20a%2012.26%25%20increase%20from%202017.%20More%20

[7] https://www.nfib.com/content/legal-compliance/money/credit-card-surcharges-and-cash-only-discounts-what-you-need-to-know/

[8] https://www.paypal.com/us/smarthelp/article/can-i-cancel-a-paypal-payment-faq637

[9] https://www.thebalance.com/venmo-scams-315823

[10] https://www.nytimes.com/2018/04/22/business/zelle-banks-fraud.html

[11] https://www.thebalance.com/western-union-scams-315825

[12] https://www.thebalance.com/ach-vs-wire-transfer-3886077

7

ANTI-SOCIAL MEDIA
You Are Posting Too Much Sh*t Online

A Couple Stories

A friend of mine told me that he was about to hire a babysitter that both he and his wife liked after interviewing her. On a whim, he looked her up on the most popular social media site, Facebook. She was underage but had pictures of herself drinking and otherwise partying. My friend called her the next day and told her he would not be needing her as a babysitter. He did not bother to tell her why.

Another friend had some rental properties and was trying to collect rent from a tenant that was past due. His wife looked her up on Facebook and found postings of how she was "going to get a gun and f**king kill her landlord if he didn't quit bugging her about rent." They took screenshots as evidence if they ever had trouble, but fortunately that renter eventually just left.

These are examples of morons, but you can bet a potential employer will look you up for stupidity. There is nothing illegal about it if you leave your account public. It is not even illegal in most states for an employer to request your username and password for any social media account, though I would consider that a major red flag for you. These are not cyberattacks per se, but something to think about when using social media.

The Internet Is Forever

Something I want to drive into your head (and hope that you drive into your children's heads) is that once something is put on the internet, there is a good chance it will be out there forever.

I know some high school teachers, and the most terrifying thing I have heard is about kids (mostly girls, but of course boys can be victims too) being pressured to send pictures of themselves seminude or nude. This is often called *sexting* because it is often by text, but can be email or social media. You must make your children understand that the second they hit Send, that picture can be accessed by anybody and exist forever. The internet duplicates content over and over through legitimate backups, web crawlers (like Google), websites scraping each other, and people downloading images to their personal devices and computers. Law enforcement and expensive lawyers may be able to get it removed from legitimate sites, but there is no way to ensure that those images are destroyed everywhere.

Social media companies make their data feeds available through something called *application programming interfaces* (APIs). Basically, companies, universities, governments, or anybody can programmatically connect to them. Even without the APIs, the websites can be *scraped*, meaning robots scan them and pull down the data that way. Through APIs or scraping, people or organizations can search for pictures from Instagram, your friends on Facebook, keywords in your Twitter account. Virtually anything. Most of these feeds are used for advertising. Some uses are good, like tracking coronavirus,[1] and some things are hideous, like facial recognition company Clearview AI that reportedly has three billion pictures from the internet and can scan them almost instantly for law enforcement.[2] Whether these are good or bad uses, my point is that if you ever had a picture or embarrassing comment on social media and it was set to "public," it is now in hundreds of other databases. There is no way to know who owns them or what they do with them. It no longer matters if you delete your original post or turn your post private now, those posts are out there forever.

The original purpose of Snapchat was to be able to send short videos that self-destructed. Teenagers thought it made them safe. It later came out that Snapchat kept all those videos on their servers, which is bad enough, but at least they could be sued or even prosecuted if you found out they still have something. The more insidious problem is that it was easy to record a snap with another phone or recording device. In any case, it was such a lie that Snapchat does not even pretend their videos are deleted anymore.

The flip side of this is that people found with compromising pictures can be prosecuted. So let your children know that they can get in trouble if they are the bully or even get illicit photos or information sent to them without requesting it. If they receive anything like this, they should report it to you, and you should report it to the authorities immediately. Do not wait for the authorities to find you and think you can talk your way out of trouble later.

Back to Security

Actual criminals used to have to stake out a place by spying on the victim's house and learning if they had anything valuable, their schedule, whether they left their keys under the mat, and any other good information to help them rob the joint. Today, people just post that kind of information on Facebook for them. People post what they got for Christmas, how they redecorated their house, when they are going to go on vacation, when the kids will be left with the babysitter, where they work, freaking everything. For the love of God, think about what you are broadcasting to the world. Not only about the posts themselves, but who will see them.

I have no idea why anybody would post to Facebook and leave any of the settings set to "public." Yes, I get the idea of social media—to connect with friends and relatives. Having said that, do you really need people in Russia, China, and Kenya to know your hometown, who you are dating, and your favorite movie? Do you like them targeting you with fake news (from Democrats or Republicans; they both do it)? Do you want to prime them with information so they can guess your password or security challenge questions?

Facebook, for Example

There is much too much to cover here, but I am going to pick on Facebook just because it is the most ubiquitous. Once you go through what you want to do there, then you will have to revisit every social media account you have and think about how these concepts apply to all of them.

Facebook seems to have a scandal every few months, and people threaten to delete them. If that is your decision, here is how to download all your data and delete your account. (I know most people use their phones for Facebook, but it is far easier to do this on a computer.)

> In the top right, click the **chevron** (down arrow) **> Settings and Privacy > Settings**. On the left is **Your Facebook Information > Download Your Information**. Set the date range to "all my data" and then hit the **Create File** button. If you have a ton of data, it could take quite a while. Facebook will provide instructions on downloading the file once it is created.

If you dare to delete your account:

> In the top right, click the **chevron** (down arrow) **> Settings and Privacy > Settings**. On the left is **Your Facebook Information > Deactivation and Deletion**. Select **Permanently Delete Account** then **Continue to Account Deactivation.** You can download your data

here if you did not already **Delete Account.** You will have to enter your password for freedom. You get one final warning:

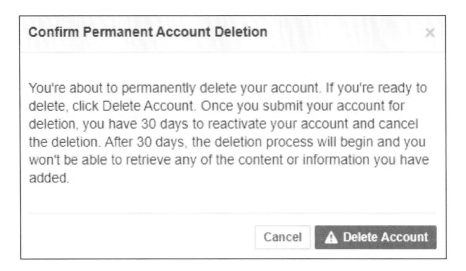

However, many people will find losing Facebook too difficult, and I am not here to lecture you on the time you waste or politics or any of that. I am only looking at the security aspect.

Assuming you will keep using Facebook, let us cover seven aspects: (1) who you consider "friends," (2) who sees your About information, (3) who sees your posts, (4) location, (5) face recognition, (6) advertising, (7) Facebook sharing their data with apps and websites.

Real Friends

The most fundamental part of Facebook, of course, is who you "friend." Often people get hung up on having as many friends as possible, so they accept every request and even reach out to people they do not know. According to Pew Research, the average Facebook user has 338 friends. The reality is that we do not have that many intimate friendships.

To get started, the easiest to unfriend are businesses. It seems to go without saying, but businesses are not really your friends, and they are truly on Facebook to harvest your data and target you for ads.

When it comes to humans, you really must think about what you want to accomplish on Facebook. Is it truly where you want to post your newborn baby or your drunken weekend pictures? Do you want all those people to know where you are almost 24/7? Think about what you want to put on Facebook, and then go through and unfriend all those that you might have second thoughts about sharing the same things with in-person.

In researching this book, I created a fake Facebook account, which the founder Mark Zuckerberg says they fight against. There was no confirmation of anything, and I was able to start friend requests immediately. So obviously, Russian propaganda machines can do this too, but by the millions. Several things creeped me out in this experience, but the one that got me was that I lied about my birthday and said I was a teenager. So what did Facebook do? It provided a list of random teenagers that I should friend. Of course, they are public, so I had access to all their About info, friends, and posts.

About

When somebody visits your profile on Facebook, the first thing they can see is the About information on the left side. You get to choose what information you put there, but also for every piece of information, you get to select if it is "public," "friend only," or "just you" who sees it. The default, of course, is public. My suggestion is to go through and delete all these entries. This is a great way for a hacker anywhere on earth to get information for guessing your security questions, so selecting "public" is plain stupid. Then "friends only" might be okay, but don't they already know this information about you? Or if they need it for some reason, they can ask you. And of course, if it is for only you to know, then why stick it on Facebook at all? There is just no good reason to fill this information out.

> From the Facebook homepage, on the left menu, click **Your Name**. A new screen is shown with your profile picture. Under your picture, click **About**. Delete it all. If you cannot bring yourself to do that, at least set everything to "friends" There is an icon right next to each item that you can click to set this.

Public or Private

The next thing to consider is if your posts should be public or friends only. Facebook lets you choose on a post-by-post basis if it is public or friends only. This is nice if there are benign posts that you want to broadcast to everybody. Just be aware that it defaults to the last one you chose. If you pick "public" for this post, you must remember to switch back for the next "friends only" post.

> In the top right, click the **chevron** (down arrow) **> Settings and Privacy > Settings**. On the left is **Privacy**. I suggest going through all the Your Activity and make sure none are "public."

Even with all of this, you still do not have the ability to stop your friends from reposting. You should still carefully consider what you post and when. For example, do not announce your vacation or even work travel dates ahead of time because it is telling everybody that you will not be home. Even when you are on vacation, if you think it is a good idea to take some photos from your phone, it will tell people you are not home, and worse, it will post your location. (We talk about that next.)

Post those pictures when you get back and make it clear you were there last week. Also think about discussing where and when your kids are at daycare. Think about if you should really post those pictures of the nice jewelry or new entertainment system you just bought. Just think, when posting, about who would want that information and why.

Location

When you load photos to Facebook, they supposedly strip the geolocation information from them. When everybody on earth downloads your photo, they cannot pull the location off it. Instead, if you have Facebook on your phone, it will pull the GPS information directly and put it in the title of your post.

You can turn this off in Facebook:

> In the top right, click the **chevron** (down arrow) **> Settings and Privacy > Settings**. On the left is **Location > Edit**. Select **Off** in the drop-down.

I would also go right to the source and turn it off in your phone. Open the Facebook app:

Click the three lines ☰. Scroll down to **Settings and Privacy > Settings**. Scroll down to **Location.** Turn off both the **Device Setting** and the **Facebook Setting for This Account Location History.**

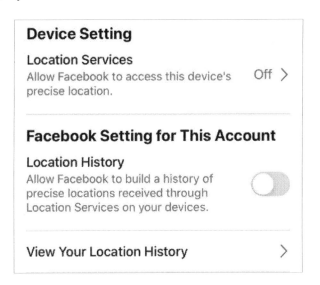

If you have been using Facebook and are just now turning off location history, then it might be a good idea to see what history they have:

> **Click on View Your Location History**. You can scroll back in time to see that Facebook has been tracking you everywhere. To delete this data, in the top right, click the three dots (**...**). Some options pop up, and **Delete All Location History** is what you are looking for.

If you are wondering why Facebook would want to track you, it is because they make billions off it. If you were walking by a McDonald's (I have no idea if McDonald's uses Facebook or location, this is just an example), then Facebook could charge McDonald's more to send you an ad right at that moment. Conversely, if Facebook sends you a McDonalds ad in the morning and then can show McDonald's that you went there for lunch, then Facebook can tell McDonald's the ad worked and charge accordingly. The security issue is that Facebook, McDonald's, McDonald's ad agency, and who know how many others know where you are constantly. Not only that, but if any of them have a data breach, then there is no telling who has that data.

Face Recognition

For the love of God, turn this off. From the browser:

> In the top right, click the **chevron** (down arrow) **> Settings and Privacy >**

Settings. On the left is **Face Recognition**. You might get a warning. If it is already off, make sure to keep it off. If it is on, click **Edit** and select **No** in the drop-down.

×

Please Review the Face Recognition Setting

Your face recognition setting is off. We want to let you know what face recognition is and how we use it, and then you can decide whether to turn it on or keep it off.

How We Use Face Recognition

If you turn this setting on, we'll create your face recognition template and use it in the following types of ways:

- Find photos and video you're in so we can help you review or share content, suggest tags, and provide more relevant content and feature recommendations.

- Help protect you and others from impersonation and identity misuse, and improve platform reliability.

If you turn this setting on, we'll create your face recognition template and use it in the following types of ways: ×

- Find photos and video you're in so we can help you review or share content, suggest tags, and provide more relevant content and feature recommendations.

- Help protect you and others from impersonation and identity misuse, and improve platform reliability.

- Provide accessibility features by telling people with visual impairments who's in a photo or video.

What We Collect

Face recognition is a technology that analyzes photos and videos you're in to calculate a unique number, called a "template." When your face recognition setting is on, we create and use your template to compare it to analyses of other photos or video to recognize if you appear in that content.

We don't share your template with anyone. We'll keep your template while your account is active but will delete it if you turn your face recognition setting off.

Image from the Evil Facebook

Facebook Advertising

Then there is the advertising. Facebook is free to use, but they make billions of dollars, and advertising to you is how they do it. Let us be clear: if you are on Facebook, they can and will use your data to advertise to you. These are the terms of using Facebook. The only control you have here is how much of your data they use to customize those ads, but that does not even reduce the number of ads.

> In the top right, click the **chevron** (down arrow) **> Settings and Privacy > Settings**. On the left is **Ads**.

There is an entire page here where you can tune what Facebook uses to direct ads at you. For example, in the Interest section, you can decide if you want more ads based on cooking, mountain biking, whatever you are into and told Facebook about. This is up to you.

Of course, all of what you allow is up to you, but Facebook really makes one of them a massive pain. Under the Advertisers and Businesses section, there are three tabs. In the first tab is a pretty big list of companies, and you cannot turn them all off at once. Instead, you must find **View Controls** under each of them and turn them off one at a time. They are especially devious because when you open them, the box says Don't Allow. I would think that is the setting, but that is not the case. You must click **Don't Allow** to make that the setting. Then you get an annoying pop-up that makes you click **Don't Allow** again. Plus, you must do it twice for each company, once to stay off a list and once to not be excluded. The only relief is that you can check the little box that says **"Don't show this again"** so that it stops. The fact that Facebook is so evasive about this tells me it is a massive moneymaker!

Facebook Data Shared with Applications and Websites

The primary thing we will concern ourselves with here is the other apps and websites you use your Facebook account to access. You know when you see one of these:

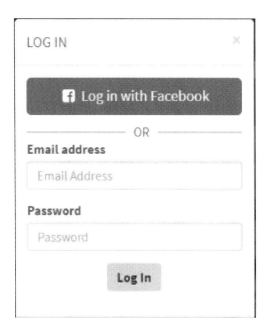

In the first chapter I advise you to never use your Facebook account (or Google or any other) and instead create a new account with your email and password generated by your password manager. When you do use your Facebook account, you are giving this application access to information on Facebook. You can see what that information is:

> In the top right, click the **chevron** (down arrow) **> Settings and Privacy > Settings**. On the left go down to **Ads and Websites**.

There are three tabs across the top, Active, Expired, and Removed. Go into the **Active** tab. Here is a list of all the applications that can still use your Facebook account and the exact data they can access. Some people have hundreds of applications listed. You can open them one at a time and dial in exactly what you will allow each of them to see.

Another alternative is to check them off one at a time and then hit the **Remove** button. Keep in mind that removing these accounts means you may not be able to access those applications or websites in the future. If you still want to use them, then you will have to go log in one last time with the Facebook login, then create a username and password. Then come back here and delete them.

There is an even bigger move that you can do here. Scroll down to the bottom where it says Preferences. There is a box titled "Apps, Websites, and Games." There will be a button labeled **Edit,** and when you click it, you will get this warning:

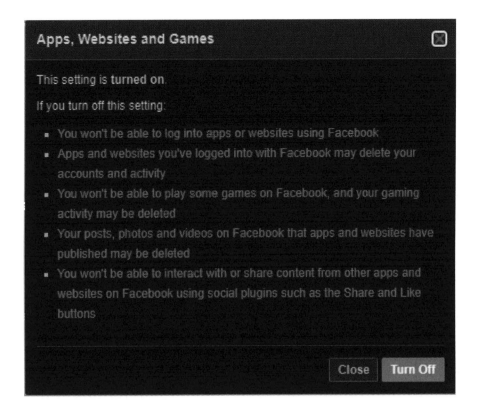

So if you hit **Turn Off**, all those warnings are true. But you are no longer giving your Facebook data to any outside apps.

You are not done yet. On the left menu is **Instant Games** and **Business Integrations**. They all must be removed too. I do not know why Facebook makes these differentiations; they are all just places you used Facebook to log in.

There is a caveat to this, however, and it is that any data those other companies have already harvested is not deleted. If you want to track that down, you must go back to the top and select the **Removed** tab. In each one, Facebook provides you with a link to their privacy policy. In theory, you can contact them and ask for your data to be removed. I have no idea where you would even start with that.

Back in the "Preferences" section, there is a box titled "We Removed Apps Others Use." Until about 2014, Facebook allowed these linked applications to see your entire Facebook feed, including anything your friends posted. In other words, you may never use the app, but if your friend did, the app could see your Facebook feed. This is what led to the Cambridge Analytica scandal where, because of this feature, 87 million US Facebook users were targeted in the 2016 presidential campaign.[3] Originally, a guy wrote an app that gave online quizzes and got 270,000 people to sign up. Because he could see all the friends and their friends, he was able to access exponentially more feeds. So once again, Facebook shut this feature down in 2014, but the data was still being used in 2016 by the people that harvested it and not shut down until 2018. **Data on the internet is forever, and you cannot control who gets it once released.**

LinkedIn

These clowns got hacked in 2012 and made everybody change passwords, but if you reused the same password on some other account, then go back to chapter 1 on why password reuse is bad.

I must use LinkedIn for professional reasons, so I understand how hard it would be to turn it off. Assuming you keep it, put your professional history and interests on there, but not your personal information. Assume your next employer is looking as well as a potential criminal.

Be aware that criminals might call you up for a fake job interview to get even more information on you and your company. One more recent scam due to the coronavirus pandemic is to find people working remotely and call them up pretending to be the company IT people. They use LinkedIn information to get your trust and then ask directly or send you to a fake website to get your company VPN credentials.[4] The hint here is your IT people already know your (or at least can reset) your VPN credentials, so they should never need to call you for them.

Twitter

Twitter is a social media company that is just texting on steroids. Instead of texting with individuals or small groups of people you know, Twitter lets you text with the entire world. Why this is successful is beyond me, but I am apparently a curmudgeon.

Say you complain on Twitter that the washing machine you just bought from Whirlpool is a piece of junk and why. Then you get a *tweet* (Twitter message) supposedly from Whirlpool to call them and get a free prize or whatever. Sometimes this is Whirlpool, and sometimes this is a scam.

It turns out that legitimate companies watch Twitter (all major social media) and often try to respond to keep their image up.[5] Well, scammers figured this out and will also try to respond as if they are from the legitimate company. It would be a tweet back saying something like, "We're sorry you had a bad experience. Give us a call and we'll make it right!" Then, when they can make contact, they ask for personal information or money. Be sure to verify the tweet came from the official Twitter account of the company and not some knock-off. I would also try to verify it some other way, like by going to their real website and finding the customer support line and asking them if the offer is real.

Other Social Networks

Instagram and WhatsApp are owned by Facebook, so I imagine you will have to go through and configure all those data-stealing settings.

Of course, there are plenty more. I mentioned Snapchat previously, but there is Pinterest, TikTok, and a host of others. TikTok drew President Trump's attention because they are owned by a Chinese company. He has no more idea what it is than I do. If you are just recording yourself dancing, it is probably good safe fun. If your kids are providing personal information so pedophiles can find them, then not a good idea.

Surveys and Quizzes

Due to my curmudgeon ways, I have always hated online surveys and quizzes, so I would not have ever thought of this one. Apparently, they are big on social media, and I already told you about the Cambridge Analytica scandal. Writing this book, I stumbled across Buzzfeed, a vapid media website. It has an entire section for quizzes. Most are harmless (all of them seem asinine), but know that they track everything you enter. Quizzes are a fantastic way to collect security question data, like "What was your first job?" or "What was your first car?" or "Who was your first love?"[6] I hope by now you can see why answering these questions is a bad idea. If not, then I do not know what to say at this point.

Anti-Social Media

References:

[1] https://medicalxpress.com/news/2020-08-social-media-covid-long-haulers.html

[2] https://www.nytimes.com/2020/01/18/technology/clearview-privacy-facial-recognition.html

[3] https://www.nytimes.com/2018/04/04/technology/mark-zuckerberg-testify-congress.html

[4] https://krebsonsecurity.com/2020/08/voice-phishers-targeting-corporate-vpns/

[5] https://www.theguardian.com/money/2012/may/12/complaint-air-on-twitter

[6] https://krebsonsecurity.com/2018/04/dont-give-away-historic-details-about-yourself/

8

SOCIAL ENGINEERING

Formerly Known as Scams

Social engineering is the hacker's term for going after a human for information as opposed to finding a technical vulnerability in their computer or network. Before nerds could run rampant making billions in Silicon Valley and have all their comic books made into movies, this type of thing was simply called a *scam*. However, scams have gone into hyperdrive in tandem with technology.

If you saw the movie *Catch Me if You Can* about Frank Abagnale Jr., then you know how the best con man of the '60s and '70s did it. If not, just know Frank had to be able to smooth talk people (face-to-face) out of information; go through incredible measures to pretend to be a pilot, doctor, and lawyer; and be able to forge checks and cash them in person. Then he had to move every few years and assume an entirely new persona to avoid capture.

Think about the Russian kid in his mom's basement circa 1980. How is he going to pull off a scam in the US? The best he can do is get a few phone books and start calling. The calls are like $10 a minute, he can call maybe twenty people a day, he has no information on whoever he is calling, his terrible English would be a massive red flag, and what would he be trying to scam them out of anyway?

Today, that Russian lost the cold war and grew up broke, but his kid has far more opportunity. The kid can buy botnets for a few dollars to blast his spam to millions of people, and only a tiny fraction of them must respond for there to be a payoff. He can peruse Facebook all day and know where you live, your family members, your friends, your schedule, and whatever else you post. The number of different scams he can try is only limited to his imagination.

This chapter covers the scammer's method of communicating with a potential victim. The methods covered include email, texting, phone calls, and websites, along with some examples of how they might work. The next chapter, called "Bypassing the Firewall" is really an extension of this chapter, but focusing on some technical aspects of social engineering. After that, the chapter "Scams," is a sample of the actual scams themselves regardless of how contact is made.

Phishing

Generically, *phishing* is any kind of email, text, or phone call that temps a person to action. *Phishing* is a play on *fishing*. The "bait" is the issue that concerns you. It could be something as innocuous as, "You need to update your Google account," or something as serious as, "The FBI is going to throw you in jail." It could be a worldwide disaster like the coronavirus, or a local disaster like your kid's school on fire. The "hook" is getting you to do something. This could be opening an email attachment or clicking a link that downloads malware to your computer, or it could be a link to an imposter website that tricks you into entering your username and password.

I will even cut to the chase on protecting yourself. Before ever opening an attachment, downloading files or images, clicking a link, or even calling a phone number, be sure that you trust the sender and were expecting the message. Even if the message appears to be from a trusted friend or coworker, if they ask for personal information or money, give them a call to verify. I cannot emphasize enough that calling and talking to a familiar human voice could save you untold pain.

Email Phishing Scams

Imagine that you get an email from your bank saying there is a problem with your account. But do not worry, all you must do is log in and set it straight. They are even considerate enough to provide you with a link that takes you directly to your login page. You click the link, go to the bank sign-in page, and enter your username and password, and then the screen goes blank or locks up or you get an error or go to a different website—anything but your actual account. Stupid computers! Maybe you do it a couple more times, even trying your other passwords, and get the same results. What is going on?

There is a good chance that the email and the website you went to were fake and now the scammers have your bank login credentials. If this happens, the scammers are moving quickly, so you need to move faster! Call your bank immediately and tell them to block any transactions and get their advice on other measures. While you are on the phone with them, go to the real bank website and change your password. If you have 2FA setup, that could be saving you at this very moment. If you do not have 2FA setup, then do it now.

The bank scam is one of hundreds of angles a scammer could take to get you to click a link and give your credentials. It could be a fake governmental agency, like the IRS, FBI, CIA, or SSA; a utility like your mobile phone company; or a technology company like Amazon, Apple, Google, PayPal, or Microsoft. The possibilities are endless. The message could be as seemingly innocuous as, "You need to update your account." They could be threatening fines or jail. They could be offering a lot of money.

The range of quality of the scams amazes me. Some scammers craft emails and websites to be exact copies of the originals, while others are child-like, with horrid spelling and grammar and low-res cut-and-paste jobs.

In their September 2017 report, the company Webroot found that on average, 1.385 million phishing sites were created per month! In their June 2019 report, they found that the number of sites grew 220% in 2018. The reason so many sites are created is because companies like Webroot track the phishing websites down and provide that intel to anti-phishing tools and/or authorities to have them blocked. Well, to avoid that, many of these sites live only four to eight hours. The scammers build a website, launch their phishing emails to nail as many people as possible, and then start again the next day.

Spear Phishing

Most phishing is "spray and pray" to thousands or millions of people because even a small percentage of success can pay off. *Spear phishing*, on the other hand, simply means that scammers are targeting a specific person or group of people. This is usually enabled by information that they get from social media sites.

Professionally, LinkedIn is a treasure trove of information that scammers can use to find out a person's title, what projects they are working on, where they fit into the org chart, and even where they might physically be. For example, many people announce that they will be at a conference and would like to meet people there.

Pre-texting is a technique that goes along with spear phishing, where the scammer is using the information they can get online to make themselves familiar to the target. It could be part of a single email where they add specific information and hope to score in one attempt. But more often, it might be several emails where the scammer tries to gain comfort with the target and additional information.

For example, the scammer could get initial information on LinkedIn and pose as a potential customer as an introduction. They can see that you work on a specific project, so they can feign interest and use that as an opportunity to gather more intel on you. If they can get a conversation going, then they are also gathering trust. Then at some point, they will spring the trap and get you to open an enclosure or click a fake link, or they will even just mine you for more personal or company information. Maybe you are in the middle of the corporate ladder and they are looking to figure out who your boss is so they can go whaling.

Whaling

Whaling is spear phishing for the important people in a company, like the CEO or a VP—somebody that can get access to critical information or can authorize a big check. If you are one of these people, then obviously you need to stay on your toes.

Probably the biggest whale out there is Jeff Bezos, founder and CEO of Amazon. It has recently come to light that the crown prince of Saudi Arabia sent him a WhatsApp message that had malware in it that could track his phone and see his texts and pictures. When the *National Enquirer* tried to blackmail him because of his mistress, he assumed that the Saudis had provided them the information. Turns out his mistress gave her brother the incriminating texts and he gave (sold?) them to the *National Enquirer*. Jeff Bezos was under attack from so many directions that he could not keep them straight.[1]

Most of us are not Jeff Bezos, but this stuff affects us. Bezos had the cashola to hire a forensics expert to track down the WhatsApp malware, and now all the cybercriminals in the world know that this malware exists. Since then, Facebook (owner of WhatsApp) has patched that vulnerability, and if you have WhatsApp set to auto-update, then you have it too. If not, then you are vulnerable.

Another reason we non–Jeff Bezoses should care about whaling is that whales can be used to attack us indirectly. Do not forget that companies can have low- and mid-level people in finance that are authorized to cut checks to a big supplier, or somebody in HR who can get some good blackmail information on somebody that does have a big title.

Imagine you are the new person in the finance department of a company. You get an email from the CEO, who is in the middle of a high-pressure negotiation and needs a bunch of money transferred to some other company to make this deal happen. It is urgent! The email says the CEO normally would have called your boss to do it, but she is on vacation.

Of course, if you are sitting here reading this in the social engineering section of a book on cybersecurity, you know that it is a scam and that anybody who falls for this is a moron. However, the brilliance of a lot of scams is that they get people's emotions running so their defenses are down. A new person, contacts from the CEO, the big deal, the big money, the time crunch all trigger emotional responses. Turns out, the email itself could be from the real CEO's account if the scammers were able to break into it.

Business Email Compromise

These are called *business email compromise* (BEC) scams. This is where a scammer breaks into a business email account and tries to get others to send information or money. The ideal email account target is one that belongs to a whale because (1) that alone will provide the scammer a ton of great information, and (2) it is natural for a person to do what their boss or other company executive tells them to do.

However, if a scammer can break into the email of a coworker you trust, then it can still be effective. Think your boss, her boss, somebody from finance or human resources. An email from within has a level of trust that is valuable all by itself.

The key is to be aware that scams like this are out there and that if the CEO really is in a situation where he is emailing unsuspecting employees for huge cash transfers, then he is the moron. Still, you do not want to mess this up if it is real. If you happen to know the CEO's phone number and have heard him talk, you can call him. This is perfectly conceivable at a smaller company. If the company is bigger and you barely know what the CEO looks like, then that is the first indicator that the email is fake. But ask your boss or her boss or the CFO if they can confirm it by either knowing what the CEO is doing or calling to confirm for you. Leave it to the mini-whales to decide.

Another form of BEC is when somebody you do business with is compromised. Say a scammer can break into your personal accountant's, banker's, or lawyer's email. Then they email you to move funds for legitimate purposes to the scammer's accounts.

In the chapter on scams, we will talk about how a business email compromise can be used to scam you out of your house down payment.

Vishing

The hacking world refers to phone call scams as *vishing*, which is a play on *voice phishing*. The rest of us call these *phone scams*. I have a whole section on phone scams later.

Texting (SMS) Scams

Texting scams are also known as *smishing* which is a play on SMS and *phishing*. Again, nerds making up a name that does not need to exist.

Whatever it is called, treat texts just as skeptically as emails and phone calls. Anybody can send a text claiming to be anybody else. They can also contain links and phone numbers. As in all cases, assume it is a scam and try to find evidence that it is not. If it is supposedly from your bank, then go to their official website and figure out how to contact them from there.

Here are a couple text scams that recently came right to my phone:

> Only 4 days left to file your claim. You could collect $200-$400 in the $650M Illinois Facebook Settlement. Learn more:
> https://is.gd/d0x9v2

> Facebook Ads Team: Your activity on Facebook Ads didn't follow our Community Standards and your Business Page was disabled: https://faceboook-page28196004.com

In the first one, they do not even try to make the URL look real, but it is based on a real lawsuit in Illinois against Facebook. In the second one, they tried to put "Facebook" in there, but you can identify the improper domain after you read the next chapter on web addresses and domains. Both use Facebook references to gain trust. They didn't realize I have no friends, so Facebook to me means "waste-of-time scam material."

References:

[1] https://www.nytimes.com/2020/01/22/technology/jeff-bezos-hack-iphone.html

9

BYPASSING THE FIREWALL
Knowing Is Half the Battle—G.I. Joe

This chapter could have just as easily been called "Social Engineering Part II." It will be the most technical chapter in the Basic section of this book but arms you with things to look for when being socially engineered. So why did I instead call it "Bypassing the Firewall" then? I'll give a detailed explanation of a firewall in the chapter on networking, but the only thing you need to know about it here is that a firewall is a mechanism that blocks people on the internet from directly attacking your computer or phones or other devices. A firewall is very powerful, so bad actors have to figure out ways to get around it.

How *do* bad actors get around the firewall? They must trick you to request malware from the inside, install it yourself, or invite it in. You might be thinking, "Why would I install malware myself or invite it in?" Here are six ways we will cover in this chapter:

1. It is possible you are voluntarily planting malware on your home network by connecting untrusted devices like cameras, smart speakers, internet-connected toys, or appliances to your home network.

2. You try to install an application and it turns out to be malware, or the application is real but has malware with it.

3. You are surfing the internet with your browser and either mistype an address or click a link that takes you to a malicious site. The browser then loads the malware.

4. Emails either have enclosures with malware or have links to websites with malware.

5. You or your kids are on a peer-to-peer network getting pirated music, movies, or games. This practically ensures malware infection.

6. You are walking through a parking lot, see a USB drive sitting there, and think, "Yes, somebody's private home pictures!" Congratulations, instead of private pictures, you get a virus.

IoT Devices

The internet of things (IoT) are devices that connect to the internet. Simple as that. Today our houses can be filled with smart speakers, TVs, cameras, door locks, you name it. These devices are connected right to your home network, so if they have malware on them or can get malware on them by connecting to the internet, then the bad guys are in. I will discuss IoT devices in far more detail in the chapter on networking in the technical section, but the big thing here is, don't install these devices in your home unless you trust the manufacturer.

Installing Software

The entire purpose of your computer is to run applications or games. The only thing to say is that you must trust the company or person sending you the software. Almost nothing in life is free, so if you get an offer for a free game, computer "cleaner," or whatever they dream up, do some research on it first.

Web Surfing: Look for the Lock

If you are going to any website, you should look for the following indicators, especially where you need to log in, enter any kind of personal data, or buy something. Glance up at the top left side of your browser in the address/search bar. Make sure that there is a padlock indicator and the address starts with the protocol "https" instead of "http." (Most browsers do not show the protocol part unless you click on the address, but the lock signifies https.) Most browsers today will even say "Not Secure" if it is not https.

This is what the lock in Chrome in Windows looks like:

Bank of America - Banking, Cred   X   +

← → C   🔒 bankofamerica.com

Microsoft Edge in Windows:

Safari on Mac:

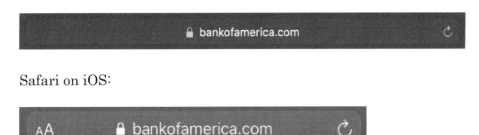

Safari on iOS:

Brave on Android:

This indicates two important things.

1. The URL you typed in was proven to be delivered from the server that has that domain. This is a little hard to understand, but when you want to go to Chase Bank to do your banking, and type "chase.com" into your browser, somebody could intercept that request and pretend to be the same website. Then they can try to trick you into giving them your login credentials. This lock and https indication means that you really went to "chase.com," but it does not prove that JP Morgan Chase Bank owns that website. We will discuss this more.

2. The connection to the Chase Bank server is encrypted, so nobody else can see the information you see or send. They also cannot modify anything without you knowing.

This is all done with something called SSL/TLS certificates. There is a lot going on with them in the background, but it is important you look for the lock and https indicators. If your browser ever gives you a warning that there is something wrong with the website certificate, then stop. Do not click Continue Anyway. Recheck that you have the right URL (i.e., chase.com), and if you do, something is wrong. Call the website owner or wait until they fix it.

Big-Time Red Flag

Links do not have to show their URL or even be text. For example, icons and pictures can have links embedded such that if you click them, they take you to another webpage. Even if a link looks like a link, say www.google.com, what is displayed doesn't have to be the actual URL and clicking could take you to another webpage. Before clicking any links, make a habit of hovering your mouse over it and the real link will be displayed in the bottom left of your browser. If the URL listed there is different than you expect, this is a huge red flag that clicking this link is a bad idea.

Web Addresses and Domains

Unfortunately, knowing about the lock is not enough. You also must know what the heck the lock means. For example, Google's website is www.google.com. To get your browser to show the lock, Google must prove to somebody called a certificate authority (CA) that they own the domain www.google.com. I will spare the details of what that takes, but when done, the CA issues Google a digital certificate that they can install on their servers. When your browser goes to that domain, it downloads the certificate and does a couple of things. One, through some cryptographic magic, the certificate confirms to your browser that you are indeed communicating with www.google.com as opposed to somebody pretending to be at that domain. Then your browser and the Google server set up the HTTPS session where both sides can encrypt all the communications between them.

Sounds good, right? Well, the problem is that a bad actor can register the www.goog1e.com (the *l* is replaced by a 1) domain, go to a CA and prove that it belongs to them, and get a certificate. If you click a link to www.goog1e.com or somehow mistype that, then the browser will show the lock and you could easily think that you are visiting Google's website when a bad actor is now downloading malware to your computer. Or they make their website look just like Google's, and they try to trick you into giving them your Google credentials.

The lock only means that if you know the right address to a website you trust and you type the address in correctly, then you have a secure connection. When we talk about spotting something suspicious in a link or an email, we must understand what makes up a web address (often called the URL, for *universal resource locator*). The following illustrates the parts of a URL:

protocol://subdomain.seconddomain.topdomain/pathname/filename.ext /sometimes crazy stuff

Protocol: There are several protocols, but the ones you see surfing the web will be either *http* or *https*. You only get the lock if the website you go to supports https.

Top-level domain: the most common by far is .com, but most of us are also familiar with .net, .gov, .edu, .org, and .mil. Since 2013, hundreds have been added such as .io, .biz, and .info. There might also be country codes such as .ca (Canada), .de (Germany), etc. The tricky ones are country codes with ".co" in front. .co.uk is a common example.

Second-level domain: This is the part that most of us will recognize as the most important identifier in a web address. Google or Amazon is the second-level domain in google.com or amazon.com respectively.

Domain: The top- and second-level domains combined. So google.com or amazon.com are registerable domains. This is the most critical part to understand because this is what the lock proves.

Subdomain: The most common subdomain is *www*, but it could be anything. Common examples are *aws* in aws.amazon.com or *mail* in mail.google.com.

Pathname: As we know, most websites have multiple pages. The pathname tells your browser what page of the website to put you on. Of course, if nothing is listed, then you are on the Home page.

Filename: This is only shown if you are literally trying to read a file from the website you are on.

Crazy stuff: There is a lot of legitimate, cool stuff that can happen here, but one example is if you go to Google's website and do a search. As soon as you hit Enter, a new page will load. The address will still start with https://www.google.com/search? and then have a seemingly random string of characters. This is how your browser is telling Google to return the results of your search. In this case, the crazy stuff is good. It can sometimes be an indicator of bad.

Here is an example web address showing Google's Gmail inbox with a specific email open:

At this point, you are probably thinking, "Why wasn't I protected by this part by the 'Nerd Alert!'?" Well, because knowing this stuff can help you stay out of trouble, and that is the point of this book.

The most important part to pay attention to in the address is the second-level and top-level domain combination. I will generically refer to this combination as the *domain*. Look for the very first single forward slash (/) and find the second- and top-level domain combination to the immediate left. If there is no forward slash, then find the rightmost parts, so *google.com* or *amazon.com*, for example. The domain is the critical part of a URL when determining if the lock means anything.

The person or organization that owns the domain must prove that they have control of any websites at that domain to get a certificate and therefore get the lock. Again, I refer to the domain as the combination of the top-level and second-level domains. Most of us would realize that www.goog1e.com (the number 1 instead of the letter *l*) is not the Google website. However, www.google.com is not the same as www.google.fr. This may be confusing because if you go to those two sites, you get to Google. However, that is because Google registered and owns both domains. A better example might be www.whitehouse.gov versus www.whitehouse.com. The former is the official US presidential propaganda machine, and the latter is an unsecure site that has this tiny disclaimer:

We are not affiliated or endorsed by U.S. Government.

Another example is www.facebook.com versus www.facebook.fr. The former is the legit site; the latter gets this warning:

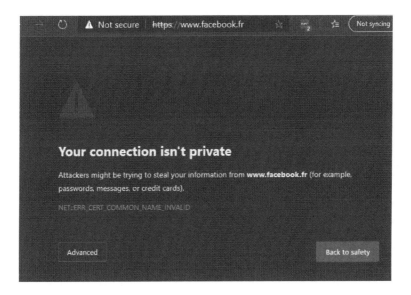

Apparently, facebook.uk is for sale and facebook.cm redirects to seemingly random offerings (some pornographic) at the time I am writing this.

As common thing that scammers will do is register a domain with a trusted second-level but use the top-level .cm. The country code for Cameroon is .cm. Bad actors know that when typing the address we trust, we will accidently type ".cm" instead of ".com" If whoever has facebook.cm wanted to get a ton of Facebook credentials, they could make their site look like Facebook and probably harvest thousands of logins. Of course, Facebook would eventually get that shut down, so they are probably happy with the tons of accidental traffic they are getting now.

Once a person or organization has a domain, they can make any subdomains or paths they want. Most of the time, the www subdomain simply takes you to the same website as the main domain. For example, www.google.com and google.com take you to the same website because Google set it up that way. They do not have to, but the point is that Google owns the domain. Therefore they can add any subdomain they want, and any subdomain can be assigned to a different website. A legitimate example here would be www.gmail.google.com, where millions of people get their email instead of doing a search at www.google.com.

Let us say I got the domain jokey.com and wanted to trick people that come to my website. I could create a subdomain like google.jokey.com or gmail.jokey.com or even layers of subdomains like www.gmail.google.jokey.com. You can see how somebody not paying attention might think they are going to their Gmail account. I can also use the paths to try a similar trick, for instance, www.jokey.com/google/gmail. Therefore, I emphasize being able to identify the domain.

To put a real-world example to it, let us talk about Equifax again. If it is not obvious, Equifax screwed up constantly both during and after their breach. After their massive breach became public, they repeatedly tweeted to go to securityequifax2017.com to learn about what you should do if you fear were a victim. However, the real website was equifaxsecurity2017.com. Keep in mind that Equifax's main website is at equifax.com. It turns out that a software engineer saw that they had taken out this entirely new domain that could be easily confused. So, to make a point, he bought the fake domain and copied their website. Then, whoever was doing the tweets at Equifax got confused somehow and tweeted out the fake address. The fake site got over two hundred thousand hits before it was taken down. The article covering this in the *New York Times*[2] asked a security expert if they could have done something better. He said they should have used a subdomain of equifax.com so people could see that Equifax owned it. If anybody at Equifax reads this book, I suggest: wesuck.equifax.com.

One thing that hoses up the ability to check out the domain is a URL shortening service. These services give people the ability to take an exceptionally long URL and reduce it to a short one that is easier to handle, especially in something like a text message. Of course, bad guys can disguise their URL doing this. The most popular one is Bitly, but others include Rebrandly, TinyURL, and others. As an example, I went to Bitly's website and entered a Google search result for the White House. I got back https://bit.ly/37HcRSm. The way to find the real URL without going there is to copy that and put it in a browser address bar and add a "+" to the end. You are taken to the Bitly website and shown the actual link. You must be careful, because it is easy to accidently click it instead of copying it and to hit Enter instead of adding the "+" once you get it into the browser bar. Here is the same one for TinyURL, https://tinyurl.com/y5werfrg, and they work the same way. It is probably best to only click shortened links when you trust whoever sent you the link.

Email

Email is, by far, the most effective way for bad guys to get malware on your computer. According to the Verizon 2019 Data Breach Report,[1] the median company received over 90% of their detected malware through email. The Verizon report is specifically investigating businesses, but the point is that employees using email are the biggest cyber threat businesses face. You do not want to be patient zero for a malware infection at work, and all the lessons are the same for your home system. The two ways email can deliver malware are through enclosures and links to bad sites.

As you know, we can use email to send each other virtually any file or program that resides on our computers through enclosures. The enclosure could be an executable (.exe, .dll, .vba extensions) that is the malware itself. Because this is the most straightforward method, this used to be the most common technique. However, it is generally the easiest for antivirus programs to catch. Enclosures can also be documents, spreadsheets, presentations, pictures, or videos that are infected with malware. This is much easier to hide from antivirus programs and therefore is now the most common method.

Email can also have links to websites that when clicked, download malware to your computer. One clue can be to hover your mouse over the link and look at the bottom left corner of your browser or email window. The actual web address of the link is displayed. If the link says it is a site you trust, but then when you hover, the actual link is something else, then this is a dead giveaway that the link is bad.

The primary thing to keep in mind here is that you should never open an enclosure or click a link in an email that you do not trust. Make sure the email is from somebody you know, and even then, if you are not expecting it, pick up the phone and call them. "Hey, Bob, did you send me that 'How to Enlarge Your Penis' Email?"

We are focusing here on malware delivery. Email is also great for scams of all kinds. You can get fake emails that are supposedly from your bank, Google, the FBI, the IRS, your boss, the CEO, or your company, and from Nigerian princes. We will cover all kinds of email scams in the chapter on scams, but here we discuss some technical indicators of a fake email.

First, and just like with websites, you can look at the domain of an email address. It turns out they are connected. When Google registered the website google.com, they also got the rights to use @google.com for their email addresses. Notice it is generally much easier to see the domain in an email address because it is simply whatever is after the @ symbol. If you get an email from somebody claiming to work at Google and their email ends @google.com, then that confirms that the email did come from a Google account. It is not the end-all tell, unfortunately, because it could also be that somebody at Google had their email compromised.

In Gmail, there is a chevron (down arrow thing) at the top of the email by the sender address that you can click for details.

 Google Analytics <analytics-noreply@google.com> Unsubscribe

to me ▼

Here are the details of an email I pulled out of my spam box that claimed to be from Google:

from: vancannon <AAT91D5SF9KRJFS81B3M@aat91d5sf9krjfs81b3m.edu>

reply-to: bq@biopascualhaw.com,
holamundo12@yandex.com,
amendis45@yandex.com,
bq@quechuaua.club,
3032716965@qq.com,
db@hingwangnong.best,
holamondo@foxmail.com,
3485906504@qq.com,
holamundo94@protonmail.com,
holamondo.fred@vp.pl,
alljust4u@asia.com,
alljust4u@usa.com,
holamondo@mail.com,
bq@chinafendamental.club,
sfsdfsfqsdfq@yandex.ru,
mz@amendis.co.uk,
tk@honkongchiflo.club,

to: "97,190.ci45.inbox@amfd02.alpha-mail.net> <"
<vancannon@i3u0s.18kxm.s00ob.__rand>

date: Jan 24, 2020, 6:45 PM

subject: Suspicious connection to ███████████ {My actual email}

security: topukmarket.club did not encrypt this message Learn more

The "from:" field: The address has a form of my name and then has a ridiculous email address. Obviously, I did not send myself this email, and if I had, I would not have sent it from that email address. In general, the name can be anything the scammer wants it to be, but the email address with it is more difficult to spoof. Make sure the email makes sense and pay particular attention to the domain. Legitimate email domain examples would be @netflix.com, @paypal.com, @amazon.com, and the like. Look for suspicious characters or added words. Not @paypal-compliance.com, for example.

The "reply-to:" field: Should be the same as the "from:" This spam has a big list of nonsense email addresses.

The "to" field: Should be to me, not another list of crazy email addresses. Notice there is one with a form of my name, but then a ridiculous domain after the "@."

The "security" field: Unfortunately, whether the email was encrypted is not a good indicator of fraud, but the fact that the "topukmarket.club" is mentioned as the one who should have encrypted this email but is not same as the sender is a good indicator of fraud.

The "mailed by" and "signed by" fields: Are missing. They should be from the email provider. If another Gmail user sent this email, these fields would say "gmail.com." If it was a Hotmail user, it would say "hotmail.com," and if it came from a business, it would be the business domain. On this last one, if a Google employee sent it, their email would be joe@google.com, and these fields would say "google.com."

Contrast this to a legitimate email from Google:

from:	Google Analytics <analytics-noreply@google.com>
reply-to:	Google Analytics <analytics-noreply@google.com>
to:	▉▉▉▉▉▉▉▉▉▉▉▉▉ {My actual email}
date:	Jan 15, 2020, 9:49 AM
subject:	$150 Google Ads credit from Analytics, just for you
mailing list:	<8cdcb30347beda7d3f5c060e8e49087653116b72.googl e.com> Filter messages from this mailing list
mailed-by:	scoutcamp.bounces.google.com
signed-by:	google.com
unsubscribe:	Unsubscribe from this mailing list
security:	Standard encryption (TLS) Learn more

Microsoft's Outlook does not make it as easy to see the email details as Gmail, but still look at the sender email address and that the "to:" field is you and your email address.

Peer-to-peer (a.k.a. Torrenting)

Using a peer-to-peer (p2p) network is often called *torrenting*. If you do not know what torrenting is, then you probably are not doing it. But there is a chance somebody in your household is. It is most often used to download music, videos, and games illegally. Napster was the original music p2p sharing platform and was shut down years ago because most of the music was protected by copyright.

Bypassing the Firewall

Most of the time when you download something from the internet, you are downloading the entire file from one server (big computer). For example, if you watch a video on YouTube or Netflix, they have a big server farm somewhere, and one of those servers is delivering that video to your computer. P2p file sharing works slightly differently in that there is no central server providing everybody the files. Instead, your computer and many "peers" (other people with a home computer) create a torrent network. The files are all broken into smaller pieces, and then you download all the pieces from several different peers. To be a good member of this network, your computer is also uploading these file pieces to other computers. It is an extremely efficient way to distribute large files to many people, and the technology itself is not illegal. Governments, universities, and corporations can use closed p2p networks to take advantage of their efficiency. However, they are simply a bad idea on the internet when you do not know who is on the other side.

Torrenting requires a program (called a client) on your computer, and the most popular ones are uTorrent, BitTorrent, qBittorrent, Vuze, and Deluge. There are also websites that serve as the basis for all this, and they are often shut down by authorities somewhere and restarted somewhere else. The Pirate Bay is the most popular one, but there are also RARBG, 1337X, ExtraTorrent, Zoogle, TorrentDownloads, and the list goes on.

The first thing to worry about is that it is illegal to download copyrighted material. The Recording Industry Association of America (RIAA) and Motion Picture Association of America (MPAA) are no longer suing individual teenagers for tens of thousands of dollars as a scare tactic (yes, they did this),[3] but they are still cracking down through something called *copyright trolls*. Copyright trolls are people that make money by suing huge numbers of people for copyright infringement. They are overly aggressive and often intimidate people into settling out of court because people are embarrassed, do not know their rights, and/or cannot pay for lawyers. If you want to learn more about the trolls, see the EFF's website: https://www.eff.org/issues/copyright-trolls.

From a security perspective, p2p networks on the internet are a disaster. For one, everybody in a p2p network can see everybody else's IP address. This is a great way for the copyright trolls, RIAA, and MPAA to find people to sue. It is also a great way for every hacker on the planet to get your IP address and probe it for any vulnerabilities. In the chapter on networking, I talk about routers and the great firewall rule. To get p2p to work, you must disable that feature through port forwarding or UPnP. Now by definition, you are downloading files from computers all over the world, defeating your own firewall, and have no idea who they are. I honestly cannot think of a better way to invite hackers into your computer and deposit whatever viruses, malware, keystroke loggers, and whatever else they can think of to infiltrate your computer and then the rest of your network.

This is an easy one! Instead of using p2p networks, go out and buy your music, TV shows, movies, and video games. It is way less expensive than lawsuits, being robbed, and identity theft.

Candy Drop

If you saw candy lying on the ground, would you pick it up and eat it? Does it depend on if the wrapper is still on? No! Well then, do not pick up a USB drive (sometimes called a thumb drive or flash drive) from the parking lot and shove it into your computer! Time to learn about a form of social engineering called the *candy drop*.

I used to have to go to military bases, and there was always a ban on people bringing floppy disks, CDs, memory cards, or USB drives into any building. Most of the computers even had the CD readers removed and USB ports epoxied over. The reason is because one day at some base somewhere, a hacker threw a bunch of USB drives into the parking lot. People who worked on the base picked them up, walked into the building, and shoved them right into their computers. Of course, they had malware on them.

Hackers call this attack a *candy drop*, and it is my absolute favorite form of social engineering. *Social engineering*, as we've covered, refers to anytime hackers trick people instead of attacking computers or networks directly. I say it is my favorite not because I want anyone to be harmed, of course, but because it plays so well to human nature. The excuse most people have for putting these drives in their computers is that they want to see if there is any information that will help them return the drive back to the original owner. That is usually partly true, but we all know they were looking for embarrassing pictures. You know it is true!

This attack has been around for a while but is still highly effective. A study by some people at the University of Illinois, University of Michigan, and Google dropped 297 flash drives around the Illinois campus. Of those, 135 (45%) of the flash drives "called home," meaning the researchers could tell the drives were plugged into internet-connected computers and a file opened by a person. And 98% of the drives were taken.[4] This means that way more than 45% of the drives could have delivered malware (had this been their intent). This is because USB drives can deliver malware to a computer without the need for either an internet connection or a person to manually open a file.

This is how the Stuxnet malware was launched against the Iranian nuclear program. Starting in about 2005, the United States and Israeli intelligence agencies (it is widely believed, though never publicly acknowledged) created Stuxnet. Its aim was to continually propagate itself through computers and other USB drives until it could identify the specific equipment the Iranians used for purifying uranium. The entire point of using USB drives was that the final targets (the Iranian processing facilities) were not connected to the internet. Around 2010, the malware could identify that it found its targets. It then caused the nuclear centrifuges to spin out of control until they broke, but at the same time, report to the equipment operators that everything was normal. Stuxnet took down an estimated 20% of Iran's centrifuges.[5]

Let us be clear. If the NSA is after you, this book will be virtually worthless. But for the rest of us, keep unknown candy out of your mouth and USB drives out of your computer.

References:

[1] https://enterprise.verizon.com/resources/reports/2020-data-breach-investigations-report.pdf

[2] https://www.nytimes.com/2017/09/20/business/equifax-fake-website.html?auth=login-email&login=email

[3] https://www.eff.org/wp/riaa-v-people-five-years-later

[4] https://elie.net/publication/users-really-do-plug-in-usb-drives-they-find/

[5] https://en.wikipedia.org/wiki/Stuxnet

10

SCAMS

An Explosion of Dirty, Rotten Scoundrels

This is the chapter where we bring it all together. To identify and understand the scams, you had to know how scammers break your passwords, look you up on social media, dig through your trash, and infiltrate your computer. You also must know what the various forms of social engineering are, and even the various payment methods. It is only after knowing all of that that you can understand what the scammers are doing.

When I was in college, I would sign up for credit cards to get free T-shirts (I guess this was a thing in the early '90s?) and then cancel the card. I do not remember it hurting my credit, but it could have. In any case, I got a call one day (on my home landline from a human) telling me that I had won a trip to Florida. All I had to do to get the tickets sent to me was to pay a deposit that would be refunded later. I remember being excited, dropping the $400 check in the mail, and realizing it was a scam several months later. You can be judgmental of my naivete, but it can happen to anybody.

As a matter of fact, being overconfident and thinking "this can't happen to me" might be the biggest threat. In a weird way, reading this book might make you more vulnerable if it makes you cocky.

I know there have always been scams out there. But between the internet, social media, smartphones, and all the breaches, bad actors have so much more opportunity. Their anonymity and reach along with their access to information are all factors driving this phenomenon. The number of scams and variations are massive, and there is no possible way I could cover all of them. The best defense is just to know that they are out there and keep your defenses up. There is no possible way I could cover all of them.

There are two basic techniques in a scam. One is to gain trust in some way. The other is to put the victim in a high-pressure fog so they cannot stop and think about what they are doing. Many scams use both techniques.

To try to establish trust, the scammer might claim to be from the government or a large well-known company, or to be a relative, coworker, church member, or any person you might defer to. If you get an email from the CEO (or pastor or relative or friend), you might not stop to think that the email is fake. I have read about church members getting scammed because a fellow churchgoer got scammed first and told the next person about the "opportunity" without yet realizing it was a scam.

Scammers want to use extreme emotions to put you in a fog where you cannot make logical decisions. They usually give their claim some sense of urgency, like you will go to jail, a loved one might be in trouble, or even the scammer needs help, if they can get you to care for them for some reason. They also like to add scarcity to the urgency. "This is a once-in-a-lifetime opportunity to buy this rare gold coin before somebody else does" is a classic one. If somebody is really putting the pressure on you, it is almost never a bad idea to step back (hang up the phone if this is the case) and think for a while. The scammer will do everything possible to keep you in the fog. Remember, if the deal is so great, the scammer should buy it. If you are going to jail, you should get off the phone and then call a lawyer.

Romance scams, which we will cover, use both trust and urgency. Maybe the scammer will spend months romancing you; then one day they are in an urgent situation and need money now.

One good source of education for a lot of different scams is the AARP. Here is the link: https://www.aarp.org/money/scams-fraud/. Unfortunately, seniors are often targets of fraud for various reasons, but any of us can fall for scams if the scammer's timing is right. I have read lately that millennials are just as likely to be scammed, just with different approaches.

In the stories on the AARP website, the victim will often talk about how they stayed on the phone with the scammer while they guided them to a store, told them how to buy gift cards, and then had the victim read the card numbers to them. I could not believe this was possible, but then it happened to my friend's parents! Or the scammer stays on the phone to guide them to the bank and initiate the wire transfer. This can often be over the course of several hours and multiple phone calls. In any case, gift cards and wire transfers are fast and untraceable, so scammers like them. Legitimate government agencies or companies will not even take gift cards or demand wire transfers.

Another source is the FBI website at https://www.fbi.gov/scams-and-safety/common-scams-and-crimes..

To determine which ones to cover here, I am starting with this list of the 2019 Top 10 scams on seniors according to the US Senate Aging Committee.[1] I will then discuss a few more scams after that.

1. Social Security impersonation scam

2. Robocalls and unsolicited phone calls

3. Sweepstakes scams

4. Romance scams

5. Computer tech support scams

6. Grandparent scams

7. IRS impersonation scams

8. Identity theft

9. Debt scams

10. Elder financial abuse

Social Security and Internal Revenue Impersonation Scams

I put these together because they are the same scam, with the only difference being which governmental agency is coming after you.

In the chapter on opening online accounts, I advise that you should open an online Social Security and IRS account before scammers do. But this is different because they are not attacking those accounts. Rather, they are trying to use the names of the government agencies to engender trust and fear to get money from you directly. These attacks are executed through robocalls, email phishing, and maybe even text messages.

Regardless of the form of the message, they are often ominous, saying that there has been suspicious activity detected on your Social Security number. Or that you owe the IRS and that you could be fined, jailed, and/or have your Social Security number revoked.

Know that the SSA or IRS almost always contact you through the mail. If the issue is so extreme that something like jail is involved, they will certainly not call you ahead of time and let you know that agents are on the way to your house. The best thing to do when these calls, texts, or emails come is to ignore them, unfortunately.

Unsolicited Calls – Robot or Human

Just being called by a robot or a stranger is not a scam by itself, but over the last couple of years this has become a real menace to society. Years ago, the national Do Not Call Registry was created, and it reduced the number of telemarketing calls substantially. It is still a good idea to put yourself on there at www.donotcall.gov. Unfortunately, it only stops legitimate business from calling. Today's scammers do not care who is on the list.

I have received a crazy number of scams phone calls from people trying to sell me car warranties. I have no idea how I got on that list, and even called the dealership to accuse them of selling my information. They swear they did not, though I have my doubts. The dealer did tell me that car registration is public, so anybody can see when and what kind of car I bought. I have not investigated if that is true, so I will have to do that one day. One thing I have learned is that the scammers have an amazing operation going on, because sometimes the call is from California and sometimes it is from Florida, but most of the time they use a local phone number. They imply that they are connected to my car manufacturer by saying they are a Honda service provider, but then when I push them on that, they admit that they are not connected to Honda. When I ask them the name of their company, they are rather good at making one up or have a system, because I never get the same name. By the way, even "legitimate" third-party car warranties are scams in the sense that the premiums you pay are way too high relative to the coverage you get. Your car practically must explode the day you buy the insurance for it to be worth it.

At least the car warranty calls to me were from actual people. Robocalls have run out of control—to the tune of five billion a month.[2] Robocalls are either computer-generated or voice recordings that play when you answer the phone. No government agency is going to use robocalls to say you are going to be fined or go to jail (though they do use robocall for public service announcements like bad weather approaching). They usually use regular mail if they need to contact you, and provide numbers for you to call.

I have read about "yes" phone scams.[3] They usually start off with, "Can you hear me?" Then when you respond affirmatively, they have it recorded and try to use that recording to authorize payments for whatever they are trying to steal. The articles I have read do not give details about how hackers use your voice, so I am not sure how that works. I have had to say yes when setting up my cable (TV/internet) accounts, as well as with some financial transactions. It is just odd to me that the operator would be talking to the hacker to get to that point then not notice when the hacker played a recording to say "yes."

Some people think that they are helping the rest of us by answering and trying to waste the callers' time. I admire the sentiment, but first, if it is a robot, you are not really tying any of their resources up. Second, that is probably true of human callers, but the scammers are often trying random numbers and really like to know when one is legitimate and even better, if the person will answer. Even listening to their pitch without hanging up makes you a valuable number. A great trick on their part is to tell you if you want to be removed from their list, to type 2 on your keypad or say something. The scammers sell each other these lists of phone numbers and verified numbers with humans that answer. They are worth more even if you never get scammed! In the end by responding in any way, you get yourself put on more call lists.

The best thing to do is let any calls that you do not know or are not expecting go to voicemail. Any legitimate caller will leave a voicemail. The fake calls that do leave a voicemail are generally easy to identify once you read this book.

The first thing that makes these effective is the fact that scammers can show just about anything they want on your caller ID. Amazingly, there are services you can buy on the internet where you can input the fake caller ID number. You can even have it say "IRS" or "Suburban Police," providing credibility to those of us that do not know this. Scammers can show a local number even if they are from a foreign country. There have even been reports that some put your number in the caller ID just because that sparks enough curiosity to get you to answer. "Hey, how am I calling myself?"

The phone carriers might help by putting up "Possible Scam" on caller ID but are pathetic about it. As far as they are concerned, they get paid for calls by the scammers just like any other customer, so have no financial motivation to stop them. However, the government signed the Telephone Robocall Abuse Criminal Enforcement and Deterrence (TRACED) Act in late 2019.[2] It puts the telecoms on the hook to work together to implement technology to stop caller ID spoofing and gives the FCC some power to go after the scammers themselves. It is believed, however, that many of the scammers are overseas, so we will probably have to wait until the anti-caller ID spoofing technology comes out to really be able to stop this craziness.

Phone companies are slowly rolling out a technology called the SHAKEN/STR protocol that will slow or stop caller ID spoofing.[4] They could have done this years ago, but, as I mentioned, they make money off the scammers, too, so they are in no hurry. It will literally take another act of Congress to force the phone companies to implement this.

Nigerian Prince email and Sweepstakes Scams

The Nigerian legal code section 419 apparently defines fraud, and since this type of scam originated there, it is often called *419 fraud*. Today any scams run by Nigerians are known as 419 fraud.

The original scheme was something along the lines of a Nigerian prince that needed to smuggle his fortune out of the country because his government was being overthrown. He needed to deposit the fortune in your bank account until the coast was clear, and then when he got out safely, he would claim his fortune. But he would leave a sizable bit of it in your account as gratitude. Of course, the scam was that they got your bank account information, and instead of making a massive deposit, they made a withdrawal.

The sweepstakes scam is the exact same idea. You won a gazillion dollars from someplace you have never heard of, but you need to send them a check to cover transfer fees, taxes, prove it is you, or anything they can imagine.

Other variants might be a United States IRS or FBI agent charged with helping the prince escape, so he does not have access to the money. But if you send some of your money, then they can get it freed up.

The question you should always ask yourself is, if they have millions, why do you need to send them a check? I do not know who falls for these scams, but the fact that they have been going on for so long tells me that enough people do to keep them going.

You can see below one I recently dug out of my Gmail spam folder. They are trying to convince me to send $120 to get my $4.5 million. Notice the warning Google is giving me at the bottom of the email.

--

The Economic and Financial Crimes Commission (EFCC)

Urgent Attention:
I am , Ibrahim Magu the acting Chairman of the EFCC in conjunction with International Police, The Economic and Financial Crimes Commission (EFCC.We got a report from director of UBA bank in Nigerian, person of Mr.Kennedy Uzoka/Mr. Morgan Daniel. The Economic and Financial Crimes Commission (EFCC) is a Nigerian law enforcement agency that investigates financial crimes such as delayed transaction, abandoned fund etc. The EFCC was notified that sum of 4,500,000:00 USD is being pending on your data and will be confiscated in next few days if you the beneficiary failed to claim it. He informed us that you have not claimed your fund yet. He claimed that you refused to come up with $120 needed for the transaction to be completed. However, we only heard from him, therefore we really want to hear from you as well to know exactly what transpired between you and UBA CEO Mr.Kennedy Uzoka and why you did not claim the fund up till now. We will like you to explain to our humble understanding as soon as possible why haven't have the fund in your possession. As you can see we're already on this issue and will see to successful end of it this time, we have not come for threaten or arresting anybody yet but to settle the case amicably so we will appreciate it if you honor us, I assure you we will definitely come to resolution point of the whole matter.

Mr. Ibrahim Magu
Economic and Financial Crimes Commission - EFCC

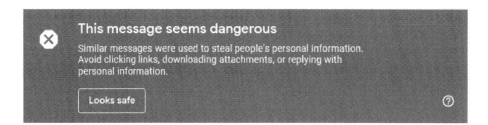

This message seems dangerous

Similar messages were used to steal people's personal information. Avoid clicking links, downloading attachments, or replying with personal information.

Looks safe

Romance Scams

The internet can be a great way to take charge of your social life, whether looking for friendship or love, rather than relying on pure chance. It might be that the biggest threat to online dating is that you can fill the unknowns in your own mind. In real life, you can see that dude lives in his mom's basement and does not know how to use silverware. Online, he might not even have to weave you a tale; you might very well put that together in your imagination. The biggest thing with any scam is to know that they exist.

There are plenty of stories of people finding love on the internet and one of them turning out to be a con. This is often called catfishing, and there was even an MTV television show with that name where they would try to bring the people together and expose the catfish. There are two ways to look at this.

The first is if the other person does want to meet in the real world, then you must protect yourself physically. Only meet in public places, do not give them clues to where you live, the same advice that anybody should heed whether you meet the person online or at the grocery store. I have no good advice on when you can start to trust the other person in this case other than to always be on the lookout for things that do not make sense or conflict.

The other way to look at this is if the other person does not want to meet but at some point asks for money, the scam alerts should be blaring. The scams are everything from their business needs a bridge loan due to extraordinary circumstances, to they are stuck in a foreign country and need some cash to get out, to they have health issues and need money for that. It really does not matter what they need money for. If you have not met them in person, it is a scam.

Computer Tech Support Scams

My father-in-law has received several phone scams where they say they have noticed that his computer is running slow or has an issue and they would like to walk him through how to fix it. The first time they got him to log into his computer, and then he realized something was not right, fortunately, before he went to a website or anything. The lesson from this one is that no legitimate company (Microsoft, Dell, Apple, whatever) is going to proactively call you to help you fix your computer. NEVER.

If you have ever been surfing the web and come across a big warning like the one, then you know what this scam is. This one was put up by somebody with a brilliant grasp of the English language.

The next one is much better and is made to look like a Microsoft site. It is difficult to see in the picture, but there is no lock in the address bar (it says "Not Secure"), and the domain is "oob004.site." If you paid attention to the "Bypassing the Firewall" chapter, you can tell that isn't Microsoft's domain.

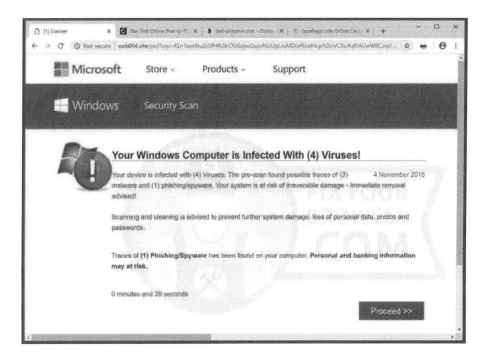

Image courtesy of www.fixyourbrowser.com

For the love of all things holy, do not click on anything or call them. They may or may not actually download a virus to your computer with this screen. But they are also trying to get you to call them so they can "help" by selling you fake software to remove this virus or even get you to download more software from them. This new software more than likely will stop the warnings, but also allow them to remotely access your computer and do whatever they want. On YouTube, there is a person that goes by the alias Jim Browning. This guy is my hero because he proactively calls these fake tech support people, and when they try to connect to his computer, he counter-attacks by installing his own remote access software on their computers! The videos of him then watching the bad guys are simply amazing. He has successfully busted a few of them even though they were in India.

Close the browser as fast as you can, but sometimes these fake sites make it impossible to close the browser window.

For Windows, my first attempt is usually **Alt+F4**, which will force the closure of whatever window is active. If that does not work, then you need to use Task Manager. To do so, type **CTRL+Alt+Delete**. The screen turns blue, and you have several options. Click on **Task Manager** then select the browser that has the locked-up window and click **End Task** in the lower right. This will kill all your browser windows, not just the bad one.

For Mac, the equivalent of the Task Manager is the Activity Monitor. Press **Command+Option+Escape** for a list of programs running, select the bad one, and then click **Force Quit** in the lower right of the window. This will kill all your browser windows, not just the bad one.

If closing the window makes the problem go away, then you are probably okay. However, if the warning keeps popping up, then they probably installed some adware on your computer despite Windows Defender (or XProtect on Mac). A good option is to try Malwarebytes. They have a powerful free adware cleaner at https://www.malwarebytes.com/adwcleaner/. Unfortunately, though, the only sure way to get rid of any malware is to reinstall your operating system.

This scam can start with a cold phone call, too, as I mentioned earlier with my father-in-law. They can say, "Hey we are from Microsoft (or Apple or such-and-such security company), and we see that your computer has a virus or is otherwise compromised, and we can help you out." Then they will tell you to just give them some information (that they can use to attack your computer remotely or for identity theft later), or even go to a website and install the remote access software I just discussed above. They might even try to guide you through your computer to "remove the virus," when they are really guiding you to open your computer for them to attack. Just hang up. No company or organization on earth will initiate the call with you to help with your computer legitimately.

Grandparent Scams

This one is particularly evil. The scammers will often find a younger person on social media and try to figure out who their grandparents are. Then they call the grandparents and pretend to be their grandchildren in trouble and desperately needing money.

Think about this possible scenario. The kid posts on Facebook that he cannot wait to go to spring break in Mexico with his best buddy Joe. And of course, he provides details on where they are staying and how they are getting there. In the meantime, Grandpa is probably vaguely aware of the trip and that punk Joe that is always getting his grandchild into trouble.

One night, grandpa gets a call from his hysterical grandchild that he and Joe were partying on vacation in Mexico and got pulled over and given a DUI. He pleads with grandpa not to tell his parents and send money now. Then the call is taken over by a supposed police officer or defense attorney to corroborate the story and guide Grandpa on the payment.

If you are Grandpa reading this, then the best thing to do while on the line is just have Grandma call your grandson's phone. He will probably be fine and wonder why you are calling him on vacation. If that fails, hang up and call his parents. Let them deal with it if it is true. You have done your part in life.

General Financial Scams

The scam list has identity theft, debt scams, and elder financial abuse listed separately, but they all seem like variants to me. They are all different ways scammers try to get bank account, credit card, mortgage, estate, Medicare, Social Security, or tax information from the victim and then either steal their identity, drain their accounts, or con them out of money outright.

The scammers might claim that you or a relative owe a big bill and need to pay it now. They might claim to help you with debt consolidation or "notice" that there is something wrong with one of your accounts and if you provide the information and/or a payment, they will take care of it for you.

The *elder abuse* variant often is somebody who knows the victim and has a lot of information already, like what assets they have and how to manipulate them. They often also have the advantage of trust as it can be a family member or home care provider. There is not much information I can provide in a bad situation like this.

Overpayment Check Scams

I have personal experience with this one. In 2018, a coworker of mine got a message from a LinkedIn connection about a marketing side job. He investigated it because the message came from somebody he knew. The idea was to be something like a secret shopper and write up reviews. Since he wrote the company press releases, this type of thing was right down his alley, so he investigated it. They said to start out, he needed to buy an iPhone (I have no idea why), but not to worry because they would send him a check to cover his expenses. He gave them his address and waited for the check.

In the meantime, his friend on LinkedIn sent a note telling everybody that her account was hacked and that the marketing gig was a fraud. The checks that he ended up getting were on the order of $2,000, which even though iPhones are disgustingly expensive, was double what one costs. It was very curious because the checks looked entirely legitimate. The scammers, not knowing the gig was up, then sent my coworker a message that they had indeed messed up and sent too much, but to go ahead and cash the checks, buy an iPhone, and send them a check for the excess.

At this point, since my coworker had been warned, he investigated the scam and found out that this is somewhat common. Had he cashed the check, his bank would have deposited the money into his account. It would look as good as the rest of the money in his account. The scammers hoped that he would send a real check to them for $1,000 (whatever the difference was), and they would be quick to cash it. The scammers' check would, of course, bounce, but it takes a couple of weeks or more for the average bank to figure it out. When they did, my coworker would have been liable for the entire $2,000.

In the chapter on payments, I discuss how the delay in verifying checks (it does not matter if they are personal or cashier's checks or money orders) has been used for scams for decades.

Variations of this include getting a check in the mail and a letter explaining that you won a foreign lottery, government grant, or scholarship and you need to send money back for taxes and fees.

Just keep in mind that nobody is sending you a check for no good reason. Did I really have to say this out loud?

Mortgage Scams

This is a big-time scam that can be life impacting.

Say a hacker can break into a mortgage company, brokerage, or real estate lawyer's email account and monitor emails. They can then watch for people who are about to close on a house, and when it comes time to send the down payment, they swoop in. They use the actual email account of the person they broke into and tell the home buyers where to send the down payment, complete with account details, almost certainly by wire transfer. The timing of the email might be before the real transfer email, in which case, the bad guys are trying to get your money before the transaction should happen, but more likely, they will wait until the real email goes out. Then the bad guys create a fake email saying that the first one was wrong, or that the details changed, and because of the delay, it is urgent that the payment be made immediately, or the house will not close.

There are several things to point out here. The first point is that it uses the business email compromise attack that we discussed in the social engineering chapter, where hackers break into legitimate email accounts and use them to gain the trust of employees or customers. The second thing is that it relies on wire transfers. In the chapter on payments, we discussed that banks use this method because it is fast and almost irreversible. Banks use this for most mortgage down payments to ensure they cannot be scammed. Unfortunately, this is also ideal for scammers to receive funds. Finally, scammers love it when there is a lot on the line and they can pressure you into action without thinking. People do not buy houses very often, so they have no idea what is normal, and there is a lot of emotion to take advantage of.

To protect yourself, the most important thing is when it comes time to send the down payment; do not trust any email. Call the business that sent the details using a known phone number, or better yet, drive to the place of business and get the transfer details directly. If something changes or is "urgent," be especially vigilant in verifying that it is a legitimate change. Also, I said wire transfers are almost irreversible. If you can notify your bank of fraud fast enough, then they might be able to reverse the transfer. How fast it needs to be, I do not know, but every minute counts in this situation.

Money Mules

When bad guys steal money or goods, they need to hide the trail to them. After all, if they buy something illegally and have it sent to their house, then it is easy for the police to figure out where to go.

If we are talking money, they are trying to send you stolen money and then have you send them a prepaid card or wire transfer—the untraceable and irreversible payments, of course. If we are talking about stolen goods, they want you to receive the packages at your house and then reship them, often to another country. These might be goods they stole directly, but they could also be goods bought with stolen credit cards.[5]

We talked about romance scams where the bad guys are conning you out of your money, but they could meet you the same way and then start sending you money and having you resend it. They might even let you keep some of it, initially anyway.

With the COVID pandemic came millions of layoffs. What a great opportunity for scammers. They could make this sound like a job offering, and now you are often receiving money or goods and sending them somewhere else. They will use you and maybe even pay you a bit, but because it is a "job," they can ask for your Social Security and bank account numbers to "prove eligibility" or for "direct deposit" of your paychecks. When they are done with you, then they can steal your identity and try to drain your bank account. What a holiday bonus!

Pharmaceutical Scams

Brian Krebs wrote a book call *Spam Nation* where he tells the story of the Russian underground that flooded the world with fake Viagra and penis enlargement emails. They made untold millions, and many of them operate to this day.

I worked at a cybersecurity firm that did research to create tools called *secure email gateways* and *secure web gateways*. Companies buy these to protect employees' email and web browsing, respectively. Without a doubt, many spam emails and scam websites are for cheap drugs.

That these are so successful probably says something about our society, but I will avoid that discussion here. All I have to say is there is absolutely no quality guarantee on any of these drugs. Some may be the real thing smuggled right off the real assembly lines, others may be knock-offs in some dirty factory, and some may be outright fakes. There is no way to know, and using these is gambling with your life.

Sextortion

In 2015 a website name Ashley Madison was breached. Most of the users' real names, emails, home addresses, search history, and credit card transaction history was stolen and eventually showed up on the dark net. Ashley Madison was a website that enabled extramarital affairs (as if you did not know). There was intent by several people and even organizations to use this data to blackmail the website customers. It is unclear how many were blackmailed, but I am sure there were quite a few people sweating this one out.

As mentioned in the first chapter on passwords, there have been so many breaches of usernames and passwords, that bad actors can use that information for other blackmail. One of them is to send an email to a potential victim and claim to have hacked their computer. They show the victim the breached username and password to "prove" they hacked their computer, then proceed to tell them that they turned on their video camera and recorded them watching porn and masturbating at the same time. Of course, the blackmail is that they will release the video to their spouse or publicly if the victim does not pay, usually in Bitcoin. In theory, this hack is possible, but more likely it is just a scam. In either case, paying the blackmail is only going to encourage the bad actors to come after you again. Once they see you are willing to pay $1,000, why not ask for $2,000 next week? It is not a good idea to pay scumbags here because, well, they are scumbags.

Ransomware

Ransomware is a computer program that finds all the files on your computer and encrypts them. You can see them sitting there, but you can't open them…because they are encrypted. Then the ransomware shows a big banner that says your files have been encrypted and the only way to get them decrypted is to pay the bad guys, usually in bitcoin. This is a disaster.

Most of us don't have bitcoin setup, so we would have to figure that out. Then there is the issue of if you even bother. If you pay them $1000, then they can come back and say they were kidding, it is now $2000. They are scammers after all. Many businesses quietly pay when it happens to them. The FBI wishes nobody paid, because it obviously encourages more of this, but they can't tell somebody who will go out of business otherwise not to pay.

The best way to handle ransomware is to not be a victim in the first place. By a mile, a phishing email is the #1 way of getting ransomware, either because you download an attachment or click a link that downloads it. A far second place is you come across a bad link in your regular internet browsing and download it that way. This is usually done on shady sites and/or clicking on ads. In the Technical and Advanced sections, I offer several technical layers of defense for malware. Implement as many of them as you can.

PayPal Scams

PayPal is so ubiquitous today for online payments that there are bound to be scams involved. We will start with those that are not even due to the payment system itself, but rather scams that could involve any payment system. The PayPal website lists many common email scams,[6] but remember, they could be texts or any other communication.

<u>Advanced fee</u>. For this one, refer to the Nigerian prince/lottery scams. You are told that there is a fortune just waiting for you, but first send a fee through PayPal to get the money freed up. You send the money and never hear from them again.

<u>High-profit, no-risk investments</u>. Exact same as above, send us money, you will never hear from us again.

<u>Fake charities</u>. Often people take advantage of disasters and send out emails, texts, and the like asking for money—pay with PayPal! If you want to give to a cause, do not respond to the solicitations directly. Investigate charities through other channels. Here are some resources:

http://www.charitynavigator.org
http://www.bbb.org/us/charity
http://www.charitywatch.org

<u>You have been paid</u>. You sell something online, and the buyer claims they paid you. Do not take their word for it. Check your account for the actual payment before you ship.

<u>You have been paid too much</u>. This is just like the check overpayment scam. You sell something, and the buyer "accidently" sends a PayPal payment for more than you asked and then sends an email and wants you to wire the extra amount back. Chances are the buyer was able to hack somebody's PayPal account and is trying to buy stuff with it and get some cash too. The problem for you is that once the real owner figures it out, they will complain to PayPal and have the charges reversed. You will be out the merchandise, PayPal payment, and money you wired. It is rare people will overpay, so if this happens, do not send the merchandise. Refund their entire payment and find a new buyer.

There is a variant to this where the bad guys not only hacked a PayPal account, but one of your friend's Facebook, WhatsApp, email, or text accounts. Pretending to be your buddy, they tell you their PayPal account is somehow broken, but they just sold something and need to take payment. They then send a payment from the hacked PayPal account to yours. You see the payment and wire the bad guys' bank account (though you think it is your friend). The bad guys have the money at this point, and later, the legitimate owner of the PayPal account has PayPal reverse the charges on you.[7] If you have a buddy that asks for anything even remotely like this, give them a call and ask what the heck they are doing. There is a good chance you will be the one showing them they have been hacked.

Your account is about to be suspended (or any other issue). Any email that tries to look like it came from PayPal with warning or call to action that includes a link. When you click the link, it takes you to a fake website clone of the PayPal login page. This is a classic phishing scam, and they hope to get your credentials. Go to https://www.paypal.com/us/signin directly instead of clicking the link and check your account for any issues.

There are apparently several variations of PayPal scams involving shipping. To qualify for PayPal's Seller Protection Policy, you must ship to the address on the Transaction Details Page. (If you are selling with PayPal, I am going to assume you know what this is.) Then you must be able to prove that the goods indeed were shipped to that address. The bad guys have several ways of making it look like they did not receive the goods you sent them:

The buyer has you use their shipping account. The buyer says they can get a lower price or theirs is more reliable. They can come up with any reason why. The problem is that they then have control over where it is shipped, no matter what address you initially use, and you have no way to prove it did not get to them. Only use your own shipping company.

Pre-paid shipping label. Just like the above scam, now the buyer controls where the product is shipped, and you have no receipt that the product went to the address in the Transaction Details Page.

Package rerouting. The buyer provides a fake address and then watches the online tracking. When they see the failed delivery, they reroute it to their real address. When they enter the complaint to get the payment reversed, you cannot prove it made it to the proper address due to the reroute. Even if you can see the rerouted address, it is not the one on the Transaction Details Page. The only real advice PayPal gives is to tell your shipping company to block buyers from rerouting packages. Return them if undeliverable.

Venmo and Square Cash App Scams

These apps are only for small payments to friends and family. Using Venmo or Cash App for buying and selling goods is against their terms of use. If using these, reread that last sentence.

An interesting scam I found could, in theory, happen to any payment system on your phone, but Venmo and Cash App might be the easiest to do this through. A stranger approaches you on the street and needs to borrow your phone to make a call. They have an emergency of some kind. You unlock your phone and hand it to them. They pretend to make a call but say the person did not answer so they want to send a text. This ends up just being a cover while they open your Venmo or Cash App and send themselves some money.[8]

If somebody sends you money from their Venmo or Cash App, either out of the blue or because they have an issue with their account, and then asks for it back, they probably hacked somebody else's account or funded theirs with a stolen credit card. Either way, they get your money, and then the charges are reversed when the legitimate owner sees the fraud.

A popular scam is a variant of the advanced fee scam. The scammers will say, "If you send me money, I will send ten times the amount back." For some reason people will try it with $1 and to their amazement, get $10 back. "What the heck? It is real!" they think. Then they send $100, and it goes bye-bye.

Another one is Cash App Fridays on Twitter. These are lotteries where you play by sending a dollar. Somehow, nobody ever wins these.

Finally, neither Venmo nor Cash App have call centers. Yeah, you can Google them and find all kinds of phone numbers, but they are fake. Call one up and complain about something, and they will ask for your account number (Cash App symbol, whatever), phone number, password, and whatever else you will give them and will then go take over your account. If you need real help, use the Venmo or Cash App app and chat through it.

Scams

References:

[1] https://www.aging.senate.gov/imo/media/doc/Fraud%20Book%20%202020.pdf

[2] https://abcnews.go.com/Politics/law-robocalls/story?id=68008423

[3] https://www.usatoday.com/story/tech/talkingtech/2017/03/27/dont-say-yes-when-robocall-scam-rings/99709634/

[4] https://www.redcom.com/stir-shaken-overview/

[5] https://www.consumer.ftc.gov/blog/2020/03/whats-money-mule-scam

[6] https://www.paypal.com/us/smarthelp/article/what-are-common-scams-and-how-do-i-spot-them-faq3176

[7] https://www.forbes.com/sites/zakdoffman/2020/03/09/alarming-paypal-scam-alert-this-stupidly-simple-new-hack-puts-you-at-risk-heres-how-it-works/#7aae0b584436

[8] https://www.lifewire.com/top-venmo-scams-4782833

Technical

This section of the book is probably what you initially thought this entire book was going to be about: the technical stuff. But do not worry, most of the security features on your computer are turned on by default, and therefore most of that is informational. It might get a bit harder in the networking part but stick with it. Learn the things in this section, and you will be in better shape than all your neighbors.

By no means does "technical" mean you have to be an IT pro or software developer. If you are handy with email, word processors, and spreadsheets, you can handle this. In the Advanced section of this book, I show how to add more layers of security, but they do require more technical ability.

Some of the more technical features that I recommend will have warnings that look like this:

🚫 **MAY BREAK THINGS:** Then I try to explain what it might break.

If you see this, read through the section first, and if you think that you can handle any issues that come up, then implement it. If it seems far too complicated, then it is. Ultimately, you must be able to use your computers and smartphones. I would much rather have you implement what you are comfortable with than to have you throw your arms in the air and ignore the whole thing because one aspect drives you crazy.

What I want to impress upon you, the reader of this book, is that no technology can substitute for a careless human operator. The only way to make a computer 100% safe is to lock it down so tight that it cannot do anything: including run programs or reach the internet. You might as well buy a brick and set it on your desk if that is the intention.

11

YOUR COMPUTER
No Smart Aleck Comments

When your computer asks if something should be allowed, you must pause and think about why you were asked that and if it is what you intended. Not only do some people ignore their computer warnings, but they also often do a Google search to learn how to turn them off. Or their kid turns off the warnings because they are slowing down their mayhem. Many of the features we talk about here are simply the computer asking you if you *really* intended to do that. If you are not sure, default to "**Don't Allow**."

What About Antivirus Programs? Glad You Asked

There are several issues with antivirus programs, from the highly technical to economics.

I will spare you the details of highly technical parts, but at a high level, antivirus programs often conflict with the security measures that the operating systems have in place. Maybe the antivirus program can stop a given virus, but in doing so defeats the security measures of your browser or operating system and therefore opens other vulnerabilities. Then there is the fact that there are tens of thousands of types of malware out there with new versions every day. The antivirus companies can only respond to existing malware, not new ones they have not seen yet. Finally, viruses are only a small part of the hacking game. If you get antivirus software and then use weak passwords, for example, there is little the antivirus can do for you.

On the economics, the antivirus industry is so competitive that most companies include their own spyware to monitor you and get you to buy upgrades from them. Some even use the information to advertise to you. This practice is not only ethically questionable but also opens privacy and security issues.

Cybersecurity experts believe that keeping your software updated with the latest patches is far more important than antivirus software. Google did a survey of regular web users and cybersecurity experts.[1] They found that the regular web users believed antivirus to be the most important measure you can take to be safe online. The security researchers placed software updates as the top priority:

> 35% of experts and only 2% of nonexperts said that installing software updates was one of their top security practices. Experts recognize the benefits of updates— "Patch, patch, patch," said one expert—while nonexperts not only are not clear on them but are concerned about the potential risks of software updates. A nonexpert told us: "I don't know if updating software is always safe. What [if] you download malicious software?" and "Automatic software updates are not safe in my opinion, since it can be abused to update malicious content."

> Meanwhile, 42% of nonexperts vs. only 7% of experts said that running antivirus software was one of the top three things they do to stay safe online. Experts acknowledged the benefits of antivirus software but expressed concern that it might give users a false sense of security since it is not a bulletproof solution.

Keep all of this in mind when I recommend what to do for antivirus in each operating system. But the preview is that this book will pay for itself by allowing you to avoid paying for antivirus, let alone the better security you will have.

General Software Rules

Brian Krebs is well-known in the cybersecurity world for his investigative reporting on the latest breaches and cybercriminals. When it comes to software, Krebs lays out three rules:[2]

1. If you did not go looking for it, do not install it.

2. If you installed it, update it.

3. If you no longer need it, remove it.

The basic idea is that software often creates a way for attackers to get into your computer or leaks data out to them. Let us visit each of Krebs's rules.

If You Did Not Go Looking for It, Do Not Install It

I will repeat this repeatedly. When your computer asks if you really want to download software, or allow an application access to something else, stop and think about if you even asked for it. Many times on the internet, companies or people will want to get you to install software that sounds good. Would you like this new toolbar? Would you like to be protected from viruses? Would you like this alternative search engine? If you were not out looking for it, the answer is almost surely no. Later, we discuss Windows UAC and/or Mac Gatekeeper, which provide these warnings when software is about to be installed. No really, are you sure?

Update It (The Race You Did Not Know You Were Losing)

There is an entire ecosystem of researchers (software manufacturers themselves, universities, private individuals, cybersecurity companies, nonprofits, and governments) looking for security vulnerabilities in software on every computer, phone, and device out there. A vulnerability is any way a criminal could take control of the device and/or access the information on it. The idea is to find vulnerabilities before the bad guys do. There are several organizations that track and maintain databases on security vulnerabilities. Two of the best known are OWASP and MITRE, both nonprofits.

Ideally, when vulnerabilities are found, the software manufacturers are quietly told about them to give them a chance to fix the issue. There is usually a deadline for when the vulnerability will be announced, so they have a sense of urgency. The specific software company may be able to negotiate the deadline if they can show a good-faith effort that they are working on it. However, the vulnerability is usually published at some time, and the software manufacturers may or may not have a patch by the time the vulnerability is disclosed.

Hackers are constantly scanning the internet to "fingerprint" your system. They are looking for the type of computer you have, the operating system, and what applications you use, and cataloging it. Sometimes this is detectable directly because that information is sent over the internet and some information is discovered indirectly, say by the protocols being used or how they are implemented.

This is the crazy part. When a vulnerability is published by the "good guys," there is a race between the bad guys and the rest of us. The bad guys are trying to exploit the vulnerability before we get our software patched. The problem with this race is that most of us have no idea it is going on! The way to "win" is to enable auto-updates on your software. The operating system, browsers, and all applications running on your computers, phone, and devices all need to be set to auto-update.

If You No Longer Need It, Remove It

Finally, even if old software does not end up becoming a security concern, it can slow down your computer and waste hard drive space. It is good hygiene to clear out programs that you no longer use. Some software once popular but now riddled with vulnerability software includes Java, Adobe Flash, Adobe Shockwave, Adobe Reader, and Microsoft Silverlight.

A bit of a warning here. The internet is filled with programs that say they can clean your computer or fix all your registries and restore your old performance. I have never seen these tools make an improvement in performance, and they are often outright scams. If your computer is running slowly and you suspect it is because of all the old programs and changes they made over time, then I recommend reinstalling the OS.

When you buy legitimate software, make sure you keep the media or more likely today, the access keys, so that you can download and reinstall it later. Then, if you want to try to restore your computer performance with a cleaning, you can reinstall Windows or macOS from scratch and then reinstall the software you need.

Getting Rid of Computers

Do not throw away, give, or sell your computer without thinking about the sensitive information on it. Your entire browsing history might be in it, along with credentials for email and social media sites. A lot of important old documents and photos are probably on there. All your contacts may be in there, so a bad guy can impersonate you to try to scam them.

It is critical to know that it is not enough to delete files. The first problem is that files you delete are simply pushed to the Recycle or Trash bin. You might think that emptying the trash would delete them forever, but it's not so. Your computer only deletes the file name from the directory, but the actual file is still there. There are many programs out there that can find old files and restore them on your computer. This is a godsend if you want to retrieve the files one day, but it is also a major security issue.

Additionally, even if the computer does not work, a hacker can pull your drive out, connect it to his computer, and find files.

If you are going to throw your computer away or recycle it, then the easiest thing to do is open it up, find the hard drive (or solid-state drive), and smash it with a hammer. (I am not kidding.) If you happen to have encrypted your hard drive (see encrypting your drive in the PC or Mac sections later), then that is probably good enough.

In the individual chapters on Microsoft Windows and Apple Macintosh, I provide details on how to prepare your computer for selling or giving away.

Operating Systems

We are going to start by looking at the most important software on every computer, and that is the operating system. The four primary computer operating systems in the world are Microsoft Windows, Apple macOS, Google Chrome OS, and various forms of Linux.

Google's Chrome OS comes on lower-priced machines, called Chromebooks, and has a bit of a different philosophy. It is not really meant to run any programs nor save files of any substance. Rather, it assumes that you are connected to the internet and run all programs and save all files there. This inherently makes Chrome OS more secure because it cannot run malware if it is not running any downloaded programs, but this also limits them a bit for home use. For example, a Chromebook is worthless if your internet connection goes down.

Chromebooks (laptops that run Chrome OS) are popular in education, at least in the K-12 levels because of their lower prices, higher security, and the assumption that the school provides all their materials online. Due to the nature of Chromebooks, I will not cover them in the Basic section of this book, but in the Advanced section, I suggest having a Chromebook dedicated as the only machine in your household used for accessing critical accounts such as banking and brokerage accounts.

Linux is incredibly popular among IT professionals, programmers, and people like that, but we will skip that entirely in this book.

Most of us deal with Windows or macOS, so we will discuss them in the next couple of chapters. If you only use Windows (PCs) then you do not need to read about Macs and vice versa.

We will discuss smartphone and tablet operating systems, of which there are two. Android by Google is about 85% of the market, and iOS (and iPadOS) by Apple has the other 15%. If you only use one of these, then you can skip the chapter on the other.

References:

[1] https://security.googleblog.com/2015/07/new-research-comparing-how-security.html

[2] https://krebsonsecurity.com/2011/05/krebss-3-basic-rules-for-online-safety/

12

MICROSOFT WINDOWS

How Bill Gates Implants Chips in Your Vaccine

Windows by Microsoft is by far the most common operating system on personal computers. Therefore, it is also the most attacked.

Just knowing why the heck your computer is asking you questions like, "Are you sure you want to download XYZ file?" or telling you, "Website ABC wants access to your microphone," will put you far ahead of the game. Here we are simply learning the features that are on (or should be on, in my opinion) by default and making sure your kids did not turn them off because they are "annoying."

Get to Windows 10

Windows almost always comes preinstalled on a new computer. However, in the old days, if you wanted to upgrade, you had to go buy a physical CD at the store. Updates came in the form of *service packs* and would come out every few years. Windows 10 is a new paradigm, where instead of new versions or service packs, it is constantly updated for new features and, more importantly, for security patches.

Pay attention here: Windows XP, Vista, and 7 no longer get security updates. The only way computers with these operating systems are safe is if you can disconnect them from the internet. Windows 8 (really 8.1) is still under extended support, so it is not as risky. (Note there was never a Windows 9.) In any case, I cannot stress enough that you should be on Windows 10 with the latest updates to take advantage of its built-in security features.

Here is some great news: If you are on Windows 7, 8, or 8.1, then you might still be able to upgrade to 10 for free. Fairly decent instructions are here: https://www.microsoft.com/en-us/software-download/windows10/.

If you are not sure what version of Windows you are running right now, here is how you can find out:

1. Hold down the Windows key and at the same time, press "r."

2. In the window that pops up, type "winver."

3. Another window will pop up with the Windows version you are running.

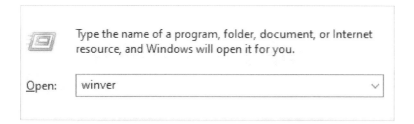

The only thing this does not tell you is how to get your current product code. You might not need it, but to be safe, make sure you can get it before you start the upgrade. Older computers have it on a shiny sticker somewhere on your computer (laptops may have it in the battery compartment) or CD box. They look like this:

An alternative to the sticker for finding the code is to look it up. This is a little technical, but doable.

1. Move your mouse to the bottom left of the screen, and in the search box, type "powershell." It should be the first match in the results.

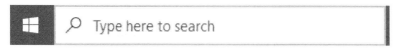

2. Click on the result. A blue window with white letters will appear. Click on it.

3. Type this obscure command into the blue window:

(Get-WmiObject -query 'select * from SoftwareLicensingService').OA3xOriginalProductKey

4. Your product key should be returned. It is twenty-five characters long and displayed as five sections with five characters in each section. Write the code down in case the Windows 10 upgrade needs it.

If you cannot get it free anymore, then consider that Windows 10 Home is $120, but a new decently-powered computer with Windows 10 already installed is $500. Economically, it probably makes sense to just get a new computer. The other aspect to consider is that an older computer (before Windows 7 for sure) may have trouble running Windows 10 and most likely not have all the hardware needed to support the new security features.

Nerd Alert! Windows Security

Microsoft was a little slow to go on the offensive, but when they built Windows Vista, security was finally a major consideration. However, attackers keep getting better and Microsoft keeps learning, so each release of Windows gets better.

The latest release is Windows 10, and it is by far the most secure. I am sure some people reading this will point out that Windows 10 has had a slew of security and general issues in 2019 [1] and continuing into 2021. This is true, but nobody would say going back to an older version is more secure.

Require Login

First, your Windows PC really should require a password when you are away. You could make an argument that a desktop that never leaves your office is safe. That is fair, but at the same time, you should be used to having to log in every time you come back to your computer at work, so it should not be a big deal. Of course, if you have a laptop that you carry out of the house, then it should be clear it needs to be protected with a login.

Windows defaults to requiring a password whenever the computer boots up or when you wake it from sleep. If you do not have this, then to turn it on:

Push the Windows button ⊞. Then click the ⚙ icon > **Accounts > Sign-In Options**. Look under "Require Sign-In" and in the drop-down box, select **When PC Wakes up from Sleep**.

Auto-Update

Keeping your operating system updated is the single most important item for security on your computer. Once you have Windows 10, it will be set to auto-update by default, and you no longer even have a choice to turn it off. To check for updates manually:

> Push the Windows button ⊞. Then click the ⚙ icon > **Update and Security**. (You will land on Windows Update.) It will indicate "You're up-to-date" unless there are pending updates waiting for you to restart your computer.

While you are here, click **Advanced Options.** Then flip the top switch that says, "**Receive updates for other Microsoft products when you update Windows**." Like it says, it will check any other Microsoft programs for updates and install them automatically too. Also flip the switch on for "**Show a notification when your PC requires a restart to finish updating**," so you know to do that.

Nerd Alert! Pause Auto-Update

The second Tuesday (and sometimes fourth Tuesday) of every month is Microsoft's Patch Tuesday. This is when Microsoft releases patches to their Windows operating system and Office suite of tools (Word, Excel, PowerPoint, etc.). On a biannual basis, they have bigger "version" releases that are named by year and month. So version 2004 was intended to be released in April 2020 (though they often come a little later than planned).

Unfortunately, these updates go wrong occasionally, and you must uninstall them to get things working again. If there is an issue with a regular Patch Tuesday update, you can uninstall them by doing the following:

Push the Windows button 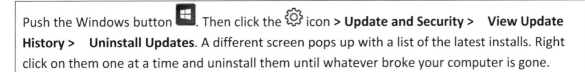. Then click the ⚙ icon > **Update and Security** >   **View Update History** >   **Uninstall Updates**. A different screen pops up with a list of the latest installs. Right click on them one at a time and uninstall them until whatever broke your computer is gone.

If one of the biannual version updates breaks your computer, then you can roll it back:

Push the Windows button . Then click the ⚙ icon > **Update and Security** >   **View Update History** >   **Recovery Options**. Under "Go back to the previous version of Windows 10" click **Get Started**. > Another screen pops up asking why you want to roll back, and you can start.

Automatic updates cannot be turned off, but they can be paused. Pausing is for when you have issues with an update and have to uninstall or roll back to a previous version. You do not want to auto-update right back to the same state that caused the problems. Fortunately, you can pause updates and hope that Microsoft fixes the issues in the meantime. There is no way to pause forever.

Push the Windows button . > Then click the ⚙ icon > **Update and Security**. Here you can pause for seven days, or click **Advanced Options > Pause Updates > Select a Date**.

Free Windows Antivirus

I railed on the antivirus industry already, but I do recommend Windows Defender. Windows Defender is the free antivirus software that comes with Windows 10, and it is on by default unless you or the computer manufacturer added a third-party antivirus. When Defender first came out, it was not as good as the third-party antivirus products, but it has since caught up.[2] So it is just as good, and free, and because it is made by the same people making the operating system, it should not conflict with other security features.

Push the Windows button . Then click the ⚙ icon > **Update & Security > Windows Security > Virus & Threat Protection** (new window pops up). Under Virus & Threat Protection settings, click **Manage Settings** and make sure all switches are on.

If you do have third-party antivirus software, I recommend uninstalling it (never run two antivirus programs at one time; they will fight each other), so it stops bugging you to buy/renew and generally wasting computer resources. To do that:

Push the Windows button . Then click the ⚙ icon > **Apps**. Scroll down until you find the third-party antivirus program and click on it. **> Uninstall**.

If it asks which things to uninstall, select every box. It will probably give warnings like, "This subscription is still active," if you are still paying for it. That is a good reminder to turn off any auto-payment you have with them.

Do Not Even Trust Yourself – Use Standard Accounts

Ⓞ **MAY BREAK THINGS:** The users that are given standard accounts might be upset that they cannot install software, make changes, or in some cases, even access some applications that the admin installs.

When you buy a computer, the makers assume that you will want the ability to do whatever you want to it. This makes sense in every way except when it comes to security and privacy.

When you initially set up your computer, you will be granted full administrative rights. This means you can install any software you want (good or bad) and can make any configuration changes you desire. However, most of the time you will not be doing these things. Most of the time you will turn your computer on to check email, surf the web, and maybe create a document or spreadsheet. In this case, you will want to restrict your own rights so you do not accidentally install malware or make configuration changes.

Beyond yourself, you might have family members or other guests using your computer. Since they are most likely computer illiterate compared to you (you are reading this book, after all) and highly likely to mess something up, it is a fantastic idea to restrict what they can do.

There are different Windows 10 accounts, and it can be very confusing because they purposely do not make it clear. First there are online versus offline accounts, and then there are administrator versus standard privileges.

Online vs. Offline Accounts

Microsoft provides a way for you to create an internet account with them and then use that account to log into your computer. This is an online account because you must have internet access to create and use it. The details of your account are in Microsoft servers somewhere. You can use this same account to log into multiple Windows computers, and if you do, some things are synchronized across those computers (the desktop background, for example, how nice). If you use any Microsoft services like Office, Outlook, Hotmail, or even Xbox, then you already have a Microsoft account.

An offline account means that no internet connection is required. It exists on a single computer and is only good for logging into that one computer. This type of account is also called a *local account.*

For consumers, these are the only two types. At work, your account could also be a *domain account* that enables you to log into other computers at your organization. But we will not worry about that here.

Administrator vs. Standard Privileges

An *administrator account* enables the user to do anything they want to the computer, from installing any software to changing critical system files and registries. If they change the wrong ones, the computer can become unstable or even useless. Administrators also have access to all the files that other users have on the computer. Administrators can add other accounts to the computer.

A *standard account* restricts what software can be installed (though not all) and cannot access or edit many critical system files and registries. A standard user can only see their own files and cannot add other accounts to the computer.

Mix and Match

Now that we defined the different account type privileges, we need to understand that a Microsoft account can exist on multiple computers and have either administrator or standard privileges on any given computer. A local account, by definition, can only exist on one computer but can also have either administrator or standard privileges.

Every computer requires at least one account with administrator privileges. This is done when Windows is first installed, and that administrator can add other accounts to the computer.

Confused? Even though I knew the basic ideas here, when I was researching this for the book, I found Microsoft's documentation to be thoroughly crappy. I had to learn mostly by trying different things. It is especially upsetting to know that they are playing games. They want every account to be a Microsoft account so they can monitor you and try to push advertising to you. How do I know this? Because when you first set up your computer, if it is connected to the internet, then you do not even get the option to create a local account. They force you to use an existing Microsoft account or create a new one. The only way for the first account (remember it must be an administrator) on the computer to be local is to disconnect the computer from the internet, create a local account, and then reconnect to the internet.

Here is how you add additional accounts to your PC:

Push the Windows button ⊞. Then click the ⚙ icon **> Accounts > Family & Other**

Users > Add Someone Else to This PC (pop-up window appears).

If you are adding a Microsoft account, you can enter the email or phone number here and you are done. That user can log in to your computer and is set to a standard user by default. You can make them an administrator by clicking on **Account Name** and then **Change Account Type** (pop-up window) and selecting Administrator from the drop-down.

With a Microsoft account, you can use your email or phone (assuming you provide a phone number) to reset your password if you forget it.

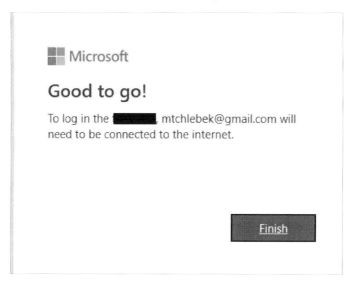

If you are adding a local user, you start in the same way:

Push the Windows button ⊞. Then click the ⚙ icon > **Accounts** > **Family & Other Users** > **Add Someone Else to This PC** (pop-up window appears). Now click the **I Do Not Have This Person's Sign-In Information**. A pop-up window appears wanting to create a new Microsoft account. Click **Add a User without a Microsoft Account.** Then assign a username and password and security questions.

A warning about any local accounts. If you lose your password, then the only mechanism Microsoft has available to let you in is to answer security questions. When you create a local user, you are required to create these. Just like with all passwords and security questions, I recommend generating them in your password manager and storing them there. Then you do not have to worry about losing them. Of course, if you are locked out of your computer, you would have to access your password manager through another computer or your phone.

Recommendations with a Microsoft Account

If you trust using a Microsoft account, then you can make that the administrator account of your computer. I then recommend creating a local/standard account for day-to-day usage. This protects against accidental malware installation, for example, when downloading an email attachment.

The single Microsoft account is nice if you oversee multiple computers in your household. If each person has a computer, then you can use the Microsoft account to be administrator of all of them and give each person a local/standard account to use every day.

For shared computers, you can set up the local standard accounts any way you want. For example, if you have a computer the entire family uses and it is fine for them to share files and photos and everything, then just have a single "Family" local/standard account everybody uses. Or you could have "Parents" and "Kids" accounts, which might be a good way to go. Or you could give every person their own local/standard account ("Dad," "Mom," "Tommy," "Little Twerp," etc.), and everybody can have their own logins and spaces.

If you go with the Microsoft account in any capacity, then set a PIN for each computer the Microsoft account is on. This is easier and more secure than using the password every time. This is because the password works everywhere, but the PIN only works on a given computer and has all kinds of protections built in. Among them is that the attacker must be physically at your computer and type guesses one at a time.[5]

Push the Windows button ⊞. Then click the ⚙ icon **> Accounts > Sign-In Options > Windows Hello PIN.** Set a 6-digit PIN.

If your computer is so equipped, then face or fingerprint recognition is also a convenient option.

Recommendations without a Microsoft Account

If you do not trust Microsoft, then you can set up a local administrator account at installation (disconnect from the internet as mentioned above.) If you already have a Microsoft account on your computer, then you can use it to create a local account, make it an administrator, then switch to that local account and remove the Microsoft account. Tedious but doable.

Then, create local standard accounts that you and others use daily just like I outline above, as if you have a Microsoft account. There is only a little added work in tracking all your accounts, but store them in your password manager, and it is not too bad.

Microsoft Family Accounts

In theory, you can also let your household members have Microsoft accounts and put them on your computer as standard users. I do not really see a need for that unless you want Microsoft to help you monitor them. Microsoft certainly tries to push you in this direction because that is the first thing you see in the area where you manage accounts.

In this case, every family member must have a separate Microsoft account. I mention in the preface of this book that I do not see a lot of value in doing this, but it is up to you.

Universal Access Control

A key security feature in Windows is called Universal Access Control or UAC. Whenever there is an attempt to install software or change critical settings, a window pops up that asks if you want to allow it. If you are the one that initiated the change, then you might think this is just annoying. However, the idea is to prevent malicious software from making changes without you knowing it.

If you are logged in with an administrator account, then you get this yes/no prompt:

If you are logged in with a standard account, you get a similar prompt, but it also requires an administrator login to continue. In other words, a standard account will be blocked for doing whatever brought this warning up.

UAC should be enabled by default, but to be sure, here is how to check:

Move your mouse to the bottom left of the screen, and in the search box type "control panel" without the quotes. **Control Panel** will show up in the search results, so click it. Go to **User Accounts** and then **User Accounts** again > **Change User Account Control Settings.** When the window pops up, make sure the slider is on the first or second (recommended) rung from the top. Then click **OK.**

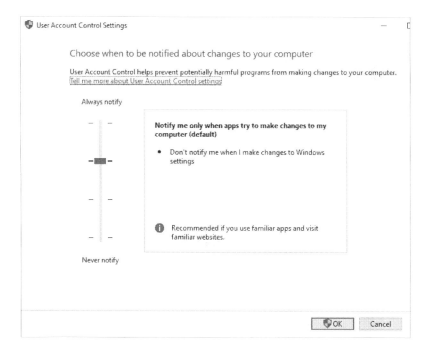

Blow Away the Bloatware

⊘ **MAY BREAK THINGS:** You might delete something you wanted or needed to keep. In most cases, you should be able to reinstall it.

What is bloatware? When most of us get a new PC, it already has Windows installed. But what most of us do not think about is the fact that the manufacturer has installed a bunch of additional software on it. Some of it is useful like drivers that control devices connected to your computer. Or a limited-time deal that you might like but wastes hard drive space and can slow your computer. One example is the McAfee antivirus software HP offers for free for a limited time. Once that time is up, you will constantly be bugged to pay for a subscription. As we discussed earlier on antivirus, Windows Defender is a better and free-forever choice. Yet other bloatware can be outright dangerous. Back in the 2015 timeframe, Lenovo computers came installed with adware called Superfish that would inject advertising into websites as you browsed them. Even worse than this invasion of privacy, was that to do this, they had to defeat your browser's built-in security.[4]

The reason PC manufacturers do this is simply because they are in a competitive market, so they are happy to have the bloatware companies pay them to have their software preinstalled. We do not care about HP's, Dell's, or Lenovo's profits. We want to get rid of the bloatware. This gets back to Krebs's first rule on software: if you did not go looking for it, do not install it.

The biggest problem here is that it is hard to tell bloatware from the valuable stuff. Microsoft came out with an option called Fresh Start that I was excited about at first. It promised a new installation of Windows 10 (complete with the latest updates) that would keep your settings and files but remove the bloatware that your manufacturer installed. It sounded perfect, but I am sorry to point out three major issues: (1) The manufacturer does add valuable software, most specifically drivers (applications that allow your computer to use other hardware). When I tried Fresh Start, it blew away my audio, graphics card, wireless network, docking station, and fingerprint reader drivers. (2) Microsoft blows away all the software I installed. (3) Microsoft itself has a ton of bloatware of their own that Fresh Start does not remove.

The Fresh Start method is therefore aggressive and then leaves the Microsoft garbage. I am surprised how many websites urge this route. If you decide to use Fresh Start, make sure you have a backup, despite there being an option to keep your files in case anything goes awry. You can reinstall the drivers either from your computer manufacturer (i.e. HP, Dell, Lenovo, etc.) or the manufacturer of the installed hardware. (For example, if you have a Nvidia graphics card, go to their website for drivers.) Also make sure you have the media (CD/DVDs) or download/activation keys for the software you must reinstall yourself. Finally, do not confuse this with "Reset this PC" because this reinstalls your computer back to what your manufacturer originally installed.

Probably better for most of us is to uninstall the bloatware manually. In general, removing software is done here:

> Push the Windows button ⊞. Then click the ⚙ icon **> Apps**. A big list comes up. Click on a given app. Then options appear to Modify or **Uninstall**.

The following is a noncomprehensive list of applications that may be on your computer, are older, and have had vulnerabilities in the past. If you are not using them, you should certainly uninstall them.

- Java
- QuickTime
- Microsoft Silverlight
- Adobe Shockwave
- Adobe Flash
- Adobe Reader

As mentioned, the following are things your computer manufacturer may have added:

- Third-party antivirus (McAfee, Symantec, Bitdefender, etc.)
- Limited offers, free samples, etc.
- Facebook
- Shazam
- iHeartRadio
- Pandora
- Netflix

The following is Microsoft garbage. These do not hurt anything, but I want them off my computer. Your mileage may vary. Some of them Microsoft does not give the option to uninstall.

- All Microsoft games (Solitaire, Candy Crush, Caesars Slots, Minecraft, NYT crossword, etc.)
- All Xbox-related items
- All Bing items (Travel, Food, Weather, News, Sports, etc.)
- 3D Builder
- Zune Music, Zune Video
- Phototastic Collage (What the hell is this?)
- Windows tips, feedback, communications
- Windows email, calendar

If something breaks, you should be able to reinstall it in the Windows store.

Unfortunately, there will be a lot of other stuff that you will not know if it is good or bad. If you have an Intel or AMD processor, then you should probably keep anything with their names in it. Same with Nvidia or AMD graphics cards. If you do not know, then leave it. If you are more cavalier about it, you can Google them and try to figure out what they do.

This recommendation is strictly to get rid of the bloatware. If your computer is not running right because of some change to the settings or registers, or even malware that you cannot get rid of, removing the bloatware manually will not be as effective as a clean install. It is also not what you want to use if selling or giving your PC away. For those cases, you do want to do either a "Reset this PC" or even reinstall from a USB drive. Details at: https://support.microsoft.com/en-us/windows/recovery-options-in-windows-10-31ce2444-7de3-818c-d626-e3b5a3024da5#bkmk_section2

Encrypt Your Disk

🚫 **MAY BREAK THINGS:** This should not break anything, but there is the risk that you will lose the encryption key and then your data will be locked forever.

Full disk encryption is important if you ever lose your device. You may have a good password protecting the operating system. But if a bad actor physically has your computer, then they can pull the hard drive out, shove it into their computer, and start reading everything.

Macs, iPhones, iPads, Chromebooks, and Android phones all include full disk encryption by default. Microsoft is complicated.

Microsoft Windows 10 Home has something called *device encryption* included, but it works if and only if your hardware supports it. The easiest way to know is to look for it.

Push the Windows button ⊞. Then click the ⚙ icon **> Update & Security**. On the left menu, look at the bottom option. If **Device Encryption** is there, click it. Then click **Turn On.** Follow the steps.

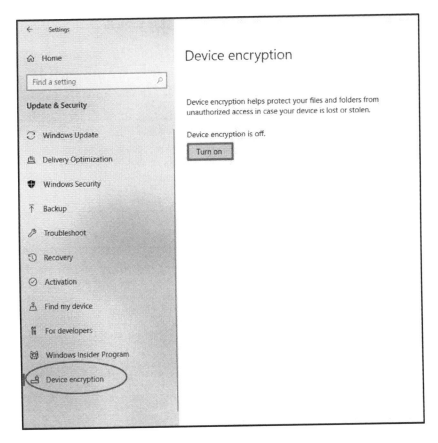

Image courtesy www.windowscentral.com[3]

If your computer supports device encryption, then enable it. If not, then you must ask yourself, "If my PC were lost or stolen, how bad would it be if somebody could read it?" Here are the options:

1. Windows 10 Pro, Enterprise, and Education all have a feature called BitLocker. Most of us have Windows Home, and upgrading to Pro costs $99. If your computer has a trusted platform module (TPM) version 1.2 or later, it is quite easy. If not, you will either need an external USB thumb drive or must enter a key (beyond your regular login) every time the computer starts.

2. VeraCrypt is a free open-sourced application. It requires a separate password (beyond your regular login) every time your computer starts.

If you have a TPM, I would go with BitLocker because it is much easier once you set things up. If not, I would use VeraCrypt to save money. Here is how you tell if you have a TPM:

> Press the **Windows key** and **R** at the same time. A little window pops up. **>**   Type in
> **tpm.msc**, and another window pops up.

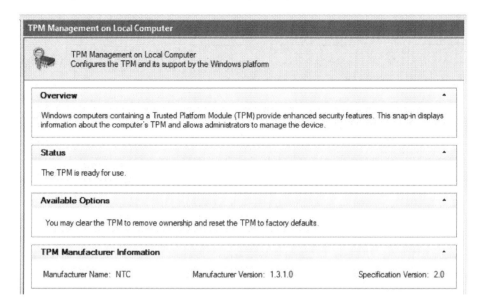

Under **Status**, you will see "The TPM is ready for use," and the version is in the TPM
Manufacturer Information.

3. Or figure it is not worth the effort. For desktop computers that do not leave your home,
    at least you also have the physical security. For laptops that you carry around, this is a
    risky option.

BitLocker

If this is your route, upgrade to Windows Pro here:

> Push the Windows button 🪟 . Then click the ⚙ icon **> Update & Security > Activation
> > Go to the Store**. Follow the instructions to upgrade.

Once you have Windows Pro, then you can get to BitLocker.

> In the search bar, type **Control Panel**, and it will show up in the results. Click it. Then
> click **System and Security >BitLocker Drive Encryption > Turn on BitLocker**.

When you turn BitLocker on, you have the choice of saving the encryption key in your Windows Account (if you use one), printing it, or storing it in a file. I think the best bet is to make an entry in your password manager and cut and paste the key into the notes.

BitLocker To Go

You might notice that in the same place you can turn BitLocker on for your main drive, you can also encrypt removable USB drives. This is a great way to ensure the security of any of those drives you might use. If you are backing up your computer this way, then I recommend encrypting that drive also.

VeraCrypt

If paying Microsoft for something they should provide for free makes your stomach turn (I am with you), or your computer tells you that you do not have the right hardware (like a TPM), then you can also try an open-source tool called VeraCrypt. It does require an additional password whenever you start your computer. I will skip the instructions here, but this article has detailed instructions: https://www.techspot.com/guides/2069-how-to-encrypt-windows/.

Windows Firewall

🚫 **MAY BREAK THINGS:** Some programs might stop working because they will be denied access to your network or the internet. The application can be granted access, but the hard part is sometimes your computer will not tell you why the program is not working. If the firewall is blocking the program, it might be difficult to figure out.

We will talk about a network firewall in detail later in the chapter on your home network. When there is a firewall on your computer, it is referred to as a host-based or personal firewall. The purpose of a firewall of any kind is to control what and how devices or software can communicate with each other.

The first time an application on your computer tries to communicate to another computer or the internet, you will get a pop-up window asking if this is okay. Just like with the UAC, if you did not expect this, click **No**, and investigate. The reasons you would expect this is you just started some new software and it is trying to communicate to another device or the internet. It could even be old software that you are just now trying to use to connect to another device or the internet. Conversely, if you are surfing the internet or downloading an email attachment and this pops up, you probably just did a bad thing. Click **No**.

Windows has a concept of public or private networks. A *public network* is when you are connected to the internet along with strangers, such as the Wi-Fi network at Starbucks or the airport. A *private network* is your home or work network where you are supposed to know and trust the other people on the network. In the public network, the firewall is going to have stricter settings and assume that you do not want to talk to other computers or share devices like a printer.

When you first connect to any network, Windows will ask if it is a public or private network. When we talk about Wi-Fi in the chapter on networks, I tell you never to use public networks and instead use your phone. But if you must, use "public" in that case. Only select "private" when you are connecting to a truly trusted network.

The Windows firewalls should be on by default, but check to make sure:

> Push the Windows button [■]. Then click the [⚙] icon**> Update and Security > Windows Security > Firewall and Network Protection**. Check that both **Private Network** and **Public Network** say the firewall is on. If not, then click on the respective title and you will then be able to turn them on.

Ransomware Protection

🚫 **MAY BREAK THINGS:** This feature will block applications from your files. Most of them will tell you so you can go into the settings and grant permission to that specific app. However, I ran into a problem where I could not access an external SD card drive to format an SD card because of this feature. The computer did not tell me that was the reason, so it was difficult to troubleshoot.

Windows 10 now has a defense for ransomware. The short version is hackers will use malware to encrypt your files. They will then try to charge you, usually demanding a Bitcoin payment, for the keys to decrypt them. For more information on ransomware, see the chapter on scams.

The protection is called Controlled Folder Access. The idea is that ransomware needs access to the files it wants to encrypt. Therefore, Windows can stop ransomware by not allowing unapproved software to have access to your files. For reasons beyond my comprehension, Windows 10 does not turn this on by default. To do so:

> Push the Windows button [■]. Then click the [⚙] icon **> Update and Security > Windows Security > Virus & Threat Protection** (new window pops up). Under Ransomware Protection, click **Manage Ransomware Protection > Controlled Folder**, and flip the switch to **On**.

Once controlled folder access is turned on, Windows selects all your personal folders for protection. To see them, from the screen where you turn the switch on, click

Protected Folders. You will see a list, and it looks like there are at least two of each, but they are separate folders—one for your personal folders and one for the public folders. If you have more than one user set up on your computer, then public folders can be accessed by all the users. Otherwise, each user can only see their private folders. If there are any other folders you want to protect, then add them here.

Microsoft does a good job determining what applications should be allowed to access your files. They certainly allow Microsoft products—Word, Excel, and PowerPoint—to access your files through controlled folder access, but many other popular tools as well. However, if you are running software that Microsoft does not allow and you are confident that it can be trusted, then go to the screen where you switch controlled folder access on and click **Allow an App through Controlled Folder Access**. The next screen has a big "**+**" where you can add your app.

If you are trying to format a USB drive, Controlled Folder Access may block it but not tell you directly. It will just say it does not have permission. You must go back into the controlled folder, access settings, and look for the tool that was just blocked and grant it access.

Privacy Settings

🚫 **MAY BREAK THINGS:** The entire point here is to prevent applications from accessing things like your camera. Most of the time, the program will tell you to give it access, so it is not an issue. But sometimes the program will just fail, and it might be difficult to figure out it was denied permission.

Windows 10 provides a massive number of privacy settings. They can be divided into two parts. The first is privacy from Microsoft, and they call this part Windows Permissions. The second part they call App Permissions, and this controls the ability of applications to access features/functions on your computer. For example, can Zoom access your microphone and camera? It all starts here:

Push the Windows button ⊞. Then click the ⚙ icon**> Privacy**. Along the left, you can see the Windows Permissions and App Permissions.

146

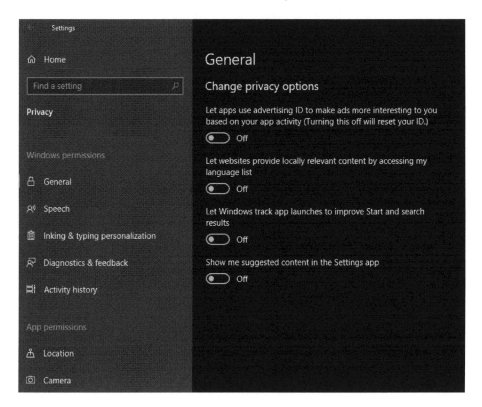

Windows Permissions

You can dial down (but not completely stop) the data Microsoft collects on you. My policy is to turn everything off until it breaks something I use. Of course, this is different for every person, but since I do not want Microsoft "optimizing" anything based on my data, I can turn it all off.

Go down that left menu and at every stop, flip every toggle **off** and uncheck every box and delete everything they already have on you.

If turning any of these off breaks something you use, then you are free to evaluate if it is worth it to keep it on. For example, if you want to talk to your computer, then for Cortana to be better, you must enable the speech recognition. It is fair if you think this feature is cool enough to allow Microsoft to listen to you the entire time your computer is on. It is not for me.

Apps Permissions

This is where it gets trickier. Zoom, of course, needs access to the camera and microphone because the entire point of Zoom is video calls. But you do not want malware turning those things on and spying on you in your underwear or hearing your intimate conversations. All those items under App Permissions are computer functions that malware might be able to use to spy on you, steal data, or attack you or your computer in some way. The idea is to limit this ability only to applications you know are running and you trust.

When you click into the specific app permissions, it is initially very confusing because it seems as though Microsoft is asking the same question multiple times. To understand this, you must know the layers that Microsoft (wrongly) assumes everybody understands. Refer to this picture as we move through the sections of each feature.

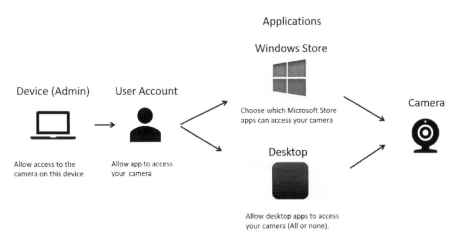

As the administrator, you can decide if any user or application can use the protected features at all. In this picture the camera is the example feature. When you click **Camera** under App Permissions, the very first section is, "Allow access to the camera on this device." If this is off, then nobody and no application can use the camera. In the case of the camera, most of us will turn this on. For some strange reason, you must click **Change** and then flip the toggle to **On**.

The next section down asks, "Allow apps to access your camera." Here is where the account of the person logged in can decide if they will allow usage of the camera. So even though you are the admin and you allowed this computer to use the camera, you can still turn it **Off** anytime you are logged in. However, other users on this computer could still use the camera if they log in with a separate account and switch this to **On**.

Assuming that whoever is logged in has the camera enabled, the next two sections are about specific applications. The first says, "Choose which Microsoft Store apps can access your camera." In this case, you can select the applications individually from the list. The next section says, "Allow desktop apps to access your camera." Desktop applications are effectively any programs that you did not download from the Microsoft store. In this case, there is a list of desktop applications, but they cannot be selected individually. Either all of them have access or none of them do.

The Microsoft Store is Microsoft's attempt to copy Apple and Google in providing a set of standards and approvals around "official" applications. It is accessed by clicking the [icon] icon in your tray at the bottom or from the Start menu. In the past, Microsoft just provided the operating system and let software developers provide whatever software they could sell. They still allow this in the form of "desktop" apps. The reason Microsoft differentiates between the two kinds of apps is because then they can say they have checked the ones in the Windows Store for malware and other standards. You are on your own for the others. One of those standards is granting Windows the ability to individually control them.

There are several annoying aspects to this. The first is that because of this arrangement, it is more likely that malware that can take over your camera will be on a desktop app that does not come through the Microsoft Store. But you cannot individually control them. If you have the camera on for any desktop application, then it is on for your malware. Also, there is a disclaimer right under the toggle switch that some desktop applications might not appear or even be affected by this. There is then a link to a webpage that details this more, but the bottom line is that Microsoft really has no control over any desktop apps that you install deliberately or by accident. The final piece to this is that they consider Microsoft Edge (their own freaking browser) to be a desktop app. If you want to use Microsoft's browser, that by the way can be downloaded from the Microsoft Store (confusing), then you must turn all desktop apps on to use it. It is hard to understand what Microsoft thinks at times. Oh, and if you think using another browser solves this, it does not. Microsoft considers all browsers to be desktop apps.

Speaking of web browsers, they have an additional complication. Even if you give the browser access to the camera, each website you visit with the browser must be enabled at the browser level. We discuss that in the chapter on browsers, but here is the modified picture for browser and website permissions.

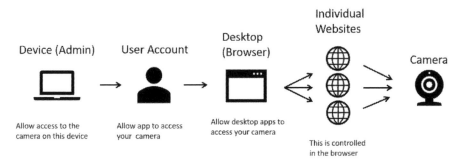

Given all that background, I recommend going through the entire App Permission section of the Privacy settings and turning everything off until it breaks something. Do it at the highest level and work your way down. I found it pretty amazing how many I could completely shut down: Notifications, Account Info, Contacts, Calendar, Phone Calls, Call History, Email, Tasks, Messaging, Radios, Other Devices, App Diagnostics, Pictures, Videos, and File System. The only reason I do not have Background Apps and Documents completely off is because Windows Security is included, and I want that to run. In this case, I turned it **On** at the device and user levels. Then in the Microsoft Store section, I turned all the other apps **Off**. It turns out that most of the apps Microsoft gives permission to by default are the asinine built-in programs nobody uses.

You might think, "How can email work in general if that is turned off?" It is because most email, including Outlook 365, is cloud-based. Your email is not directly handled on your computer. Same with most contacts and calendars.

Another interesting aspect is access to the File system. You would think this is like the Controlled Folder Access feature we enabled to protect from ransomware. Well, earlier I mentioned these privacy settings may not apply to all desktop applications. But Controlled Folder Access is far more comprehensive and can block most or all applications from access to folders.

When you do need access, most apps will tell you the issue, or at a minimum, you will get an error. That is the entire purpose of this section: You decide when your camera, microphone, location, documents, etc. are being used—not malware running in the background.

File History Backup

Computers break. The biggest surprise for most people is often that the hard drive simply fails. Hard drives are mechanical wonders that rely on tight tolerances and parts moving at high speeds. Unfortunately, that makes them unreliable. Other ways computers break are not so surprising, such as being dropped or having coffee spilled on them. If you lose your data (and photos and videos), it is just as devastating if it is due to a hacker in Russia, your kids, or plain bad luck. Therefore, it is important to protect against all the above.

The simplest way to provide backups is to get an external drive that connects to your computer and use the built-in capabilities of your Windows machine. The drive should be at least the same size (memory, not physically) as the built-in drive of your computer, and preferably twice the size. The prices have dropped so much in recent years that 2-terabyte drives on Amazon are around $60, which is a tiny investment if it saves just one important file in the future. You can either use a USB-attached drive or if you know how, a network-attached drive.

Windows provides an immensely powerful and convenient feature for backing up your data called Windows File History.

For a USB-attached drive:

Push the Windows button ⊞. Then click the ⚙ icon > **Update & Security > Backup**. Under Backup using File History, click **Add a Drive**. Select your drive from the list.

For a network-attached drive:

Push the Windows button ⊞. Then click the ⚙ icon >**Update & Security > Backup**. Under Backup using File History, click **More Options > See Advanced Settings** (a new screen pops up) **> Select Drive**. Select a network drive or add one.

Once you select a drive, the "Add Drive" option will be replaced with a switch that indicates backup is now on. See the next figure.

Here you can click **More Options** to configure File History. The first thing I noticed when I did that was close to the top, it said, "Your data is not yet backed up." I imagine that at the next scheduled interval (1 hour is the default) the first backup would start, but I am impatient and clicked the **Back Up Now** button to kick things off.

If you have a lot saved, it will take a while for the complete backup to run. But you can go work on other things while this is happening.

On the external drive, a new folder will be created called File History. Under that, a folder for each user is created so each user's data can be backed up separately. Under that is a folder for each device that user has, so that one external drive can be used for several devices. Finally, under each device folder is a Configuration folder and Data folder. The Data folder will have folders in it that match the folders you are backing up.

In the Data folder, files that are backed up will have the same name as the original but will have a date and time stamp added to the name. After a while, the files you have modified will show up with multiple entries but newer time stamps. This way, you can go back to any of the old versions you wish, not just the last one.

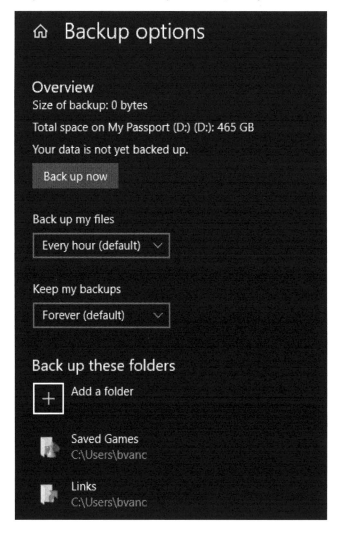

Back in the Backup Options, you can set how often you want the backup to run. Hourly is the default and a good choice. You can also set how long you want to keep the backups. Remember that on your main drive, there will only be one copy (the latest) of each file, but on the backup drive, there will be multiple copies, and how long those are kept is determined by this setting. If you run out of space on the hard drive, then you are warned that there will be no more new copies made. The best setting is "Until I need space," and File History will keep everything until space is needed and then selectively delete the oldest versions to make room for the newest ones.

Below that you can see which folders are backed up and can add or remove them as you see fit. Note that if you have OneDrive set up, then it is in the backup list by default, but only files synced to your computer are backed up, not everything else on OneDrive.

If you have a laptop that you drag around to different places, then I highly recommend a docking station of some kind. The reason is that you only need one plug to use a bigger monitor, charge up the battery, and maybe use the wired network and a full-sized keyboard and mouse. But most importantly, the docking station connects to this external drive so File History can do its thing when you are home. Obviously, it could miss the most recent hourly backups. But you do not want to travel with the backup drive because of the odds that you would lose both the laptop and the backup drive.

I read 4% of computer users backup their computers (I can't for the life of me remember where, so I apologize for not having a reference). Therefore, this would be a huge improvement for most people, and everybody must decide how much risk they are willing to live with. Using an external drive protects well against accidents and hardware failures, but there are other things to be concerned about because the external drive is still sitting next to your computer. Therefore, this does not protect against things like fire, flooding, and a thief taking all your equipment.

External drives also do not protect against most ransomware because that malware is often programmed to look for external drives and encrypt them also.

One way those issues could be mitigated is by unplugging your external drive and putting it in your vault. If the vault is fireproof, waterproof, and in a completely different room, it could help protect against all the physical threats and malware. Then, you would have to remember to periodically get your drive and plug it in and make sure File History runs. This is very inconvenient, however, and you would obviously have gaps in your backup corresponding to how long it has been since your last backup.

File History does not back up your applications and Windows configurations. Windows has other ways of doing that, and many experts think that must be part of the backup plan as well. However, my experience has been that if disaster strikes, then I always end up reinstalling Windows and all my applications anyway. As I mentioned before, keep all your CDs (if anybody still buys software that way) or better yet, your license keys (your password manager is a good place to keep them) so you can just download and reinstall your applications.

In the Advanced section of this book, we revisit Windows and discuss cloud backups that mitigate both the physical and ransomware risks. The other thing to point out is that the backup drives are not encrypted by default, but you can do that with BitLocker To Go or VeraCrypt.

File History Recovery

When something happens and you need to retrieve a file or files, there are several ways to do so.

If you know exactly which version you want to restore, go to File Explorer, find the folder or file you want, and right-click **Restore Previous Versions**. A list from which you can select will pop up. Select the version you want and then either click **Open**, which will open a new read-only instance, or **Restore**, and Windows will replace your current version with this older one.

If you want to browse old versions to determine the one to restore, go to File Explorer, find the folder or file, right click it, and this time select **Open in File History**. Now you have a list of versions and can pick **Restore** to replace the current version or save a copy in the same location as the original. You can also browse here by selecting a version. Click **Open in File History**, and you will see a preview. You can even scroll back to other versions from here to get the preview of them.

Finally, if you are restoring folders or multiple files because something big happened, like your old drive died, or you reinstalled Windows, then:

> Push the Windows button ⊞. Then click the ⚙ icon **> Update & Security > Back Up > More Options** (new screen pops up). At the bottom, click **Restore Files from a Current Backup** then choose the external drive or network location.

The File History application will show multiple windows that you can scroll left or right with the arrow buttons at the bottom. The time of the backup is shown at the top. In each time frame, all the folders and files are shown. You can also select individual files or folders here. But for a wholesale recovery, be sure you are on the right timeframe (usually this will be the latest one, but if you do go back, keep in mind any changes will be lost) and hit the big green button with the circular arrow. That version will be restored to your main drive without the time stamps added to the files just as nature intended them.

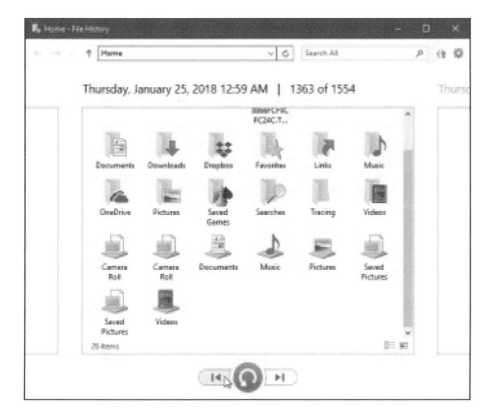

Windows (PC) Disposal

If you are going to throw your computer in the trash or recycle it, first pull out the hard drive and smash it with a hammer. I mentioned this earlier, but I was not kidding then, and I am not kidding now.

If you are giving away or selling the computer and using Windows, then you will have to completely reinstall your operating system.

If you have Windows 7 or previous, you will need to create a system repair disk (instructions here: https://support.microsoft.com/en-us/help/17423/windows-7-create-system-repair-disc) then use a third-party tool like Darik's Boot and Nuke to completely erase your drive. Then reinstall Windows 7 for the next user. Since this is difficult to do right and a Windows 7 machine is not going to be worth much, it might be best to go with the throw-away/recycle route and just smash the hard drive as mentioned before.

For Windows 8/8.1, here are the instructions: https://support.microsoft.com/en-us/help/17085/windows-8-restore-refresh-reset-pc. Make sure you choose to reset (remove everything) and not refresh (keeps your files).

For Windows 10, here are the instructions: https://support.microsoft.com/en-us/help/10547/microsoft-account-selling-gifting-windows-10-device-xbox-one.

For external drives, find their icon in Windows File Explorer, right click on it, and select "format." Uncheck the "Quick Format" box to perform a full wipe. Just like it says, the quick option is faster, but not a full cleaning.

References:

[1] https://www.techradar.com/news/another-microsoft-mess-as-windows-10-november-2019-update-breaks-file-explorer

[2] https://www.av-test.org/en/antivirus/home-windows/

[3] https://www.windowscentral.com/how-enable-device-encryption-windows-10-home

[4] https://www.pcworld.com/article/2886357/lenovo-preinstalls-man-in-the-middle-adware-that-hijacks-https-traffic-on-new-pcs.html

[5] https://www.bruceb.com/2016/08/logging-in-with-a-pin-is-easier-than-a-password-and-safer-too/#:~:text=A%20PIN%20is%20four%20or%20more%20numbers%2C%20exactly,a%20PIN%20is%20safer%20than%20using%20a%20password

13

APPLE MACINTOSH
Job's Revenge

To Apple's credit, they have taken security seriously longer than Microsoft. When it comes to security settings, Macs are more straightforward because they tend to simply decide for you if a feature should be on. For most of us, this is probably the better approach, at least when it comes to security.

Initial Settings

When you first set up your Mac, you are forced to create an administrator user and a password. (This is not the same as your Apple ID account, which we will talk about in a bit, though your Mac will also ask you for that in setup). Macs have a feature called "automatic login" which is exactly that. Do not use it. Yes, it is annoying, but you must require login. Go to:

System Preferences > Security & Privacy > General.

1. Make sure the "Require password" box is checked and set to as low a time as you can tolerate for locking the screen.
2. See that "Disable automatic login" is checked.
3. The lower half is Gatekeeper settings. We will discuss that later, but the recommended setting is "App Store and identified developers."

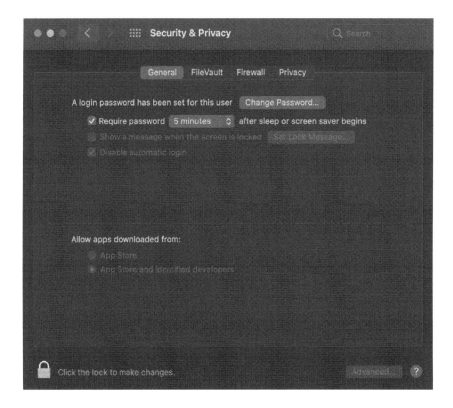

These should all be the default settings, but if you need to make changes to any of the grayed-out settings, then click the lock at the bottom. Enter the administrator password, and then you can make the changes.

If your Mac has a fingerprint scanner, you can set it up at **System Preferences > Touch ID**.

Do Not Even Trust Yourself – Use Standard Accounts

🚫 **MAY BREAK THINGS:** The users that are given standard accounts might be upset that they cannot install software, make changes, or in some cases, even access some applications that the admin installs.

When you buy a computer, the makers assume that you will want the ability to do whatever you want to it. This makes sense in every way except when it comes to security and privacy.

When you initially set up your computer, you will be granted full administrative rights. This means you can install any software you want (good or bad), and you can make any configuration changes you desire. However, most of the time you will not be doing these things. Most of the time you will turn your computer on to check email, surf the web, and maybe create a document or spreadsheet. In this case, you will want to restrict your own rights so that you do not accidently install malware or make configuration changes.

Beyond yourself, you might have family members or other guests using your computer. Since they are most likely computer illiterate compared to you (you are reading this book after all) and highly likely to mess something up, it is a fantastic idea to restrict what they can do by providing them with their own accounts. Setting them up as other users also separates all their files and many settings such that it seems like you have different computers despite using the same physical machine.

A nice thing about a Mac is when an application is installed, it is available to all users.

macOS has several account types and they are: Administrator, Standard, Sharing only, Guest, and Group.

Administrator

As mentioned above, the initial user is automatically set up as an administrator. As the one in charge of this machine, you should use this account to install software, make a lot or all the changes I suggest in the book, and then not use it.

Standard Account

A standard account gives a user access to their own Home folder but nobody else's. They can make harmless preference changes like the desktop screen and light or dark mode, but anything of any consequence, including installing software, is off-limits to them. Therefore, for everyday use, you should use a standard account to avoid a malware download or accidental changes of real consequence.

It is then up to you how you want to handle other users that want to use your computer. You could share your standard user account with them and intermingle all your files and perhaps call this account "Family." Or you could create two standard accounts, perhaps calling one "Parents" and the other "Kids." Or you could even give every person in the family a separate account. That part is up to you, but the takeaway here is that you cannot trust them or even yourself in everyday usage with an administrator account.

To create a standard account (you must do this as an Administrator):

> Click **System Preferences > Users and Groups**. Click the lock at the bottom > Click the lock icon at the bottom > Enter your password > You now have control of the Users and Groups panel. To add a user, it is somewhat hidden, but under Login Options is a **+**. Click

it.

At the top, select **Standard**. Then fill out the name and then create and store a password with your password manager, but here you can turn the length down to eight characters. I say this because you will have to manually enter this password often, and it has other protections like lockout that will prevent brute-force attacks. Then **Create User.**

If a standard user wants to do anything like download new software or make a settings change, they will require an Administrator to log in to allow the change.

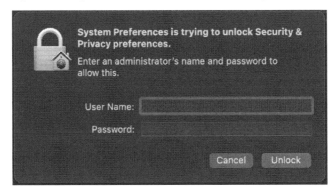

Guest Account

The guest account is a great feature, and you do not have to set it up other than to set a password. It is just sitting there for you to share with others. Say your perverted brother-in-law comes over every Christmas and wants to use your computer. If there is anybody you want to restrict, it is this guy. He surfs the exotic areas of the internet, tries to download who knows what files, and changes your background screen to pictures of cats like all weirdos do. When he finally logs out, your Mac wipes that account clean, just as if he had never been there.

Sharing and Group Accounts

The Sharing only and Groups account I will not cover. They are mainly for an office environment where you might allow others to access your computer for file sharing and/or have several teams to control.

Updates

Apple has been on macOS X since 2001 and only very recently went to version 11, named Big Sur. They were far ahead of Microsoft in realizing that constant updates online are better than making everybody buy CDs every three to five years. If you use a Mac, make sure it is on Big Sur. (It should be by default.)

> Click **System Preferences > Software Updates > Advanced >** Check all the boxes and click **OK.**

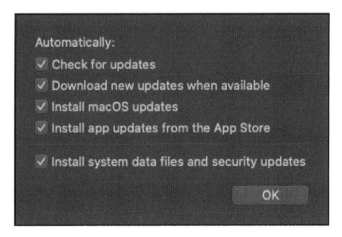

If your Mac cannot support the latest macOS release, then it is starting to get old. Apple is cagey about when they stop security support for any given version, but it seems that they support the current and last two versions (sometimes this is called N-2). As of this writing that would include macOS 10.15 Catalina, 10.14 Mojave. In the Apple world, the only reason not to be on the latest version is if your Mac is too old to support it. Once the latest macOS your computer supports is N-3 (macOS

10.13, a.k.a. High Sierra), then you are on your own. This Apple page https://support.apple.com/en-us/HT201686 enables you to look up what computers support each macOS release. If you cannot get to High Sierra, it means your computer is around ten years old, so from a security perspective, it might be time to get a new one.

Free Mac Antivirus

Macs come with a rudimentary antivirus called XProtect by default and cannot be turned off. I do not recommend any additional antivirus on a Mac. XProtect can stop the most well-known viruses, so there is that, but the bigger thing is Apple makes it difficult for you to accidently install any software, and especially software not vetted by Apple.

Apple ID

Apple ID is an account you have with Apple, not the account on your computer. Apple ID is required for many services like getting updates, using the Apple Store to get new software, iCloud for cloud-based file storage and backups, Apple email, contacts, calendar, Find my Mac, and more.

When setting up your computer, you might have attached your Apple ID to your administrator account. It was not required (it had a "skip" option), but since we want updates and to use Find My Mac at least, we should set that up.

A different Apple ID can be connected to each different user so that everyone can have separate email and contacts and all that. When logged in as a specific user, then go to **System Preferences,** and the Apple ID connected to that user will be listed at the top. If no Apple ID is connected, it will say "Sign into your Apple ID" and provide a button to do so.

Gatekeeper – Installing Software

The first time you try to install an application, Apple has a feature called Gatekeeper that will throw up a message with the name of the app, where it came from, and when it was downloaded. This is all intended to prevent malware from being downloaded by accident or along with software you really want. Apple has an evaluation process with three outcomes.

1. *Apple checked it for malicious software, and none was detected.* This will be the case for anything downloaded from the Apple App Store or Apple-approved vendors, and it is safe to proceed.

2. *{App's Name} will damage your computer. You should move it to the trash.* Apple evaluated this application and found malware. In this case, you do get a banner, and Apple is helpful enough to provide a button to trash the application. Use it.

3. *{App's Name} cannot be opened because it is from an unidentified developer.* Apple has not evaluated the software at all. It might be good, it might not. So when that warning comes, you better be 100% certain that you trust the source if you decide to install it anyway.

If you want to ignore Apple's warnings, you must go to:

System Preferences > Security & Privacy > General. (The lower half is Gatekeeper settings.)

For about an hour after you try installing, there will be yet another warning "{App's Name} was blocked from use because it is not from an identified developer." If you click Open Anyway, you get yet another "Are you sure you want to open it?"

If that warning went away in Gatekeeper, then you must go to **Finder > Applications**. Then find the application, right click, and select **Open**.

If you find yourself skirting Gatekeeper often, then I would have to question what the heck you are doing.

Data Access Consent (Privacy)

🚫 **MAY BREAK THINGS:** The entire point here is to prevent applications from accessing things like your camera. Most of the time, the program will tell you to give it access, so it is not an issue. However, sometimes the program will just fail, and it might be difficult to figure out it was denied permission to something.

Apple will ask if you are sure you want to do something potentially dangerous to the point of insanity. It is especially crazy when your Mac is new or you freshly install the OS, because even the built-in Mac applications will ask all kinds of permission. But put up with it and pay attention. This is how Apple prevents malware from accessing features on your computer that could be used to spy, steal, or harm you or your computer in some way. It is also a general rule that you are only asked once per application and then the Mac just remembers from that point on.

Data Access Consent is a feature that requires applications (even applications built in to your Mac) to ask for consent to access information or functions. The entire list: Location Services, Contacts, Calendars, Reminders, Photos, Camera, Microphone, Speech Recognition, Accessibility, Input Monitoring, Full Disk Access, Files and Folders, Screen Recording, Automation, Analytics and Improvements, and Advertising. To control them go to:

System Preferences > Security & Privacy > General > Privacy.

When your Mac asks you if you would like to allow access, be sure it makes sense. If you are trying to use Apple Maps, it makes sense to give it location access, but not microphone.

If you do not know, then choose Don't Allow first. You can always come back to this privacy screen and enable access. For example, I denied the Weather app access to Location, but I can come back anytime and check that box to allow it.

Continuing Location, notice in the right panel of the privacy page the System Services. You can click **Details...**, but it will be grayed out. First, click that lock at the bottom of the screen and enter either an administrator password or Touch ID to get it to unlock. Then you can click on the System Service **Details...**

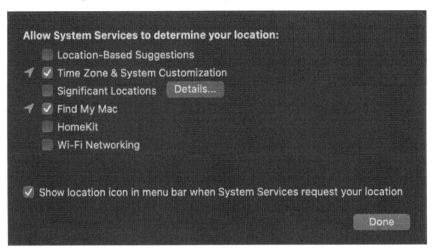

Uncheck all of them except "Time Zone and System Customization," "Find My Mac" and "Show location icon in menu bar...." Click **Done**. Location-Based Suggestions, Significant Locations, and Wi-Fi Networking are Apple spying on you. If you are using HomeKit, and whatever you are doing need location, then leave it on.

I will focus on a few specific ones after Location.

First, Full Disk Access and Folder and Files. Preventing an application from accessing files is primarily intended to stop ransomware. The short version is that hackers will use malware to encrypt your files and then demand payment, usually in Bitcoin, for the keys to decrypt them. For more information on ransomware, see the chapter on scams. If this window pops up, think about what you were doing. If you were in a program and just tried to save your work, then the window asks if that program can get access to the documents folder. In this case it makes sense to click **OK**. If you were just surfing the internet or downloaded a file in email, then this is a massive red flag. Once you allow a program to get access to a folder, you will not be asked again.

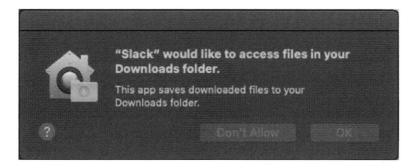

Next up are input monitoring (recording keystrokes), screen recording (screenshots or even video of your screen), and camera and microphone access. These are all things malware will want access to so they can spy on you or steal data and credentials. If any of these warnings come up, think long and hard about why you would allow an application to record keystrokes or take screenshots while logging into your computer or websites. (Hint: you normally would not.)

Finally, there is Analytics and Improvements and Advertising. I recommend going into both and turning everything off. They are how Apple monitors you and your computer and are of no good use to you.

Beyond paying attention when your computer asks, every once in a while you should click on every feature along the left panel of the privacy page and do an audit. Be on the lookout for apps you did not even know you had or apps you have not used in a long time. In the case of either, forget permissions, and go uninstall the app. And with apps you do trust, still think about if they need the specific permission you are granting.

Firewall – Turn It On

 MAY BREAK THINGS: Some programs might stop working because they are denied access to your network or the internet. The application can be granted access, but the hard part is sometimes your computer will not tell you why the program is not working, and figuring that out can be difficult.

We will talk about a network firewall in detail in the chapter on your home network. When there is a firewall on your computer, it is referred to as a *host-based* or *personal firewall*. The purpose of a firewall of any kind is to control what and how devices or applications can communicate with each other.

The idea here is when somebody or something tries to communicate with a specific application on your computer for the first time, it asks you for permission. As with all these security features, if you do not know why your computer is asking, then it is because it is under attack. Click **Don't Allow**. If you do need to allow somebody or something to get access to the application specified, then click **OK**. Your Mac will remember and not ask again.

It is odd that Apple does not enable their firewall by default. I am sure they got feedback that people find it annoying. But given Macs ask for explicit permission for applications to do all the other things—download, install, access files, and block monitoring—why not ask this also?

Make sure the Apple firewall is on.

> Go to **System Preferences > Security > Firewall**. Turn it on. Click **Firewall Options**. Check all three boxes. Click **OK**.

That last box, Stealth Mode, prevents your Mac from responding to people trying to scan for vulnerable machines. If you have no idea what an ICMP ping is, then trust me and just check this box.

FileVault

> 🚫 MAY BREAK THINGS: This should not break anything, but there is the risk that you will lose the encryption key, and then your data will be locked forever.

If your computer is ever stolen, you might think your data is safe because you have a strong password protecting it. This is necessary, but unfortunately only stops the hacker from logging in to macOS. They can still just pull your hard drive out, stick it into another Mac (or Linux) machine and start reading all the files.

To prevent this, you need to encrypt the hard drive. This is where FileVault comes in. Not only does FileVault encrypt your hard drive for you, but it does it seamlessly. When you log in to your account, it encrypts and decrypts the data for you, so you do not need to re-enter the encryption key every time.

To turn FileVault on, go to:

> **System Preferences > Security and Privacy >   FileVault**. Click the lock at the bottom > Enter your **Admin password** and then click **Turn on FileVault**.

Now you must select a backdoor method for decrypting your drive in case you forget your admin password. The two options are "Allow my iCloud account to unlock my disk" or "Create a recovery key and do not use my iCloud account." If you prefer the iCloud account, then of course you cannot forget those credentials either, but I assume you have them in your password manager. This method, should you ever need it, will assume your computer has internet access.

If you select the recovery key, it will be a long, impossible-to-remember key. I suggest you write it down on paper and put it in your physical vault *and* add it to your password manager.

If you forget both your administrator password and the backup you chose, your data is gone. You can reinstall macOS to get your computer back, but the data is gone forever.

The Apple manual says at this point you will have to have each additional user enabled by entering their password. However, on my Mac this was not necessary.

The Apple manual also says you will have to restart to get the encryption to start. When you do so, it will take your computer quite a while to encrypt everything from scratch and finish rebooting. However, my Mac just did it in the background, and I was able to continue working.

These last two items may have been improvements that came with Big Sur but had not been updated in the manuals as it was brand new at the time of this writing.

Time Machine Backup

Computers break. The biggest surprise for most people is often that the hard drive simply fails. Hard drives are mechanical wonders that rely on tight tolerances and parts moving at high speeds. Unfortunately, that makes them unreliable. Other ways computers break are not so surprising, such as being dropped or having coffee spilled on them. If you lose your data (and photos and videos), it is just as devastating as if a hacker in Russia or your kids or plain bad luck are the culprits. That is why it is important to protect against all the above.

The simplest way to provide backups is to get an external drive that connects to your computer and use the built-in capabilities of your Mac. You can use this drive for backup and other storage. You can even use one drive to back up multiple Macs. However, the drive should be at least the same size (memory, not physically) as the built-in drive(s) of your computer(s), and preferably twice the size. The prices have dropped so much in recent years that 2-terabyte drives on Amazon are around $60. That is a tiny investment if it saves just one important file in the future. Apple also offers AirPort Time Capsules for a fee which can also provide Wi-Fi and a wireless connection.

As soon as your Mac sees an external drive, it asks, "Do you want to use {name of drive} to back up with time machine?" Either click Yes when this happens or go to:

System Preferences > Time Machine. Then select the external drive. If you have FileVault on, then it will be assumed you want to encrypt the backup drive too. Use your password manager to create and store a good password, and enter it here.

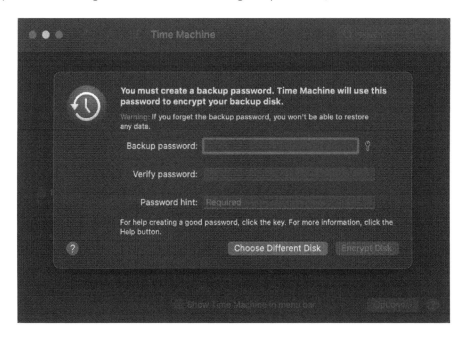

Check the box that says **Back Up Automatically**.

macOS will immediately go to work. This first backup could take hours because it is copying everything—all your files, programs, and configurations. You can work on other things while this goes on or go watch Netflix until it completes.

After that, macOS checks for any changes every hour and only records the changes, so these backups are fast. As it says in the Time Machine screenshot, you can go back to any hour in the last twenty-four, any day for the past month, or any previous week until your hard drives fill up. After that point, the oldest backups are deleted to make room for new ones.

If you have a laptop that you drag around to different places, then I highly recommend a docking station of some kind, so you only need one plug to use a bigger monitor, charge up the battery, and maybe use the wired network and a full-sized keyboard and mouse. But most importantly, that connects to this external drive so Time Machine can do its thing when you are home. Amazingly, when you are away, Time Machine will keep making backups on your local drive. Then, when you do reconnect to the backup drive, it merges them all together as if you never left. If something happens to your local drive before you get back, you do lose the backups in-between, but still sweet! The other option is to have both a travel backup drive and one at home. Time Machine will let you set up two backup drives. Go back into Time Machine, have the other drive connected, and select it as well.

Time Machine really makes all this easy.

This would be a huge improvement for most people and everybody must decide how much risk they are willing to live with. Using an external drive protects well against accidents and hardware failures. But there are other things to be concerned about because the external drive is still sitting next to your computer. Therefore, this does not protect against things like fire, flooding, and a thief taking all your equipment.

External drives also do not protect against most ransomware because that malware is often programmed to look for external drives and encrypt them too.

One way those issues could be mitigated is by unplugging your external drive and putting it in your vault. If the vault is fireproof, waterproof, and in a completely different room, this could help protect against all the physical threats and malware. Then, you would have to remember to periodically get your drive and plug it in and make sure Time Machine runs. However, this is very inconvenient, and you would obviously have gaps in your backup corresponding to how long it has been since your last backup.

In the Advanced section of this book, we revisit doing cloud and physical backups that mitigate both physical and ransomware risks.

Time Machine Recovery

Okay, something bad happened and now you need to either retrieve a file, folder, or your entire computer.

Open Time Machine from the Dock. The entire screen fades back, and a stack of windows opens. On the far right of the screen is a timeline, and just to the right of the stack of windows are buttons with up and down arrows.

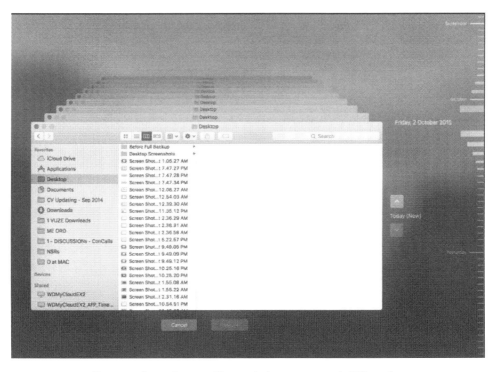

Image from https://i.stack.imgur.com/aEOve.jpg

There are four ways to navigate. First, you can just click through the windows, but this is not very efficient. Second, you can use the timeline on the right as a dial, which is ideal if you know exactly where you want to go. Third, if you select a folder or file in the top window and then hit the arrow buttons, they will take you to the last version where there was a change from the one you have now. These arrows and the fact that you can preview the files are a powerful combination that allows you to find your changes quickly. Finally, you can go into the search bar in the window and do a search.

When you finally find the file or folder and version you need, click it to highlight it, then click the **Restore** button at the bottom of the page.

If your hard drive dies, you might need to get a new one (you will have to do an internet search or call Apple for that) and then reinstall macOS or even get a new computer. At some point during setup there will be an option called **Restore from a Time Machine Backup** that you select. Then, select the backup drive, then the latest version (you can go back to older versions, but keep in mind that any changes will be lost).

Time Machine then restores *everything*—all files, macOS settings, applications, and even email contacts—just as though nothing ever happened to your old computer.

macOS Disposal

Apple has instructions on what to do when giving away or selling your Mac here: https://support.apple.com/en-us/HT201065. The biggest things are reinstalling macOS and deleting your startup disk.

14

IPHONES AND IPADS
Calling All Hackers (Apple Devices)

Smartphone and Tablet Operating Systems

iPhones run on iOS. (They are on version 14 as of this writing.) Until 2019, iPhones and iPads ran the exact same operating system. Now, iPads run iPadOS. For this book, however, I will refer to the iPhone, and it will be referring to the iPad also.

Accounts

It is possible to set up an Apple device without an Apple account (a.k.a. Apple ID), but I am going to assume most people reading this have already connected their device to an Apple account.

When setting up an Apple ID, Apple allows you to use any email address from other providers (Gmail, Yahoo! Mail, Microsoft Outlook, etc.) for this account. You can even access email from these other providers either through the built-in mail application or by downloading those applications (like Gmail) separately. However, to use iCloud Mail, you must use an Apple email (ending in @icloud.com). This is a little confusing, but good that you have all these options.

Note that your Apple ID password is not the same as your phone PIN (or passphrase). They are needed at different times for different things.

Once your Apple ID is set up, then all the Apple devices connected to that account share the same iCloud email, contacts, calendars, photos, and so on. This is also where you can set backups and get to Find My iPhone if you lose the device.

Apple forces you to set up 2FA. This is done either through a phone number or an additional Apple device connected to the same account. So, if you have an iPhone and a Mac, if you lose one, then you can get access to your iCloud account using your password and the other device. However, if you only have a single device, I highly recommend adding a second phone number to the account that Apple can use for 2FA. The second number can even be a landline because they offer voice calls. I say this because once I forgot my phone PIN and Apple ID password (before I had a password manager), and therefore there was no way for me to get into my phone or verify to Apple that they should unlock my account. I had to wait two days for them to see if anybody reported it stolen (I guess). Do this at https://appleid.apple.com.

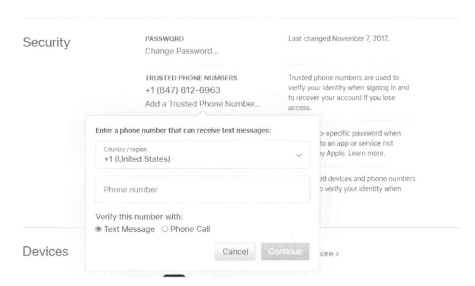

Set a Lock Screen and PIN

I know it is a pain, but you must set a PIN on your smartphone and have it lock automatically. There is a 100% probability of leaving your phone unattended at some point. After a while, you get used to entering a PIN every time and do not think about it. Also, most newer phones allow you to use a fingerprint or your face. Go ahead and set this feature up for convenience if desired. But remember, the **phone can still be opened by the PIN,** so it must be set and must be strong. Do not use all one number, like 0000 or 1111, or easy patterns like 1234 or 1793 (corners). Do not use some part of your birthday, phone number, or Social Security number. Use six digits rather than four. Put the PIN in your password manager if you might forget it.

You should set up the PIN when you set up the phone, but in case you did not.

> **Settings > Face (or Touch) ID & Passcode > Turn Passcode On >** If there are six circles, then enter a six-digit PIN; repeat to be sure you know it. If there are only four circles, look just above the keypad, click **Passcode Options > 6-Digit Numeric Code**, and enter it twice.

If you follow the above suggestions, then your PIN should be strong enough. But for those who want more than numbers, you can make it a passcode (numbers and letters).

> **Settings > Face (or Touch) ID & Passcode**. Enter your current PIN. Then click **Change Passcode**. You must enter your passcode PIN again. Look just above the keypad. Click **Passcode Options> Custom Alphanumeric Code**. Enter your new passcode.

Along with setting a PIN, you need to set the lock screen time. Obviously, the longer your phone is open, the more opportunity for someone to grab it. I highly recommend no more than a minute; thirty seconds is better.

> **Settings > Display & Brightness> Auto-Lock.** Choose the minimum you can tolerate.

Erase Data on Failed Attempts

🚫 MAY BREAK THINGS: This one could be an outright bad idea if you have kids or once in a while you get drunk and pound on your phone trying to dial an ex.

If you do backups, like I explain in a future section, then I recommend turning the Erase Data (Auto Factory Reset) feature on. This great security measure makes your phone erase itself if there are ten failed login attempts.

> **Settings > Face (or Touch) ID & Passcode**. Enter your PIN and then scroll down and toggle **On** Erase Data.

Set Auto-Updates

The iPhone and iPad should be set to auto update by default. We have discussed how critical it is to keep software updated in past chapters. To make sure:

Settings > General > Software Update >Automatic Updates; set toggle to **On**.

If you charge your iPhone at night and leave it connected to Wi-Fi, it will automatically keep you updated, though it will still notify you and ask permission to install.

Set Up Your Password Manager

As discussed in the first chapter on passwords, you need to have a password manager set up. All of them have iPhone versions that you can download from the App Store, so that is the first step. Then see the chapter on web browsers to turn on autofill so that your password manager can fill your usernames and passwords for you.

Jailbreak

Jailbreaking an iPhone means disabling the phone's built-in security. People do this for two reasons: (1) They are highly skilled and want to enable their phone to do things Apple considers harmful or cannot profit from. These people know the risks. (2) They do not know what they are doing and are enabling malware to take over their phone. At this point, the bad guys can access any data, read your emails, listen to calls, and turn on the camera and mic at any time.

If any application you want to run on your phone says you need to jailbreak (or root) your phone, **do *not* do it**.

Encrypt the Phone

If you lose your phone, the first line of defense is your PIN as I have mentioned. However, if the person who has it has some basic hacking capability, they can pull your phone apart and read the data directly off your drive. Encryption is a defense that only matters when the attacker physically has your phone, but it is an important defense.

The latest versions of iOS encrypt your phone by default assuming you set a PIN at setup. So the only thing I have to say is do not turn this off. If you do not have the phone encrypted, then when you try to turn encryption on, you will have to set a PIN (or passcode). To see that encryption is on:

Settings > Face (or Touch) ID & Passcode. Enter your PIN then scroll clear to the bottom, and in tiny letters it will say "Data protection is enabled."

Download Software from the App Store, but Not Antivirus

Apple is a closed system, meaning they make all the hardware and the operating system, and Apple does extensive vetting on applications in the Apple App Store

. Not only that, but it is almost impossible to download software outside of the Apple App Store.

Apple will not even allow developers to have applications with *antivirus* in the titles because they want people to believe that malware doesn't exist in their store. (See the next picture for their support response.) I don't recommend antivirus software for iPhones because it doesn't really even exist, or if it does, it probably does as much harm as good.

Unfortunately, though, malware *does* exist in the Apple store, so you still need to stick to reputable applications.

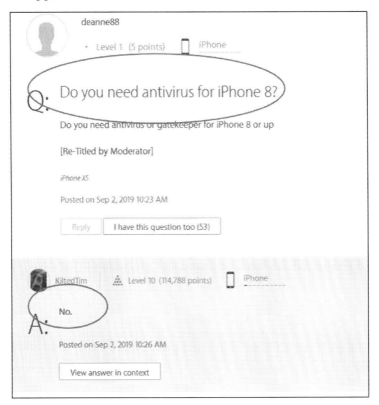

Image from Apple help page

Use a Wall Wart or Be Careful When Charging (Juice Jacking)

Be careful when using a public charging station (airports, train stations, libraries, even ride-sharing cars like Uber and Lyft) where you plug directly into a USB port. That port could try to connect to your iPhone and try to upload malware or access data. Now, your phone should detect that and ask something like "Allow Data Access?" just like when you plug into a computer USB port. If this is the case, click **Don't Allow**.

But another (and much stronger) layer of security is to simply use a regular electrical outlet and the little converter (a.k.a. wall wart) that comes with your phone or tablet to make this attack impossible.

Also, never borrow a charging cable from a stranger or one you find somewhere. It has been shown that an Apple Lightning cable can be modified to inject malware into a Mac (or PC).[1] This is an interesting twist on the *candy drop* discussed in the "Bypassing the Firewall" chapter.

Don't Use Public Wi-Fi

In a later chapter on networking, I discuss that there are simply too many ways you can be burned by public Wi-Fi. Nothing is "free," so instead pay for a data plan from your phone company that fits your needs and use LTE (the cellular network) when not at home. Heck, I do not even think it is a good idea to use your work Wi-Fi with your personal devices.

The only Wi-Fi you should use is the Wi-Fi from your home, complete with a high-strength password. It is okay to have this one network set to auto-join. But you must make sure your phone is not automatically connecting to anything without you explicitly knowing. To do this:

> Go to **Settings > Wi-Fi > Ask to Join Networks > Off**. Then go back to **Wi-Fi > Auto-Join Hotspot > Never**.

Privacy Settings

The iPhone has two aspects to privacy. One is how much data Apple can collect, and the other is what capabilities each application has access to.

Privacy from Apple

As for how much data Apple can collect on you, the data collected is used either for targeted ads, product optimization, or some mildly cool features. Some people do not mind this, but from a security perspective, the more data out there on when, where, and what you are doing is potential identity theft or stalker material. As an additional bonus, turning data collection off can save you cellular data (it sends this information regardless of if you are on Wi-Fi or not) and battery life because they are constantly sending this information to Apple.

Settings > Privacy > Tracking. Toggle **Off** Allow Apps to Request to Track.

Settings > Privacy > Analytics and Improvements. Toggle **Off** Analytics Data, Improve Siri & Dictation, and Share iCloud Analytics.

Settings > Privacy > Apple Advertising. Toggle **Off** Personalized Ads.

You also must evaluate how much you want to share with Apple on your location. This is difficult to navigate, so I will guide you here:

Settings > Privacy > Location Services > Location Services. Location Services must be toggled **On** for Find My iPhone to work, which we discuss in the next section. However, tap into **Share My Location**. In tiny print, it says, "Share your location with family and friends in Messages and Find My, make personal requests using Siri on HomePod, and use automations in the Home app." If you are not using any of these, then I recommend toggling it **Off.**

Settings > Privacy > Location Services >System Services. There is a dizzying list of reasons Apple is sending your location data to these services. The only necessary ones to toggle **On** are Emergency Calls and SOS and Find My Phone.

A couple of them will give vague warnings when you toggle them **Off**, but they are not necessary. Your phone will still be able to find network towers, set the time, and whatever else, but Apple just will not get the mapping data they want. Boohoo! If you do use things like the HomeKit or use your phone as a pedometer, then leave HomeKit and Motion Calibration and Distance **On**, respectively.

For sure tap **Significant Locations**. You must use Touch ID or enter your password. Then toggle this **Off**. Also scroll down and tap **Clear History** to delete the history they have already collected. This is Apple tracking your "significant" locations, like home, work, and practically every place you go. Calling them "significant" doesn't make it less of an invasion.

Go **Back.** Scroll down and under the heading Product Improvement and toggle **Off** all three: iPhone Analytics, Popular Near Me, and Routing and Traffic. These are mildly helpful for things like using Siri to find dinner suggestions, but it still works fine without knowing you are standing next to them.

At the bottom of this screen is the Status Bar icon. Toggle it **On**. Right above that is a legend showing what the various arrow ⟋ colorings mean. From now on, when your phone's GPS is used, this arrow, in its three potential forms, will show up in the top right of the screen (or by the battery indicator if it is on). It is good to know when this is happening.

App Privacy

🚫 MAY BREAK THINGS: The entire point here is to prevent applications from accessing things like your camera. Most of the time, the program will tell you to give it access, so it is not an issue. However, sometimes the program will just fail, and it might be difficult to figure out it was denied permission.

All the above was just to keep Apple from collecting data. You also want to ensure that your applications are not accessing your phone's capabilities to collect data, spy on you, or open a path to malware. You should audit all the features your applications can access, but we will focus in on some key security issues here.

If a malicious app can turn on the camera, microphone, or location without you knowing it, then it can obviously spy on you.

All the App privacy settings start here:

Settings > Privacy > All the permissions…

1. First, do you even have any idea what the app is? If you cannot remember the last time you used an app and it can be uninstalled, then forget permissions—just uninstall the app.

   The built-in apps are frustrating because it is hard to know what they are doing, and you cannot uninstall most of them. But you can turn all the permissions off.

2. For the apps you do allow, make sure the app needs to use that feature of the phone. It makes sense that the Camera app needs access to the camera. It makes sense that Google Maps, Uber, or Lyft needs access to Location. If it does not make sense, then deny the app access.

Let us look at a few specifically.

Location Access:

> **Settings > Privacy > Location Services**. Tap **App Clips**. Toggle Confirm Location **Off**. App clips are little pieces of a regular app used for advertising said app, and it is just deceitful of Apple to try to make it look otherwise.

> **Settings > Privacy > Location Services**. Review all the other applications.

> Make sure Facebook is set to **Never**. The App Store and Wallet can also be set to **Never**.

> Some apps should be set to **While Using**, like Maps and Ride Sharing (Uber or Lyft, for example) because location is the entire reason for their existence.

> You might want to have location tagged to photos, so it is up to you if Camera has access. A good compromise is for it to **Ask** each time so you can decide with every picture. If that is annoying and you want all your pictures tagged, just remember that, and set it to **While Using**.

To Apple's credit, they do not allow apps to use location at any time like Android does.

Microphone and Camera

A feature that helps was just added in iOS 14. In the far upper right (unless the battery symbol is there, then just to the left of it) an orange dot will appear if your microphone is on. If your camera is on, then a green dot will show up there. If you have the location arrow turned on and both are happening, I believe the dot wins, and then later you get the gray arrow. But if any of these indicators are on, then you should take note. Here is how to audit apps that can access the camera or microphone:

> **Settings > Privacy > Camera.** Toggle **Off** any apps that should not have access to it. Go to **App Clips** and toggle all of these **Off**.

> **Settings > Privacy > Microphone.** Toggle **Off** on any apps that should not have access to the microphone. Go to **App Clips**. Toggle all of these **Off.**

Local Network

Some applications will want to access your local network. Legitimate reasons might be to access IoT devices, like printers, TVs (Chromecast, Apple TV), your home speakers/automation (Alexa, Google Home, Apple HomeKit), or cameras (Ring, Arlo,

Nest). However, in the chapter on your network, we will discuss getting around the firewall. If a malicious app can access the local network through your phone, then it may also access these devices or your computers and wreak havoc. Make sure only trusted apps can access your local network and that you use them.

> **Settings > Privacy > Local Network.** Toggle **Off** on any apps that should not have access to it. Go to **App Clips** and toggle all of these **Off**.

File Access

A specific kind of malware called *ransomware* will need access to your files and folders. Ransomware encrypts your files and then demands payment (usually in virtual money like Bitcoin) to decrypt them. Make sure only applications that need to access your files can, like word processors and spreadsheet tools.

> **Settings > Privacy > Files and Folders**. Toggle **Off** any apps that should not have access to it. Go to **App Clips** and toggle all of these **Off**.

Prepare to Lose Your Phone

We take our phones everywhere, so there is always the chance of leaving them somewhere. Even when good people find your phone, they will automatically read your email and look through your photos to "help you" get your phone back. It is human nature for them to do so. As for the bad guys, getting into your phone is a treasure trove of information. They might get access to any of your social media, financial, or online merchant accounts. They can pull down your photos, contacts, physical location history, calendar, entire text history, and browsing history. They can attack you directly with this information or sell it online. Not only is this a danger to you, but it could be a danger to loved ones. Bad people could text or email them that you are hurt or in trouble and then rob or harm them.[2]

The PIN stops people from getting into your phone until you can get it back or decide to pull the plug on it. Before you lose it, set up your phone so you can remotely find and control it.

Find My iPhone

Before you lose your iPhone, make sure Find My iPhone is set up. These instructions are directly from the online Apple support pages:

1. On your iPhone, iPad, or iPod touch, do one of the following:

    o   iOS 13, iPadOS 13, or later: Go to **Settings** > [*your name*] > **Find My**.

    o   iOS 12 or earlier: Go to **Settings** > [*your name*] > iCloud > **Find My iPhone**.

If you are asked to sign in, enter your Apple ID. If you do not have one, tap "Don't have an Apple ID or forgot it?" then follow the instructions.

2. If Find My [*device*] is turned off, turn it on.

3. Turn on any of the following:

   o Enable Offline Finding: For a device with iOS 13, iPadOS 13, or later, Offline Finding allows your device to be found even if it is not connected to a Wi-Fi or cellular network.

   o Send Last Location: If your device is lost or stolen and its battery charge level becomes critically low, its location is sent to Apple automatically. When you use Find My (or Find My iPhone) to locate that device, you see where it was before its battery ran out of charge.

If you lose your iPhone, go to https://icloud.com/find/ and log in with the Apple iCloud account attached to your phone. Once you are logged in, it tries to find all your devices and displays all it found on a map. From there, you can try the various options.

If your phone can be found through GPS, then of course go look for it, but be careful. Have a friend come along with their smartphone to track it. If you see it traveling down the highway, don't go on a high-speed chase and risk injuring yourself or others. Be smart, look around, ask around, but if some thug has your phone, do not be a hero and start accusing anybody. Your phone is not worth getting hurt over.

Once you are in the vicinity, you can also use the website (again on your friends phone) to make your phone ring, so that prove helpful.

You also can send a phone number that you can be reached at, and the phone will display it. Hopefully, a person that finds it will call and give it to you.

If you cannot find your phone and it is not looking like you will, then send the command to remotely delete all the information. If it is off, the location services will not work and neither will the deletion, but once it powers back up, the deletion command will work. Finally, call your carrier and tell them to cancel the SIM card so it cannot be transferred to another phone.

If the device you are looking for is off, then you can set several actions to be enacted when it is back online, as this picture shows:

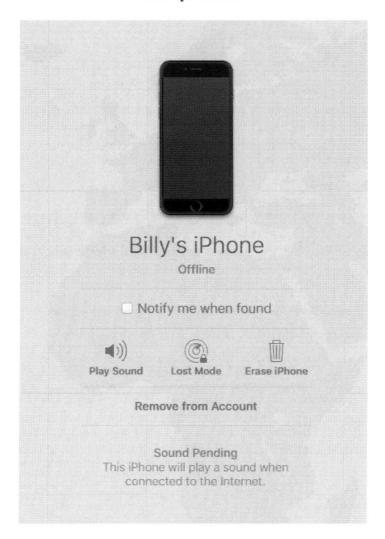

Apple has an additional feature called Activation Lock for newer devices. If you erase your phone remotely, then it cannot be turned back on without your Apple ID and password. Previously with remote erase, your data was removed, but the thief could still do a factory reset and potentially use the iPhone. Not being able to turn the phone back on drastically reduces the value of the phone to thieves.

Set Cloud Backups

In the PC and Mac sections, I talk about how important it is to back up your computers in case they break or are lost. But I personally do not back up my phones because (1) I do not keep important files on them, (2) I do not use very many apps, and the ones I do use keep the data in the cloud (like email, contacts, and calendar), and (3) I like going through and putting all the settings back to the way I like them when I get a new device. The only things I need to back up are my photos and videos, and I do that with a separate service like iCloud Photos. However, if you are not like me and losing your phone would mean losing valuable data and/or you prefer being stabbed to restoring it manually, then continue.

Apple lets you back your phone up online in iCloud or on your computer. Online is easier and set by default, so I show that here. Previously, we went through all this effort to stop Apple from collecting data, and now I am telling you how to upload the entire phone contents to their cloud. There are a few differences, but the biggest thing is that backups are encrypted and Apple claims that even they cannot access the data. Another thing is that by virtue of being connected to an Apple account, Apple already has your contacts, calendar, email, iMessages, etc. (assuming you use them). As I have said before, we must trust them to an extent. This comes down to the trade-off of using them for valuable services but not letting them generate reams of data that help them and could harm you. If you do not like this idea and still want backups, then you can look up how to back up your phone to your computer.

Connect to your home Wi-Fi. Go to **Settings > [your name] > iCloud > iCloud Backup**. Turn the toggle on and click **Back Up Now**, and then stay on the Wi-Fi network until this first backup is completed.

Going forward, your iPhone will wait until it next sees (1) you are on Wi-Fi, (2) you are connected to power, and (3) the screen is locked, and it will back up daily.

Restore Cloud Backups

Assuming you have a new device or a freshly factory reset one:

Turn on the iPhone. Follow the onscreen setup, including setting up Wi-Fi because you will want to be on it until the Apps & Data screen. Click **Restore from iCloud Backup**. Sign into iCloud with your Apple ID and password. Choose a backup referring to the date. The process starts, so stay on Wi-Fi until done. It could take a few minutes to an hour. Once completed, finish the setup process.

Giving Away or Selling Your Phone

Just like with your computer, you must make sure that there is nothing on your phone that the next person could use for fraud or abuse. The best thing to do is a factory reset, which will delete everything.

First sign out. Go to **Settings > Sign Out** and enter your Apple ID. Click **Turn Off**.

Then delete everything. Go to **Settings > General > Reset> Erase All Content and**

Settings.

Used Phones

Used phones can mean real savings, but make sure you start with a legit phone that is factory reset.

IMEI Number

Before you buy, check to see if the phone has been reported lost or stolen. Go to www.imeipro.info and enter your IMEI number.

To find your IMEI number for an iPhone, go to **Settings > General > About** and scroll down. If you cannot open the phone for some reason, older iPhones (6 and before) have it printed right on the back of the phone. Newer ones have it printed on the

SIM tray, so you need a paperclip to pop it open.

Start with Factory Reset

Buying a used phone, of course, is the flip side of selling one. You do not want to start using a phone on which the last person left data or malware. They might not have thought to reset it.

A used iPhone could have an additional issue to be aware of called Activation Lock. This is from the Apple support pages:

Before you buy an iPhone, iPad, or iPod Touch, from someone other than Apple or an authorized Apple reseller, make sure that the device is erased and no longer linked to the previous owner's account. Ask the seller whether they've turned off Activation Lock, and then follow these steps:

1. Turn on the device and slide to unlock.
2. If the passcode lock screen or the Home screen appears, the device has not been erased. Ask the seller to completely erase the device by going to **Settings** > **General** > **Reset** > **Erase All Content and Settings**. Do not take ownership of any used iPhone, iPad, or iPod Touch until it has been erased.
3. Begin the device setup process.
4. If you are asked for the previous owner's Apple ID and password, the device is still linked to their account. Hand the device back to the seller and ask them to enter their password. If the previous owner is not present, they can remove the device from their account by signing in to icloud.com/find. Do not take ownership of any used iPhone, iPad, or iPod Touch until it has been removed from the previous owner's account.

You will know that a device is ready for you to use when you are asked to "Set up your iPhone," "Set up your iPad," or "Set up your iPod" the first time you turn it on.

If you buy a device that is still linked to a previous owner's account, contact them as soon as possible and ask them to erase the device and remove it from their account.

References

[1] https://www.techradar.com/news/fake-iphone-lightning-cable-will-hijack-your-computer

[2] https://www.aarp.org/money/scams-fraud/info-07-2010/scam_alert_stranded_in_london.html

15

ANDROID PHONES AND TABLETS
Calling All Hackers (Android Devices)

Smartphone and Tablet Operating Systems

Android is on version 11 as of this writing, and it is used on phones and tablets. However, many manufacturers have their own "wrappers" on Android and must develop around and test the changes Google makes. So they tend to lag. Samsung phones, for example, are still on Android 10 as of this writing and call their wrapper One UI. In this section, I will provide directions based on Google's version (a Pixel, to be specific) and a Samsung Galaxy if different.

Accounts

It is possible to use an Android device without a Google account, but it is difficult, so I will assume that people reading this book are using a Google account.

A Google account and Gmail account are the same. In other words, you must have a username that is your Gmail account, like name@gmail.com. This account unifies all your email, contacts, and calendars across devices. You can also selectively sync files, photos, and videos. It also enables Find My Phone if you lose it and provides an easy way to do phone backup.

Set a Lock Screen and PIN

I know it is a pain, but you must set a PIN on your smartphone and have it lock automatically. There is a 100% probability of leaving your phone unattended at some point. After a while, you get used to entering a PIN every time and do not think about it. Also, most newer phones allow you to use a fingerprint or your face. Go ahead and set this feature up for convenience if desired, but remember, the **phone can still be opened by the PIN,** so it must be set and must be strong. Do not use all one number, like 0000 or 1111, or easy patterns like 1234 or 1793 (corners). Do not use some part of your birthday, phone number, or Social Security number. Use six digits rather than four if possible.

Hopefully you set up the PIN when you set up the phone, but in case you did not.

Google Android:

> **Settings > Security > Screen Lock >PIN.** Enter at least a six-digit PIN. Repeat to confirm. Then it asks what notifications to show on the lock screen. Pick either "**Show sensitive content only when unlocked**" or "**Don't show notifications at all**."

Samsung Android:

> **Settings > Lock screen > PIN >** Enter at least a six-digit PIN. Repeat to confirm.

If you follow the above suggestions, then your PIN should be strong enough. But for those who want more than numbers, you can use a password (numbers and letters) by selecting that instead of PIN.

You need the screen to lock relatively quickly to be effective. I highly recommend no more than a minute; thirty seconds is better. For setting lock screen time:

Google Android:

> **Settings > Security**. By Screen Lock, click the **Gear** icon > **Lock After Screen Timeout**. Choose the lowest time you can tolerate.

Samsung Android:

> **Settings > Lock Screen > Secure Lock Settings**. Enter your current PIN > **Lock Automatically**. Choose the lowest time you can tolerate.

Erase Data on Failed Attempts

🚫 MAY BREAK THINGS: Somebody with access to your phone (drunken you, kids, hilarious friend) might poke numbers in and end up erasing your phone.

Erasing data after failed sign-in attempts is a great security measure that makes your phone erase itself after fifteen failed login attempts. I could not find this feature in the Google Android version, but Samsung had it.

Samsung Android:

> **Settings > Lock Screen > Secure Lock Settings**. Enter your current PIN > **Auto Factory Reset**. Enter your new password.

Set Auto-Updates

We have discussed keeping software updated as critical in past chapters. Android has this on by default, but you can check manually.

Google Android:

> **Settings > System > Advanced > System Update > Check for Update**.

Samsung Android:

> **Settings > Software Update > Download and Install**.
>
> However, just below that is **Auto Download Over Wi-Fi**. Turn that on. Then not only will you be notified of updates, but also your phone will have it downloaded, and all you must do is accept.

Google only has this ability to force updates on phones it makes, like the Pixel line. Phones made by others, like Samsung, make additional modifications and cannot just push the Google updates instantly in case there is an incompatibility. Android security updates on non-Google phones may take a while longer. There is nothing you can do about this, but it is good to know.

Encrypt the Phone

If you lose your phone, the first line of defense is your PIN as I have mentioned. However, bad actors can just pull your phone apart and try to read your data directly off the hard drive.

The nice thing with the latest versions of Google Android is it encrypts your phone by default. The only thing I have to say is do not turn this off. You can see it manually.

Google Android:

> **Settings > Security > Encryption & Credentials**. It says Encrypt Phone (encrypted).

<u>Samsung Android</u>:

Samsung only encrypts the phone if a PIN is set. I am not sure if this is because Samsung is still on Android 10 or Samsung overrides this, but you must set a PIN for it to be encrypted.

> **Settings > Biometrics and Security**. Scroll down to **Other Security Settings**. Scroll down to **Strong Protection**. If it is toggled on, you are good. If not, toggle **On** and follow the directions.

Set Up Your Password Manager

As discussed in the first chapter on passwords, you need to have a password manager set up. All of them have Android versions that you can download from the app store, so that is the first step. Then see the chapter on web browsers to turn on autofill so your password manager can fill your usernames and passwords for you.

Only Download Software from the Stores, but Not Antivirus

When I talk about the "app store" here, I mean the Google Play store . Google has a far different approach than Apple. Android is an open system, in the same way Windows is for computers. Android is added to other phone makers and has looser oversight on their app store. This has pros and cons.

The pros are that developers have an easier time getting their applications into the Google Play store and therefore tend to create a more diverse set of applications. The user also has more freedom and can even download applications outside of the Google Play store. This is called *sideloading*.[3]

The cons are that with this extra freedom comes more risk. Google does not scrutinize the apps as closely as Apple. Even though Google gives you more freedom than Apple to get a virus, that does not mean you should take advantage of that freedom. If you stick to reputable companies that make apps that are in Google Play and do not sideload anything (especially free games) that you do not 100% trust, then you are not taking big risks in the first place.

Google has a feature called Google Play Protect that scans for malware on apps in their store, and even scans apps on your phone that you sideloaded for suspicious behavior. No need for an additional antivirus app.

Root

Rooting an Android phone means disabling the phone's built-in security. People do this for two reasons: (1) They are highly skilled and want to enable their phone to do things Google considers harmful or cannot profit from. These people know the risks. (2) They do not know what they are doing and are enabling malware to take over their phone. At this point, the bad guys can access any data, read your emails, listen to calls, and turn on the camera and mic at any time.

If any application you want to run on your phone comes from a source you cannot 100% trust and they say you need root your phone first (or in the process of installing the application), **do not do it!**

Use a Wall Wart or Be Careful When Charging (Juice Jacking)

When you use a public charging station (airports, train stations, libraries, even ride-sharing cars like Uber and Lyft) where you plug directly into a USB port, that port could try to connect to your phone and try to upload malware or access data. Now, your phone should detect that and ask something like "Allow Data Access?" just like when you plug into a computer USB port. Obviously, if this is the case, click **Don't Allow**.

But another (and much stronger) layer of security is to simply use a regular electrical outlet and the little converter (a.k.a. wall wart) that comes with your phone or tablet to make this attack impossible.

Never borrow a charging cable from a stranger or one you find somewhere. It has been shown that a charging cable can be modified to inject malware into a Mac (or PC).[1] This is an interesting twist on the *candy drop* discussed in another chapter.

Do Not Use Public Wi-Fi

In a later chapter on networking, I discuss that there are simply too many ways you can be burned by public Wi-Fi. Nothing is "free," so instead pay for a data plan from your phone company that fits your needs and use LTE (the cellular network) when not at home. Heck, I do not even think it is a good idea to use your work Wi-Fi with your personal devices.

The only Wi-Fi you should use is the one you set up at home yourself, complete with a high-strength password. It is okay to have this one network set to "Auto-reconnect" so it just works when you are home. But you must make sure your phone is not automatically connecting to anything else without you explicitly knowing.

Here is how to set your home Wi-Fi network to auto-reconnect.

Google Android:

> **Settings > Network and Internet > Wi-Fi.** Click the gear next to your home network > **Advanced**. Toggle **On** Auto-reconnect.

Samsung Android:

> **Settings > Connections > Wi-Fi**. Click the gear next to your home network. Toggle **On** Auto-reconnect.

Here is how you prevent it from connecting random Wi-Fi networks.

Google Android:

> **Settings > Network and Internet > Wi-Fi > Wi-Fi Preferences**. Toggle **Off** Turn on Wi-Fi Automatically.

Samsung Android:

> **Settings > Connections > Wi-Fi**. In the top right, click ⦂ **Advanced > Turn on Wi-Fi Automatically**. Toggle **Off.**

Privacy Settings

Android has three aspects to their privacy. One is how much data Google can collect. Another aspect is what capabilities each application has access to. The last aspect is how much the phone itself is tracking you.

Privacy from Google

🚫 **MAY BREAK THINGS:** Some Google services might break or just might not be as cool.

As for how much data Google can collect on you, it is all geared toward them being able to make more money off selling advertisements. Some people do not mind this. But from a security perspective, the more data out there on when, where, and what you are doing is potential identity theft or stalker material.

Maybe most disturbing is the location history. With this on, you can go to your Google account and there is a page with a date selector and map. You can choose a date, and Google will show on the map where you were all day. Mine is empty since I turned that off when I saw how boring my life was. Work in the morning, back home in the evening. My lack of social life was too depressing to document.

But whether you are like me, or have a life, letting some massive corporation track your every move is a security threat. Here is how you turn all that off.

<u>Google Android:</u>

Settings > Privacy > Advanced. Toggle **Off** Personalize Using App Data.

Settings > Privacy > Advanced > **Usage & Diagnostics**. Toggle **Off.**

Settings > Privacy > Advanced > **Ads**. Toggle **On** Opt Out of Ads Personalization. (Note: we want On because it is opt out.)

Settings > Privacy > Advanced > **Autofill Service from Google**. Toggle **Off** Use Autofill with Google. (We will use Bitwarden for password autofill.)

Settings > Privacy > Advanced > **Activity Controls**. Toggle **Off** Web & App Activity. Then it tries to tell you how horrible it will be. Click **Pause**. It goes back to the Web & App Activity screen. Scroll down a bit to Location History and toggle it **Off**. Again, you must read there might be something wrong with your mental state to turn this off, and click **Pause**. (This is what creates that tracking map above.) It goes back to the Web & App Activity screen. Scroll down a bit to YouTube History and toggle it **Off**. Read how you might be the dumbest person alive and click **Pause**. It goes back to the Web & App Activity screen. Scroll down a bit to Ad Personalization and click **Go to Ad Settings**. Toggle **Off** Ad Personalization, and you get another warning. Click **Turn Off**. You get yet another thing talking about other ad networks. Since we are going to use the Brave browser (covered in a later chapter), that does not matter. Just click **Got It**.

Samsung Android:

Settings > Privacy > Toggle **Off** Send Diagnostic Data.

Settings > Privacy > **Usage & Diagnostics**. Toggle **Off**.

Settings > Privacy > Customization Service. Scroll down and toggle **Off** Customized Ads and Direct Marketing.

Settings > Privacy > Ads. Toggle **On** the Opt Out of Ads Personalization. (Note: we want On because it is opt out.)

Settings > Privacy > Autofill Service from Google. Toggle **Off** Use Autofill with Google. (We will use Bitwarden for password autofill.)

Settings > Privacy > Advanced > **Activity Controls**. Toggle **Off** Web & App activity. Then it tries to tell you how horrible it will be. Click **Pause**. It goes back to the Web & App Activity screen. Scroll down a bit to Location History and toggle it **Off**. Again, they warn there might be something wrong with your mental state to turn this off. Click **Pause**. It goes back to the Web & App Activity screen. Scroll down a bit to YouTube History and toggle it **Off**. Read how you might be the dumbest person alive and click **Pause**. It goes back to the Web & App Activity screen. Scroll down a bit to Ad Personalization and click **Go to Ad Settings**. Toggle **Off** Ad Personalization, and you get another warning. Click **Turn Off.** You get yet another thing talking about other ad networks. Since we are going to use the Brave browser, that does not matter. Just click **Got It**.

App Privacy

◎ MAY BREAK THINGS: The entire point here is to prevent applications from accessing things like your camera. Most of the time, the program will tell you to give it access, so it is not an issue. However, sometimes the program will just fail, and it might be difficult to figure out it was denied permission.

Everything here will be done through the permission manager.

Settings > Privacy >   Permission Manager > All the Permissions...

If a malicious app can turn on the camera, microphone, or location without you knowing it, then it can obviously spy on you.

As far as permissions that apps have, you will want to go through each of the permissions and make sure of three things.

1. First, do you even have any idea what the app is? If you cannot remember the last time you used an app and it can be uninstalled, then forget permissions; just uninstall it.

    The built-in apps are frustrating because it is hard to know what they are doing, and you cannot uninstall most of them. But you can disable many of them. You can also turn all the permissions off.

2. For the apps you do use, make sure the app needs to use that feature of the phone. It makes sense that the Camera app needs access to the camera. It makes sense that Google Maps, Uber, or Lyft need access to Location. If it does not make sense, then deny the app access. Turn Facebook off so it does not post your location with every post.

3. With Location, Camera, and Microphone, there are additional choices. They are "Allowed all the time," "Ask every time," and "Allowed only while in use." (Interestingly, Samsung removed the "Ask every time" option.)

    Uber once only allowed "Deny" or "Allowed all the time." "Deny" means the app cannot work to get you rides, so you did not really have a choice. Uber wanted to be able to track you all the time, which is nonsense. There was backlash, and Uber can now be set to "Allow only while in use."

    If you want the Google (or Samsung Bixby) voice assistant to work, then you must give it microphone access all the time. I do not use them, so have it off too. However, for the most part, there is no good reason for any app to be able to track you constantly, and Google should turn this option off. Apple devices do not have the "Allow all the time" option (Siri excluded, apparently).

Device Personalization

The phone (or tablet) itself can track you. In Google's privacy statement about this, they swear the data is encrypted and it stays on the phone. But then they give some exceptions. I turn this off and do not miss anything. But the idea is the phone can watch what you do and make suggestions for typing, suggesting apps you might like, and, yes, advertising. It is up to you if you want to keep this, but if not, here is how to turn it off.

Google Android:

> **Settings > Apps and Notifications**. Under Recently Opened Apps, click **See All Apps**. Scroll down to **Device Personalization Service > Permissions**. In the Allowed section click every item and select **Deny**. When done, all the permissions should be in the Denied section.

> **Settings > Apps and Notifications**. Under recently opened apps, click **See All Apps**. Scroll down to **Device Personalization Service > Advanced> Display Over Other Apps**. Toggle **Off** Allow Display Over Other Apps.

> **Settings > Privacy > Device Personalization Services > Clear Data.** A window pops up. Select "All time" and click **Clear Data**.

Samsung Android:

> **Settings > Apps > Device Personalization Services Permissions**. In the Allowed section click every item and select **Deny**. When done, all the permissions should be in the Denied section.

> **Settings > Apps > Device Personalization Services Permissions >   Appear on Top**. Toggle **Off** Allow Permission.

> **Settings >   Privacy > Customization Service >   Customization Service**. Toggle **Off**.

> **Settings > Privacy > Device Personalization Services > Clear Data**. A window pops up. Select "All Time" and click **Clear Data**.

Prepare to Lose Your Phone

We take our phone everywhere, so there is always the chance of leaving it somewhere. Even good people will automatically read your email and look through your photos to "help you" get your phone back. It is human nature for them to do so. As for the bad guys, getting into your phone is a treasure trove of information. They might get access to any of your social media, financial, or online merchant accounts.

They can pull down your photos, contacts, physical location history, calendar, entire text history, and browsing history. They can attack you directly with this information or sell it online. Not only is this a danger to you, but it could be a danger to loved ones. Bad people could contact them by texting or using your email and rob or harm them.[2]

The PIN stops people from getting into your phone until you can get it back or decide to pull the plug on it. Before you lose it, set up your phone so you can remotely find and control it.

Before we get too fancy, the simplest pre-emptive thing to do is simply put a message on your lock screen that provides an alternative contact number if somebody finds it. A company called Asurion says this increases the likelihood of recovering your lost phone by a factor of three.

Google Android:

> **Settings > Display > Advanced >   Lock Screen > Add Text on Lock Screen**. Enter a simple message like: "If found, please call 312-555-1234."

Samsung Android:

> **Settings > Lock Screen > Contact Information**. Enter a simple message like: "If found, please call 312-555-1234."

Find My Android

First, make sure that you can log into the same Google account that is attached to your phone from a computer without your phone. You can do this at https://myaccount.google.com. This sounds trivial, but because I have been harping on you about using a password manager and setting 2FA on it, this could be an issue if the 2FA uses your phone.

Second, there are some settings on the phone that must be properly configured. The Location and Find My Phone features must be on.

To turn on Location:

Google Android and Samsung Android:

> **Settings > Location**. Make sure the toggle switch is **On**. Note that you do not have to give any applications permission nor allow Google to track your location history as discussed in the Privacy section. However, you should have the Google Emergency Location Service turned on in case of an emergency (allows 911 to find you).

To turn on Find My Device:

<u>Google Android</u>:

> **Settings > Security** (or **Security and Location**) **> Find My Device**. Make sure the toggle switch is **On**.

<u>Samsung Android</u>:

> **Settings > Google > Security > Find My Device**. Make sure the toggle switch is **On**.

> Samsung has its own version, so this can be confusing. If you prefer to use it, you will need a Samsung account. Go to:

> **Settings > Biometrics and Security > Find My Device**. You will open a new screen and move the toggle switch to **On**.

> I recommend the Google one, but regardless of the one you choose, make sure the other one is off.

Third, you must make sure Google Play has Visibility turned on. I have no idea the point of this part, but go to https://play.google.com/settings, log into the relevant Google account, and under Devices, make sure "Show in menus" is checked.

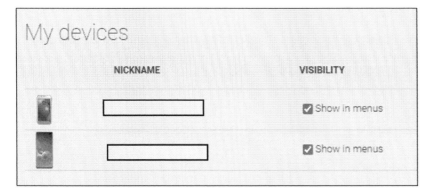

Once you have lost your phone, on your computer or another smartphone, go to https://myaccount.google.com/find-your-phone. If you use your home computer, then you might already be logged in. Regardless, you must be logged in with the same Google account that you have on your lost phone. Once you do that, then a list of devices connected to that account will show up. Pick the lost device.

If Google can contact your phone, then you get a map with your phone location highlighted. If your phone is off or out of coverage, then you will just get a map of the entire country. This is one time that letting Google track your location constantly helps, because it will show the last known location if it has it. However, I told you to turn that off previously. Apple has a feature where it will send a location right before the battery dies, but with Google, they can either track you constantly or only with Find My Device when your phone is on.

If you can locate your device with GPS, great! For the most part, you can go get it. Now, if the phone is traveling around or at least not where you left it, then obviously somebody has it. You could call a friend over and use their smartphone to log in to your Google account and then go track it down. I'd just caution that you have no idea what the person who has your phone is up to. They could be completely innocent, say you left it in their Uber, or they could be a criminal. Be smart here because no phone is worth getting hurt over.

Back to the Find Your Phone screen, on the left, you have three options. The first option is simply to make your phone play loudly so you can listen for it. This is ideal if you know you are in the vicinity of the phone (for me, usually under a couch cushion by some old Cheetos), but it is on silent or vibrate mode, so a friend calling isn't helping.

The next option is to lock the phone screen and put a message on it along with a phone number a person can call if they find your phone. Hopefully, somebody honest will find it. This message is much larger than the one we created earlier, and it even has a big Call button that allows the finder to call using your phone.

The lost option is when you have given up trying to find the phone and you want to erase it. If your Android phone is erased using this remote method, then it cannot be turned back on without you and your Google ID and password. Previously with remote erase, your data was removed, but the thief could still do a factory reset and potentially use the phone. This drastically reduces the value of the phone for thieves.

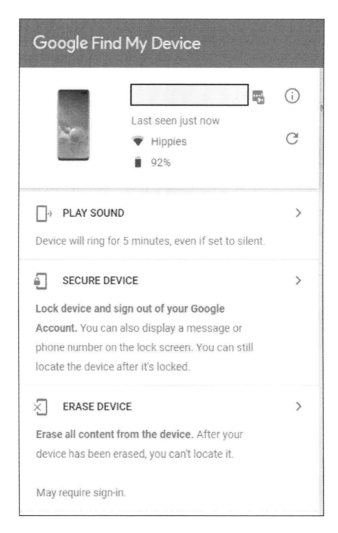

If your phone is off, then none of those options will do anything immediately. However, if it is turned back on, the lock screen will be enabled, or if you erased it, then that process will start.

Set Cloud Backups

Backups for your computers are vital in my opinion because I assume that you have data, documents, pictures, and videos that would be a disaster (or at least incredibly sad in the case of pictures) if lost. For your phone, however, you must evaluate what you would really be losing. A huge part of the information you access there is already in the cloud.

Here are the things Google backup stores:

1. Apps and apps data
2. Call history
3. Contacts
4. Device settings (including Wi-Fi passwords and permissions)
5. SMS

Notice email is not even in there. Most of us use cloud-based email, whether it is Gmail, Outlook, or Yahoo, so no reason to back this up.

Also not on that list are documents, photos, and videos. Google expects you to back your pictures up in Google Drive and Google Photos separately. There are other cloud file backup options like OneDrive from Microsoft, Box, and Dropbox. It is best to use one of these and have a comprehensive backup strategy for all your devices. I talk about that in the Advanced section of the book.

Call and SMS history, I could not care less if I lost. It might be different for you.

Contacts you want to keep. However, when you create a contact, it will ask you if you want to store it on your phone or with your Google account (or Samsung if that is your phone maker). If you keep them in your Google account, they are saved there (in the cloud). This backup is just to keep any contacts that are only stored on your phone.

Device settings might be convenient to save if you have to factory reset your phone or get a new one. When I get a new device, I like going through and setting everything how I like it, but I am not normal. As for passwords, we keep them in our password manager, so you do not need this.

The only thing in this list that might be compelling to me is app data. If I bought an app, then I would expect to be able to reinstall it later, but the data could be upsetting to lose. Fitness trackers come to mind. However, most apps store that data in the cloud as well, so you would just need to take an inventory to see if any of them store data on your phone.

If you decide to use Google to back up your phone, here is how:

Google Android:

> **Settings > System > Backup**. Turn the toggle on.

Samsung Android:

> **Settings > Google > Backup**. Turn the toggle on.

Samsung makes most Android phones, and they also offer a cloud backup. You need a

Samsung account to enable it. I do not go through this option, but you can go this route if you trust them more than Google.

Restore Cloud Backups

Since Google is on many different manufacturers' phones, I cannot give exact directions, but they will be similar. On a new or freshly reset phone, follow the onscreen instructions.

Make sure to connect to Wi-Fi when that part comes. Then at some point, it will ask if you want to restore from backup. You will need your Google account username and password. Select your backup. Stay on Wi-Fi until the process is done. Finish the rest of the setup.

Giving Away or Selling Your Phone

Just like with your computer, you must make sure that there is nothing on your phone that the next person could use for fraud or abuse. The best thing to do is a factory reset which will delete everything.

Google Android:

> **Settings > System > Advanced >   Reset Options> Erase All Data (factory reset)**.

Samsung Android:

> **Settings > General Management > Reset >   Factory Data Reset**. You get the list of all the data and applications that will be obliterated. Scroll down and when you're sure this is what you want, click **Reset**.

Used Phones or Tablets

IMEI Number

Before you buy a used phone, check to see if the phone has been reported lost or stolen. Go to www.imeipro.info and enter your IMEI number.

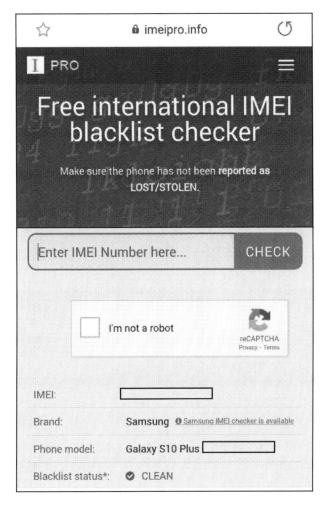

To find your IMEI number go to **Settings > About Phone**. (Most Androids will be similar.) If you cannot open the phone for some reason, then according to their website, it can be found in one of these places.

- The back of your device: If you have a removable battery, look under or below the battery for the phone's IMEI or serial number.
- The packaging: The original box may list the device's full IMEI and serial number.
- Your carrier's website: Your account details may list the device's IMEI and serial number.
- Bill of sale: Review your sales receipt or contract for your device's IMEI and serial number.

Start with Factory Reset

Buying a used phone, of course, is the flip side of selling one. You do not want to start using a phone where the last person left data or malware. They might not have thought to reset it.

Not only that, but if the phone was ever remotely erased, then only the owner can unlock the phone at all. So when physically receiving the phone, preferably with the seller present, turn on the device. If it asks for a login, then it has not been reset. Have them log in to unlock it so you can then run the factory reset (instruction in previous section).

Begin the setup process. If that starts, then you are good to go.

References:

[1] https://www.techradar.com/news/fake-iphone-lightning-cable-will-hijack-your-computer

[2] https://www.aarp.org/money/scams-fraud/info-07-2010/scam_alert_stranded_in_london.html

[3] https://ww.9to5google.com/2019/09/03/android-10-google-pixel-sideload-ota/#

16

ANDROID PHONES AND TABLETS

Calling All Hackers (Android Devices)

Smartphone and Tablet Operating Systems

Android is on version 11 as of this writing, and it is used on phones and tablets. However, many manufacturers have their own "wrappers" on Android and must develop around and test the changes Google makes. So they tend to lag. Samsung phones, for example, are still on Android 10 as of this writing and call their wrapper One UI. In this section, I will provide directions based on Google's version (a Pixel, to be specific) and a Samsung Galaxy if different.

Accounts

It is possible to use an Android device without a Google account, but it is difficult, so I will assume that people reading this book are using a Google account.

A Google account and Gmail account are the same. In other words, you must have a username that is your Gmail account, like name@gmail.com. This account unifies all your email, contacts, and calendars across devices. You can also selectively sync files, photos, and videos. It also enables Find My Phone if you lose it and provides an easy way to do phone backup.

Set a Lock Screen and PIN

I know it is a pain, but you must set a PIN on your smartphone and have it lock automatically. There is a 100% probability of leaving your phone unattended at some point. After a while, you get used to entering a PIN every time and do not think about it. Also, most newer phones allow you to use a fingerprint or your face. Go ahead and set this feature up for convenience if desired, but remember, the **phone can still be opened by the PIN,** so it must be set and must be strong. Do not use all one number, like 0000 or 1111, or easy patterns like 1234 or 1793 (corners). Do not use some part of your birthday, phone number, or Social Security number. Use six digits rather than four if possible.

Hopefully you set up the PIN when you set up the phone, but in case you did not.

Google Android:

> **Settings > Security > Screen Lock >PIN.** Enter at least a six-digit PIN. Repeat to confirm. Then it asks what notifications to show on the lock screen. Pick either "**Show sensitive content only when unlocked**" or "**Don't show notifications at all**."

Samsung Android:

> **Settings > Lock screen > PIN >** Enter at least a six-digit PIN. Repeat to confirm.

If you follow the above suggestions, then your PIN should be strong enough. But for those who want more than numbers, you can use a password (numbers and letters) by selecting that instead of PIN.

You need the screen to lock relatively quickly to be effective. I highly recommend no more than a minute; thirty seconds is better. For setting lock screen time:

Google Android:

> **Settings > Security**. By Screen Lock, click the **Gear** icon > **Lock After Screen Timeout**. Choose the lowest time you can tolerate.

Samsung Android:

> **Settings > Lock Screen > Secure Lock Settings**. Enter your current PIN > **Lock Automatically**. Choose the lowest time you can tolerate.

Erase Data on Failed Attempts

🚫 MAY BREAK THINGS: Somebody with access to your phone (drunken you, kids, hilarious friend) might poke numbers in and end up erasing your phone.

Erasing data after failed sign-in attempts is a great security measure that makes your phone erase itself after fifteen failed login attempts. I could not find this feature in the Google Android version, but Samsung had it.

Samsung Android:

> **Settings > Lock Screen > Secure Lock Settings**. Enter your current PIN > **Auto Factory Reset**. Enter your new password.

Set Auto-Updates

We have discussed keeping software updated as critical in past chapters. Android has this on by default, but you can check manually.

Google Android:

> **Settings > System > Advanced > System Update > Check for Update**.

Samsung Android:

> **Settings > Software Update > Download and Install**.
>
> However, just below that is **Auto Download Over Wi-Fi**. Turn that on. Then not only will you be notified of updates, but also your phone will have it downloaded, and all you must do is accept.

Google only has this ability to force updates on phones it makes, like the Pixel line. Phones made by others, like Samsung, make additional modifications and cannot just push the Google updates instantly in case there is an incompatibility. Android security updates on non-Google phones may take a while longer. There is nothing you can do about this, but it is good to know.

Encrypt the Phone!

If you lose your phone, the first line of defense is your PIN as I have mentioned. However, bad actors can just pull your phone apart and try to read your data directly off the hard drive.

The nice thing with the latest versions of Google Android is it encrypts your phone by default. The only thing I have to say is do not turn this off. You can see it manually.

Google Android:

> **Settings > Security > Encryption & Credentials**. It says Encrypt Phone (encrypted).

<u>Samsung Android:</u>

Samsung only encrypts the phone if a PIN is set. I am not sure if this is because Samsung is still on Android 10 or Samsung overrides this, but you must set a PIN for it to be encrypted.

> **Settings > Biometrics and Security**. Scroll down to **Other Security Settings**. Scroll down to **Strong Protection**. If it is toggled on, you are good. If not, toggle **On** and follow the directions.

Set Up Your Password Manager

As discussed in the first chapter on passwords, you need to have a password manager set up. All of them have Android versions that you can download from the app store, so that is the first step. Then see the chapter on web browsers to turn on autofill so your password manager can fill your usernames and passwords for you.

Only Download Software from the Stores, but Not Antivirus

When I talk about the "app store" here, I mean the Google Play store ▶ . Google has a far different approach than Apple. Android is an open system, in the same way Windows is for computers. Android is added to other phone makers and has looser oversight on their app store. This has pros and cons.

The pros are that developers have an easier time getting their applications into the Google Play store and therefore tend to create a more diverse set of applications. The user also has more freedom and can even download applications outside of the Google Play store. This is called *sideloading*.[3]

The cons are that with this extra freedom comes more risk. Google does not scrutinize the apps as closely as Apple. Even though Google gives you more freedom than Apple to get a virus, that does not mean you should take advantage of that freedom. If you stick to reputable companies that make apps that are in Google Play and do not sideload anything (especially free games) that you do not 100% trust, then you are not taking big risks in the first place.

Google has a feature called Google Play Protect that scans for malware on apps in their store, and even scans apps on your phone that you sideloaded for suspicious behavior. No need for an additional antivirus app.

Root

Rooting an Android phone means disabling the phone's built-in security. People do this for two reasons: (1) They are highly skilled and want to enable their phone to do things Google considers harmful or cannot profit from. These people know the risks. (2) They do not know what they are doing and are enabling malware to take over their phone. At this point, the bad guys can access any data, read your emails, listen to calls, and turn on the camera and mic at any time.

If any application you want to run on your phone comes from a source you cannot 100% trust and they say you need root your phone first (or in the process of installing the application), **do not do it!**

Use a Wall Wart or Be Careful When Charging (Juice Jacking)

When you use a public charging station (airports, train stations, libraries, even ride-sharing cars like Uber and Lyft) where you plug directly into a USB port, that port could try to connect to your phone and try to upload malware or access data. Now, your phone should detect that and ask something like "Allow Data Access?" just like when you plug into a computer USB port. Obviously, if this is the case, click **Don't Allow**.

But another (and much stronger) layer of security is to simply use a regular electrical outlet and the little converter (a.k.a. wall wart) that comes with your phone or tablet to make this attack impossible.

Never borrow a charging cable from a stranger or one you find somewhere. It has been shown that a charging cable can be modified to inject malware into a Mac (or PC).[1] This is an interesting twist on the *candy drop* discussed in another chapter.

Do Not Use Public Wi-Fi

In a later chapter on networking, I discuss that there are simply too many ways you can be burned by public Wi-Fi. Nothing is "free," so instead pay for a data plan from your phone company that fits your needs and use LTE (the cellular network) when not at home. Heck, I do not even think it is a good idea to use your work Wi-Fi with your personal devices.

The only Wi-Fi you should use is the one you set up at home yourself, complete with a high-strength password. It is okay to have this one network set to "Auto-reconnect" so it just works when you are home. But you must make sure your phone is not automatically connecting to anything else without you explicitly knowing.

Here is how to set your home Wi-Fi network to auto-reconnect.

Google Android:

>
> **Settings > Network and Internet > Wi-Fi.** Click the gear next to your home network > **Advanced**. Toggle **On** Auto-reconnect.

<u>Samsung Android</u>:

> **Settings > Connections > Wi-Fi**. Click the gear next to your home network. Toggle **On** Auto-reconnect.

Here is how you prevent it from connecting random Wi-Fi networks.

<u>Google Android</u>:

> **Settings > Network and Internet > Wi-Fi > Wi-Fi Preferences**. Toggle **Off** Turn on Wi-Fi Automatically.

<u>Samsung Android</u>:

> **Settings > Connections > Wi-Fi**. In the top right, click ⋮ **Advanced > Turn on Wi-Fi Automatically**. Toggle **Off.**

Privacy Settings

Android has three aspects to their privacy. One is how much data Google can collect. Another aspect is what capabilities each application has access to. The last aspect is how much the phone itself is tracking you.

Privacy from Google

🚫 **MAY BREAK THINGS:** Some Google services might break or just might not be as cool.

As for how much data Google can collect on you, it is all geared toward them being able to make more money off selling advertisements. Some people do not mind this. But from a security perspective, the more data out there on when, where, and what you are doing is potential identity theft or stalker material.

Maybe most disturbing is the location history. With this on, you can go to your Google account and there is a page with a date selector and map. You can choose a date, and Google will show on the map where you were all day. Mine is empty since I turned that off when I saw how boring my life was. Work in the morning, back home in the evening. My lack of social life was too depressing to document.

But whether you are like me, or have a life, letting some massive corporation track your every move is a security threat. Here is how you turn all that off.

Google Android:

Settings > Privacy > Advanced. Toggle **Off** Personalize Using App Data.

Settings > Privacy > Advanced > **Usage & Diagnostics.** Toggle **Off.**

Settings > Privacy > Advanced > **Ads.** Toggle **On** Opt Out of Ads Personalization. (Note: we want On because it is opt out.)

Settings > Privacy > Advanced > **Autofill Service from Google.** Toggle **Off** Use Autofill with Google. (We will use Bitwarden for password autofill.)

Settings > Privacy > Advanced > **Activity Controls.** Toggle **Off** Web & App Activity. Then it tries to tell you how horrible it will be. Click **Pause**. It goes back to the Web & App Activity screen. Scroll down a bit to Location History and toggle it **Off**. Again, you must read there might be something wrong with your mental state to turn this off, and click **Pause**. (This is what creates that tracking map above.) It goes back to the Web & App Activity screen. Scroll down a bit to YouTube History and toggle it **Off**. Read how you might be the dumbest person alive and click **Pause**. It goes back to the Web & App Activity screen. Scroll down a bit to Ad Personalization and click **Go to Ad Settings**. Toggle **Off** Ad Personalization, and you get another warning. Click **Turn Off**. You get yet another thing talking about other ad networks. Since we are going to use the Brave browser (covered in a later chapter), that does not matter. Just click **Got It**.

Samsung Android:

Settings > Privacy > Toggle **Off** Send Diagnostic Data.

Settings > Privacy > **Usage & Diagnostics**. Toggle **Off**.

Settings > Privacy > Customization Service. Scroll down and toggle **Off** Customized Ads and Direct Marketing.

Settings > Privacy > Ads. Toggle **On** the Opt Out of Ads Personalization. (Note: we want On because it is opt out.)

Settings > Privacy > Autofill Service from Google. Toggle **Off** Use Autofill with Google. (We will use Bitwarden for password autofill.)

Settings > Privacy > Advanced > **Activity Controls**. Toggle **Off** Web & App activity. Then it tries to tell you how horrible it will be. Click **Pause**. It goes back to the Web & App Activity screen. Scroll down a bit to Location History and toggle it **Off**. Again, they warn there might be something wrong with your mental state to turn this off. Click **Pause**. It goes back to the Web & App Activity screen. Scroll down a bit to YouTube History and toggle it **Off**. Read how you might be the dumbest person alive and click **Pause**. It goes back to the Web & App Activity screen. Scroll down a bit to Ad Personalization and click **Go to Ad Settings**. Toggle **Off** Ad Personalization, and you get another warning. Click **Turn Off.** You get yet another thing talking about other ad networks. Since we are going to use the Brave browser, that does not matter. Just click **Got It**.

App Privacy

Ⓞ **MAY BREAK THINGS:** The entire point here is to prevent applications from accessing things like your camera. Most of the time, the program will tell you to give it access, so it is not an issue. However, sometimes the program will just fail, and it might be difficult to figure out it was denied permission.

Everything here will be done through the permission manager.

Settings > Privacy >   Permission Manager > All the Permissions...

If a malicious app can turn on the camera, microphone, or location without you knowing it, then it can obviously spy on you.

As far as permissions that apps have, you will want to go through each of the permissions and make sure of three things.

1. First, do you even have any idea what the app is? If you cannot remember the last time you used an app and it can be uninstalled, then forget permissions; just uninstall it.

   The built-in apps are frustrating because it is hard to know what they are doing, and you cannot uninstall most of them. But you can disable many of them. You can also turn all the permissions off.

2. For the apps you do use, make sure the app needs to use that feature of the phone. It makes sense that the Camera app needs access to the camera. It makes sense that Google Maps, Uber, or Lyft need access to Location. If it does not make sense, then deny the app access. Turn Facebook off so it does not post your location with every post.

3. With Location, Camera, and Microphone, there are additional choices. They are "Allowed all the time," "Ask every time," and "Allowed only while in use." (Interestingly, Samsung removed the "Ask every time" option.)

   Uber once only allowed "Deny" or "Allowed all the time." "Deny" means the app cannot work to get you rides, so you did not really have a choice. Uber wanted to be able to track you all the time, which is nonsense. There was backlash, and Uber can now be set to "Allow only while in use."

   If you want the Google (or Samsung Bixby) voice assistant to work, then you must give it microphone access all the time. I do not use them, so have it off too. However, for the most part, there is no good reason for any app to be able to track you constantly, and Google should turn this option off. Apple devices do not have the "Allow all the time" option (Siri excluded, apparently).

Device Personalization

The phone (or tablet) itself can track you. In Google's privacy statement about this, they swear the data is encrypted and it stays on the phone. But then they give some exceptions. I turn this off and do not miss anything. But the idea is the phone can watch what you do and make suggestions for typing, suggesting apps you might like, and, yes, advertising. It is up to you if you want to keep this, but if not, here is how to turn it off.

Google Android:

Settings > Apps and Notifications. Under Recently Opened Apps, click **See All Apps**. Scroll down to **Device Personalization Service > Permissions**. In the Allowed section click every item and select **Deny**. When done, all the permissions should be in the Denied section.

Settings > Apps and Notifications. Under recently opened apps, click **See All Apps**. Scroll down to **Device Personalization Service > Advanced> Display Over Other Apps**. Toggle **Off** Allow Display Over Other Apps.

Settings > Privacy > Device Personalization Services > Clear Data. A window pops up. Select "All time" and click **Clear Data**.

Samsung Android:

Settings > Apps > Device Personalization Services Permissions. In the Allowed section click every item and select **Deny**. When done, all the permissions should be in the Denied section.

Settings > Apps > Device Personalization Services Permissions >   Appear on Top. Toggle **Off** Allow Permission.

Settings >   Privacy > Customization Service >   Customization Service. Toggle **Off**.

Settings > Privacy > Device Personalization Services > Clear Data. A window pops up. Select "All Time" and click **Clear Data**.

Prepare to Lose Your Phone

We take our phone everywhere, so there is always the chance of leaving it somewhere. Even good people will automatically read your email and look through your photos to "help you" get your phone back. It is human nature for them to do so. As for the bad guys, getting into your phone is a treasure trove of information. They might get access to any of your social media, financial, or online merchant accounts.

They can pull down your photos, contacts, physical location history, calendar, entire text history, and browsing history. They can attack you directly with this information or sell it online. Not only is this a danger to you, but it could be a danger to loved ones. Bad people could contact them by texting or using your email and rob or harm them.[2]

The PIN stops people from getting into your phone until you can get it back or decide to pull the plug on it. Before you lose it, set up your phone so you can remotely find and control it.

Before we get too fancy, the simplest pre-emptive thing to do is simply put a message on your lock screen that provides an alternative contact number if somebody finds it. A company called Asurion says this increases the likelihood of recovering your lost phone by a factor of three.

Google Android:

> **Settings > Display > Advanced > Lock Screen > Add Text on Lock Screen**. Enter a simple message like: "If found, please call 312-555-1234."

Samsung Android:

> **Settings > Lock Screen > Contact Information**. Enter a simple message like: "If found, please call 312-555-1234."

Find My Android

First, make sure that you can log into the same Google account that is attached to your phone from a computer without your phone. You can do this at https://myaccount.google.com. This sounds trivial, but because I have been harping on you about using a password manager and setting 2FA on it, this could be an issue if the 2FA uses your phone.

Second, there are some settings on the phone that must be properly configured. The Location and Find My Phone features must be on.

To turn on Location:

Google Android and Samsung Android:

> **Settings > Location**. Make sure the toggle switch is **On**. Note that you do not have to give any applications permission nor allow Google to track your location history as discussed in the Privacy section. However, you should have the Google Emergency

Location Service turned on in case of an emergency (allows 911 to find you).

To turn on Find My Device:

Google Android:

> **Settings > Security** (or **Security and Location**) > **Find My Device**. Make sure the toggle switch is **On**.

Samsung Android:

> **Settings > Google > Security > Find My Device**. Make sure the toggle switch is **On**.

> Samsung has its own version, so this can be confusing. If you prefer to use it, you will need a Samsung account. Go to:

> **Settings > Biometrics and Security > Find My Device**. You will open a new screen and move the toggle switch to **On**.

> I recommend the Google one, but regardless of the one you choose, make sure the other one is off.

Third, you must make sure Google Play has Visibility turned on. I have no idea the point of this part, but go to https://play.google.com/settings, log into the relevant Google account, and under Devices, make sure "Show in menus" is checked.

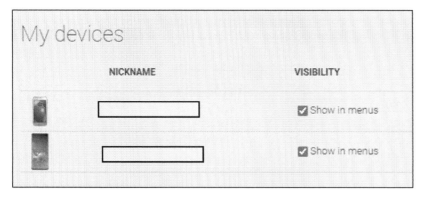

Once you have lost your phone, on your computer or another smartphone, go to https://myaccount.google.com/find-your-phone. If you use your home computer, then you might already be logged in. Regardless, you must be logged in with the same Google account that you have on your lost phone. Once you do that, then a list of devices connected to that account will show up. Pick the lost device.

If Google can contact your phone, then you get a map with your phone location highlighted. If your phone is off or out of coverage, then you will just get a map of the entire country. This is one time that letting Google track your location constantly helps, because it will show the last known location if it has it. However, I told you to turn that off previously. Apple has a feature where it will send a location right before the battery dies, but with Google, they can either track you constantly or only with Find My Device when your phone is on.

If you can locate your device with GPS, great! For the most part, you can go get it. Now, if the phone is traveling around or at least not where you left it, then obviously somebody has it. You could call a friend over and use their smartphone to log in to your Google account and then go track it down. I'd just caution that you have no idea what the person who has your phone is up to. They could be completely innocent, say you left it in their Uber, or they could be a criminal. Be smart here because no phone is worth getting hurt over.

Back to the Find Your Phone screen, on the left, you have three options. The first option is simply to make your phone play loudly so you can listen for it. This is ideal if you know you are in the vicinity of the phone (for me, usually under a couch cushion by some old Cheetos), but it is on silent or vibrate mode, so a friend calling isn't helping.

The next option is to lock the phone screen and put a message on it along with a phone number a person can call if they find your phone. Hopefully, somebody honest will find it. This message is much larger than the one we created earlier, and it even has a big Call button that allows the finder to call using your phone.

The lost option is when you have given up trying to find the phone and you want to erase it. If your Android phone is erased using this remote method, then it cannot be turned back on without you and your Google ID and password. Previously with remote erase, your data was removed, but the thief could still do a factory reset and potentially use the phone. This drastically reduces the value of the phone for thieves.

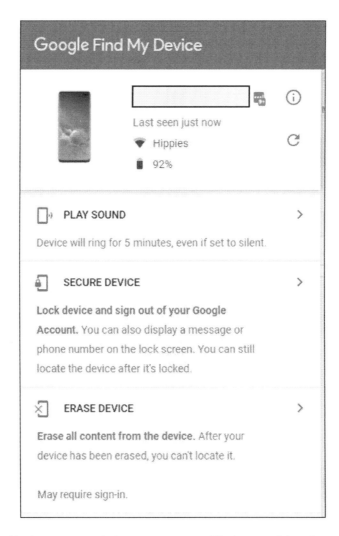

If your phone is off, then none of those options will do anything immediately. However, if it is turned back on, the lock screen will be enabled, or if you erased it, then that process will start.

Set Cloud Backups

Backups for your computers are vital in my opinion because I assume that you have data, documents, pictures, and videos that would be a disaster (or at least incredibly sad in the case of pictures) if lost. For your phone, however, you must evaluate what you would really be losing. A huge part of the information you access there is already in the cloud.

Here are the things Google backup stores:

6. Apps and apps data
7. Call history
8. Contacts
9. Device settings (including Wi-Fi passwords and permissions)
10. SMS

Notice email is not even in there. Most of us use cloud-based email, whether it is Gmail, Outlook, or Yahoo, so no reason to back this up.

Also not on that list are documents, photos, and videos. Google expects you to back your pictures up in Google Drive and Google Photos separately. There are other cloud file backup options like OneDrive from Microsoft, Box, and Dropbox. It is best to use one of these and have a comprehensive backup strategy for all your devices. I talk about that in the Advanced section of the book.

Call and SMS history, I could not care less if I lost. It might be different for you.

Contacts you want to keep. However, when you create a contact, it will ask you if you want to store it on your phone or with your Google account (or Samsung if that is your phone maker). If you keep them in your Google account, they are saved there (in the cloud). This backup is just to keep any contacts that are only stored on your phone.

Device settings might be convenient to save if you have to factory reset your phone or get a new one. When I get a new device, I like going through and setting everything how I like it, but I am not normal. As for passwords, we keep them in our password manager, so you do not need this.

The only thing in this list that might be compelling to me is app data. If I bought an app, then I would expect to be able to reinstall it later, but the data could be upsetting to lose. Fitness trackers come to mind. However, most apps store that data in the cloud as well, so you would just need to take an inventory to see if any of them store data on your phone.

If you decide to use Google to back up your phone, here is how:

Google Android:

      Settings > System > Backup. Turn the toggle on.

Samsung Android:

      Settings > Google > Backup. Turn the toggle on.

Samsung makes most Android phones, and they also offer a cloud backup. You need a

Samsung account to enable it. I do not go through this option, but you can go this route if you trust them more than Google.

Restore Cloud Backups

Since Google is on many different manufacturers' phones, I cannot give exact directions, but they will be similar. On a new or freshly reset phone, follow the onscreen instructions.

Make sure to connect to Wi-Fi when that part comes. Then at some point, it will ask if you want to restore from backup. You will need your Google account username and password. Select your backup. Stay on Wi-Fi until the process is done. Finish the rest of the setup.

Giving Away or Selling Your Phone

Just like with your computer, you must make sure that there is nothing on your phone that the next person could use for fraud or abuse. The best thing to do is a factory reset which will delete everything.

Google Android:

> **Settings > System > Advanced > Reset Options> Erase All Data (factory reset)**.

Samsung Android:

> **Settings > General Management > Reset > Factory Data Reset**. You get the list of all the data and applications that will be obliterated. Scroll down and when you're sure this is what you want, click **Reset**.

Used Phones or Tablets

IMEI Number

Before you buy a used phone, check to see if the phone has been reported lost or stolen. Go to www.imeipro.info and enter your IMEI number.

To find your IMEI number go to **Settings > About Phone**. (Most Androids will be similar.) If you cannot open the phone for some reason, then according to their website, it can be found in one of these places.

- The back of your device: If you have a removable battery, look under or below the battery for the phone's IMEI or serial number.
- The packaging: The original box may list the device's full IMEI and serial number.
- Your carrier's website: Your account details may list the device's IMEI and serial number.
- Bill of sale: Review your sales receipt or contract for your device's IMEI and serial number.

Start with Factory Reset

Buying a used phone, of course, is the flip side of selling one. You do not want to start using a phone where the last person left data or malware. They might not have thought to reset it.

Not only that, but if the phone was ever remotely erased, then only the owner can unlock the phone at all. So when physically receiving the phone, preferably with the seller present, turn on the device. If it asks for a login, then it has not been reset. Have them log in to unlock it so you can then run the factory reset (instruction in previous section).

Begin the setup process. If that starts, then you are good to go.

References

[1] https://www.techradar.com/news/fake-iphone-lightning-cable-will-hijack-your-computer

[2] https://www.aarp.org/money/scams-fraud/info-07-2010/scam_alert_stranded_in_london.html

[3] https://ww.9to5google.com/2019/09/03/android-10-google-pixel-sideload-ota/#

17

WEB BROWSERS
No Chrome Zone

Perhaps the most-used software on your computer or smartphone will be the web browser because it is the window to the internet. There are four traditional browsers to consider: Apple Safari, Microsoft Edge, Google Chrome, and Mozilla Firefox. I am going to introduce the Brave browser to the list.

You might have noticed that in my list of the major browsers, Microsoft's Internet Explorer (IE) is not mentioned. Edge is the intended replacement. Microsoft has bowed to pressure to keep IE with Windows because many companies have built legacy software that exclusively use IE. However, that does not explain why Microsoft does not just make it downloadable from somewhere.

With Edge, Microsoft tried to build a new browser from the bottom up but admitted failure when they switched to Chromium. Chromium, believe it or not, is the same code that underlies Google's Chrome browser.

Google Chrome is the dominant browser in terms of market share. This is somewhat amazing considering Windows machines come with Edge and Macs come with Safari, so Google had to convince people to use their current browser to download Chrome. But it did earn this market share by being the best browser in terms of performance, security (other than what we will talk about later), and features for several years. However, the competitors have caught up to the point where there really is not any difference in performance and security, but privacy is a different story.

Recommended Browser

My recommendation is just to stick with the browser that comes with your operating system, so Windows with Edge, macOS with Safari, and iPhone with Safari. The one exception is Android. Here I recommend Brave. Not only that, but if for some reason you do not like Edge or Safari, then I recommend Brave as the first alternative. The reason for this is threefold: (1) Windows and macOS combine with their respective browsers to provide some additional security. (2) Google makes their money by giving the software away for free and harvesting your data to sell to advertisers. (3) Accordingly, Safari, Edge, and Brave all have anti-tracking capabilities built in. Chrome will never do that.

I do not trust any of the big tech companies any further than I can throw them when it comes to my personal information and data in general. But at least Microsoft and Apple make most of their money selling software and hardware, so their livelihood does not depend on harvesting people's data. They all collect data, it is a relative thing.

A few years ago, I would have recommended Firefox for all browsing. However, Mozilla (company that makes Firefox) makes all their money by making Google the default search engine,[1] which is a weird conflict. Not only that, but also Firefox has fallen from 30% market share to almost nothing. They recently laid several people off and really seem to be struggling with direction. Their newest Firefox for Android had many technical problems. (I could not find the Back button and found it had trouble rendering many websites correctly.) It turns out that the founder of the Brave browser is a former CEO of Mozilla, so maybe he can restore his former glory.

(Not Very) Private Mode

All the major browsers come with something called Private, InPrivate, or Incognito mode. These are for preventing other people on the same computer from seeing what you have been browsing. However, these modes do nothing to prevent outside tracking. Here is Google Chrome's list of what Incognito mode does and does not do:

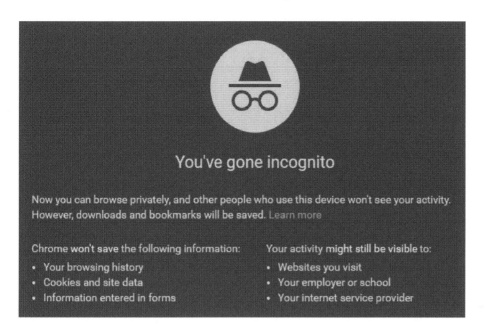

All the browsers have the same list of don'ts. Here Google tells you that your employer or school and ISP can all still track the websites you visit. They conveniently leave off that Google can track you because you are still using their browser. They also leave off that anything you download will remain on the computer and anything you copy to the clipboard will remain. Probably the funniest part is that it will save anything you bookmark. My advice is do not bookmark your favorite porn site in Incognito mode because it will show up bookmarked in regular mode.

Nerd Alert! DNS Cache

Your computer also has something called a DNS cache. To make web surfing a little faster, it will save your recent website IP addresses in memory, so if you really want to go all cloak and dagger with your spouse or kids, then Google how to look that up (and clear it).

Private mode does block first-party cookies. Cookies are tiny text files that websites store on your computer to save bits of info about you. Say you go to your favorite retailer website, Costco, and log in and put some items in your shopping cart. Then you get distracted, wander off, and come back to your computer the next day. This time when you go to Costco's website, you are automatically logged in (i.e., you do not have to enter your username and password), and your shopping cart still has the items you selected in it. This is possible due to cookies. Cookies have a bad reputation but are helpful for this type of use. Private mode removes this convenience.

I am not even going to recommend here that you need to use private mode or clear your first-party cookies all the time. Maybe just do it once in a while because the number can get big over time.

In this example, the Costco website is the first party, and you are the second party. The cookies in this case are called *first-party cookies*.

Private modes do not block third-party cookies.

Turn Third-Party Cookies Off

When you first install the browser you are using (or when you read this book), you should disable third-party cookies. The only purpose for third-party cookies is to track you on the internet for surveillance advertising. Have you ever wondered how it is possible to search for something—a pair of shoes, for example—and suddenly no matter what website you go to, there is an ad for those shoes? The answer is third-party cookies.

There are huge ad networks (Google having the largest one, followed by Facebook, but there are hundreds) that work with thousands of websites. Continuing the above illustration, say that Costco is part of an ad network. Now when you are on the Costco site, that ad network, with Costco's permission, will place a cookie on your computer that tracks what you looked at and where you are and even try to figure out what computer and browser you use. Then you head over to Walmart's website, and it turns out Walmart is also in the same ad network as Costco. Now, Walmart can see that cookie because they are part of the ad network, and can try to push things you were looking at on Costco's website. The ad network is the third party in this case, and the cookies are considered third party because they came from the Costco site and you are now on the Walmart site.

A browser security concept called *same-origin policy* states that anything that originated at one website should not be accessible by another website. When this policy can be violated, there are all kinds of attacks that hackers can try, such as *cross-site scripting* (XSS) and *cross-site request forgeries* (CSRF). Though not related to those, third-party cookies are a blatant violation of same-origin policy.

Google knows third-party cookies are ethically questionable and an outright security issue, but have I mentioned they make a ton of money off them? Google can also see the writing on the wall that governments are cracking down on them (GDPR in Europe, Consumer Privacy Act in California, antitrust investigation in the US). To side-run these regulations, Google is leading a standards group to come up with alternatives to third-party cookies. They are doing no such thing, because if Google Chrome has the dominant market share, they can simply track you using Chrome.[2]

Google is trying to have it both ways. If they can say there is an alternative to third-party cookies (a crappy one they are inventing now), with Chrome as the dominant browser, they can eliminate their competition. Well, the point of my rant here is that you should turn third-party cookies off and not use Google Chrome.

Turn Other Trackers Off

There is a lot at stake with third-party cookies, so forward-thinking ad networks have tried other methods to track you around the internet. Safari,[3] Edge,[5] and Brave (not Chrome) have implemented tools to block those as well. These protections should all be on by default but might not be set to the most stringent. I have not had any issues with the strictest settings, but I am sure they will mess up some websites. If that is an issue for you, then turn them down a notch.

Here is how to turn off third-party cookies and other trackers.

Edge (Windows) (requires two settings):

> In the top right, click the **…** > **Settings** > **Cookies and Site Permissions** > **Cookies and Site Data**. Toggle **On** "Block third-party cookies."

> In the top right, click the **…** > **Settings** > **Privacy, Search, and Services**. In the Tracking Prevention box, turn the toggle switch **On** and then click the **Strict** box.

If you would like to see the trackers Edge blocked, go to:

> **…** > **Settings** > **Privacy, Search, and Services** > **Blocked Trackers**. There will be a list ordered by how many times each tracker was blocked.

Privacy, search, and services / Blocked trackers	
Tracking prevention blocked 36.681 trackers	Clear data
Tracker	Times blocked
Google	5.624
Verizon Media	5.607
Adobe	1.369
Facebook	1.190
Twitter	1.185

<u>Safari (macOS)</u>:

In the top menu, click **Safari > Preferences**. A window pops up. Click **Privacy** and make sure Prevent Cross-Site Tracking is checked.

If you would like to see the blocked trackers, in the top menu, click **Safari > Privacy Report**. A window will pop up.

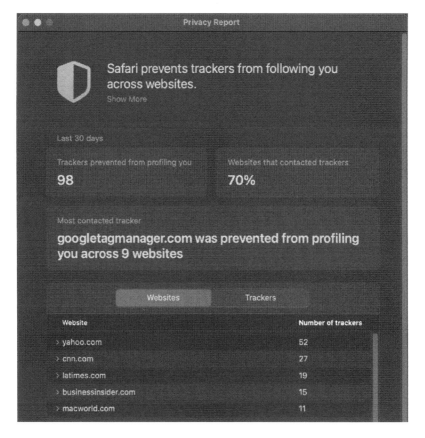

<u>Safari (iPhone)</u> (has two settings):

Open the **Settings** app and scroll down to **Safari**. Scroll down to the Privacy and Security section and toggle **On** Prevent Cross-Site Tracking.

From the **Settings** app, scroll down to **Privacy > Tracking**, and make sure Allow Apps to Request to Track is toggled **Off.**

<u>Brave (Android)</u>: Brave blocks tracking by default and assumes you would only want exceptions.

Go to a website like www.cnn.com. I pick that only because I know it has lots of ads, but any site will do.

> In the top right, click the ⬤ . There is a huge toggle switch if you want to turn protection for that site off. (Do not unless it is breaking the site and you must see it for some reason.) Go to **Advanced Controls**. You can see the toggle is **On** for "Block cross-site trackers." To continue, click **Block Cookies** and make sure **Block Cross-Site Cookies** is selected.

Ad Blockers

There are blocking trackers and there are blocking ads. If third-party cookies are turned off and you are using the browser's tools for stopping other trackers, then most of the privacy concerns go away. Without the trackers, the ads are not as targeted and cannot follow you around the internet. In other words, advertisers are shooting random ads at you. This is no different than advertising on broadcast TV.

The flip side of ads is that there are millions of content providers out there that rely on them for income. If the ad revenue dries up, so does their content. Allowing random ads supports them while preserving your privacy.

Given the above, I do not believe it is necessary to block ads strictly for security reasons. There are instances of ads being used for malware, but if you click on the ad with the pretty woman that says, "She has 10 secrets, #3 will blow your mind!" then this book is failing you. In general, just try to avoid clicking on ads.

Safari, Edge, and Brave also block ads, but not all of them. They say they block the "most aggressive" ones, but you are leaving it up to them to determine which ones are "aggressive." Some websites that depend on those ads might sense the browser blocking ads and try to stop you from accessing the content.

There are several browser extensions out there that block tracking and more aggressively block ads. Some of the popular ones are uBlock Origin, Privacy Badger, AdBlock, AdBlock Plus, and Ghostery. However, I do not know if they can be trusted not to track you themselves. I know this is cynical, but just like with antivirus and VPN providers, this market is extremely competitive, and many of them are "free." So I am suspicious for the same reasons. If you want more aggressive ad blocking than the default browsers or must use Chrome for some reason, then I would recommend Privacy Badger. It was written by the Electronic Frontier Foundation. This nonprofit group exists explicitly to fight for internet privacy and can be trusted.

To aggressively block ads at the network level, check out the Pi-hole idea in the Advanced section.

Password Fillers

All the browsers offer password-filling capabilities. As discussed in the first chapter, I recommend an independent password manager. A decent password manager works across platforms, and the browsers, practically by definition, cannot. Even the most die-hard Apple fan might need to access a password while traveling or at a friend's house, and a password manager gives them that access. (Make sure you log out when you leave.) Password managers are also more comprehensive in that you can store a lot more than just passwords. I mentioned storing your security secrets in the notes, for example. They are also not limited to website passwords, so you can use them for desktop applications, IoT passwords, physical locks that use keypads, your home vault, etc. Finally, even though they have improved recently, browsers simply do not put the effort into security they should.

Turn Off the Browser Password Filler

When you add the password manager extension, you will quickly be annoyed when there are now two applications trying to remember and autofill passwords. Here is how to turn off the browser offering:

Edge (Windows 10): in the top right, click the **...> Settings > Profiles > Passwords**. Toggle **Off** "Offer to save password" and "Sign in automatically."

Safari (macOS): in the top menu, Click **Safari > Preferences**. A window will pop up. Click Autofill and then uncheck Usernames and Passwords.

Safari (iPhone): open the **Settings** app and scroll down to **Passwords & Accounts**. Toggle **Off** Autofill Passwords.

Brave (Android): In the bottom right, click the ⋮ > **Settings > Passwords**. Toggle **Off** Save Passwords.

Beyond the passwords, the browsers will try to autofill payment card information and addresses. Again, all the major password managers will also store and attempt to autofill this information for you. Turning this off in the browsers is often right next to turning off the passwords I mention above.

Enable the Password Manager to Autofill in Smartphones

The browser extensions for desktops and laptops work great for replacing the autofill of your browsers. However, smartphone browsers do not allow extensions. Rather, you must install the password manager application, then give it permission to access and fill in data in the browser. This requires some additional settings, so here are the links to the most common password managers for setting that up.

<u>iPhone</u>:

Bitwarden: https://bitwarden.com/help/article/auto-fill-ios/

LastPass: https://www.lastpass.com/autofill/iphone

Dashlane: https://support.dashlane.com/hc/en-us/articles/360000734299-Using-Dashlane-to-autofill-passwords-with-iOS

1Password: https://support.1password.com/ios-autofill/

<u>Android</u>:

Bitwarden: https://bitwarden.com/help/article/auto-fill-android/

LastPass: https://www.lastpass.com/autofill/android

Dashlane: https://support.dashlane.com/hc/en-us/articles/202734501-Using-Dashlane-to-autofill-passwords-with-Android

1Password: https://support.1password.com/android-filling/

Default Engine Set to *Not* Google

When you do a Google search, the first few entries are usually ads where the advertisers bid to get that space based on the search terms you entered, not organic search results. This is okay by itself, but a while ago Google tried to make it hard to tell that they were ads. There was an uproar, and Google retreated. This is just an indicator of Google's evilness.

Another thing about Google is that you would think if you did a search and your whacked-out next-door neighbor did the same search, then you would get the same results. This is not even close to the case because Google does not just rely on the search you just did. Instead, it tracks all your past searches and modifies the current results around your past interests. If you ask a question about climate change and Google has you pegged as a liberal, then you will more likely be pushed to CNN. If instead Google thinks you are a conservative, then you will more likely be pushed to Fox News. If your neighbor is a "loon" from the other end of the political spectrum, it is more likely because of Google (and Facebook) manipulation than actual differences you have as human beings.

Apple also has an unholy alliance with Google[6] to block all competition. Google pays Apple many billions annually to be the default search engine in Safari. The

Department of Justice is looking into this antitrust deal given that these companies control the only two smartphone operating systems available. Tim Cook (CEO of Apple) does interviews and talks about how Google's use of personal data is evil. Then after making his customers use the Google search engine, he goes home and swims in the cash. Here is a picture sent to me by Tim's angry brother, Donald:

Tim Cook swimming in dirty Google money. Image from Disney.

In any case, you do not have to use Google search.

One alternative is Microsoft's Bing search engine. It also incorporates past searches. By most people's reckoning, it is not as good as Google. I have been using Bing on my main computer for a while, and it works. The biggest thing that annoys me is that when you find a YouTube (owned by Google of course) video, it will not take you there directly and tries to play it within Bing. Occasionally, when I am trying to find something obscure and do not get a great answer from Bing, I will try Google, just to get different results. But I cannot say either is better. The biggest reason to go to Bing is just to stick a finger in Apple's and Google's eyes. The final thing I will say here is that Yahoo! Search is powered by Bing, but now you are sharing your search data with two faceless corporations, so forget this one.

The resistance's favorite search engine is DuckDuckGo. It is based on Bing, but they act as an intermediary and don't let Bing see who is making the request. This preserves privacy and it follows that they can't use past search history to tailor the results to you. They do sell advertising, but they also say the ads and search results you get are entirely based on the search terms you just entered. I use DuckDuckGo on my smartphone and am happy with it relative to Google.

Here is how to set up the default browser:

<u>Edge (Windows 10)</u>: This one will already be set to Bing. If you prefer another, in the top right, click the **...** > **Settings** > **Privacy, Search, and Services**. Scroll all the way down to **Address Bar and Search**. In "Search engine used in the address bar," select **DuckDuckGo**.

<u>Safari (macOS)</u>: In the top menu, Click **Safari** > **Preferences**. A window will pop up. Go to **Search** > By Search Engine is a drop-down. Select **Bing** or **DuckDuckGo**.

<u>Safari (iPhone)</u>: Go to the phone **Settings** > **Safari** > **Search Engine**. Select **Bing** or **DuckDuckGo**.

<u>Brave (Android)</u>: In the bottom right, click the ⋮ > **Settings** > **Standard** tab. Select **Bing** or **DuckDuckGo**. For some reason, you can set a different search engine when using private mode. Set this to something else if you like.

Location, Camera, Microphone Access

🚫 MAY BREAK THINGS: Some websites may not work as intended, but you can allow them access individually.

All four operating systems we have discussed—Windows, macOS, iOS, and Android—have settings for allowing applications to access your device capabilities, like location, microphone, camera, and more. Your browser is an application, and therefore access to those items can be controlled accordingly. However, once you give your browser access, you can pass this access on to websites on an individual basis.

You do not want random websites to have the ability to turn your camera or microphone on and spy on you, but you do want access when you are in a video conference or something similar. In some cases, you will want to deny every website access (pop-ups and redirects), and in some cases you can allow all of them access (sound). However, in most cases, you will want websites to ask on an individual basis.

Notifications were nuisances, but now they are threats. If you allow a website to send notifications to your computer, from then on, it can do that even if your browser is not running. So of course, some hackers now sell a service to websites to allow ads and scams to be delivered right to your computer. The "tech support scam" is first, where they send you a note that your computer has viruses and you must buy antivirus.[7] In general, do not allow notifications.

Once you allow or deny a given site access, your browser will remember that setting going forward. If you ever change your mind, you can come back to these settings and change them.

<u>Edge (Windows)</u>: In the top right, click the **...** > **Settings** > **Cookies and Site Permissions**.

Location, Camera, Microphone, Notifications, Clipboard, USB are the ones I would home in on first. They can either be "Ask First" or "Deny." Click into them and check the "Allow list." Delete any sites that you do not want to grant access.

Safari (macOS): In the top menu, Click **Safari > Preferences**. A window will pop up. Go to **Websites.** Location, Camera, Microphone, Notifications, are the ones I would home in on first. When you select one, there is a list of websites that have already asked for permission along with how you responded. You must look in the bottom right to see what happens at new websites. You can set "Ask" or "Deny" or "Allow." I would never set it to "Allow" no matter how annoying it is that your browser asks you all the time.

Safari (iPhone): Go to the phone **Settings > Safari**. Scroll down to the Settings for Websites section. **Camera**, **Microphone**, and **Location** should at least be set to **Ask** or **Deny**. Safari does not remember sites and will just ask (or deny) every time. This is better from a security perspective.

Brave (Android): In the bottom right, click the ⋮ > **Settings > Site Settings**. Location, Camera, Microphone, Notifications, Clipboard, USB are the ones I would look at first. They can either be "Ask First" or "Deny." Click into them and check the "Allow list." Delete any sites that you do not want to grant access.

References

[1] https://fourweekmba.com/how-does-mozilla-make-money/#:~:text=The%20majority%20of%20Mozilla%20Corporation%E2%80%99s%20revenue%20is%20from,to%20be%20featured%20on%20its%20Mozilla%20Firefox%20browser.

[2] https://www.bloomberg.com/news/articles/2020-07-16/google-s-cookie-overhaul-could-reshape-the-digital-ad-industry?srnd=premium

[3] https://www.theverge.com/2020/3/24/21192830/apple-safari-intelligent-tracking-privacy-full-third-party-cookie-blocking

[4] https://blog.mozilla.org/blog/2019/09/03/todays-firefox-blocks-third-party-tracking-cookies-and-cryptomining-by-default/

[5] https://docs.microsoft.com/en-us/microsoft-edge/web-platform/tracking-prevention#:~:text=The%20tracking%20prevention%20feature%20in%20Microsoft%20Edge%20protects,access%20browser-based%20storage%20as%20well%20as%20the%20network.

[6] https://www.nytimes.com/2020/10/25/technology/apple-google-search-antitrust.html

[7] https://krebsonsecurity.com/2020/11/be-very-sparing-in-allowing-site-notifications/

18

YOUR HOME NETWORK
Home Sweet Penetrated Home

Most people sign up for internet service and just use whatever equipment their internet service provider (ISP) gives them. There is a lot to understand when it comes to your home network.

Here is a crude diagram of your home network:

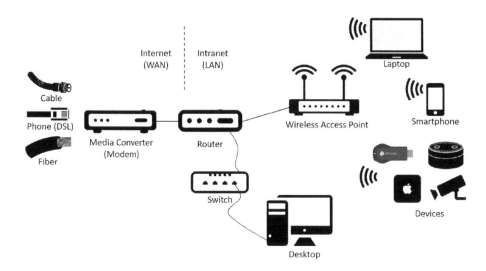

Looking at the drawing, you will most likely realize that you do not have nearly that many individual boxes. For example, the modem, router, switch, and even wireless access point are often one combined device given to you by your internet service provider (ISP) when you sign up for an internet connection. I am showing all of them individually so we can understand what each part does regardless of how many boxes they entail.

Media Converter

Regardless of the way the internet is delivered to you: satellite, cable, phone (DSL), fiber, or even wirelessly, the respective signals must be converted to digital ethernet signals your computer can understand. Generically, this is called a *media converter*, but most often you know it as a modem. There is not much to discuss about the media converter as far as security goes.

The only concern if you have an older stand-alone modem would be performance. Just make sure that if you buy a higher-speed plan (say 100 MBs or more) from your ISP, your modem can handle it.

I should note that it is possible to connect your computer directly to the modem. If you have a stand-alone modem, then there will only be one port to connect to your computer. This will work but is an awfully bad arrangement because this places your computer directly on the internet for anybody to access. It turns out this is a fundamental thing to understand. Let us discuss the router next.

Router

The router is the heart and brains (your network does not have a soul, so do not be silly) of your local network, and we will therefore spend the most time discussing it. Without a router, your computer is literally on the internet. By setting up a home network with a router, you are shielded from direct attacks because of something called *network address translation* (NAT).

NAT

To understand NAT, you must understand what an internet protocol (IP) address is. An IP address is literally a number assigned to your computer that uniquely identifies it on the network. Just like your physical home address, there can only be one home per address, or the mailman will not know where to deliver your mail. Your ISP only gives you one IP address when you sign up, so this creates an issue if you have more than one computer or device to connect. The primary purpose of the router is to create a smaller network, called a *local area network* (LAN), that is separate from the internet (a.k.a. *wide area network* or WAN). The router then takes the internet IP address for itself, so any internet communications to your household come to it. Then it assigns every computer and device on the LAN a different IP address. The router can keep track of what device is communicating to the internet and routes (get it, the router routes!) the messages to the correct device accordingly.

I have no idea if this was intentional when NAT was created, but it is a fantastic security feature. This is one of the most powerful safety features available. Feel the goosebumps? No? Perhaps I should explain more.

This is how it works. Say your router has four computers connected to it, A, B, C, D. When computer A connects to a website, say YouTube, so we can watch cat videos for eighteen hours, the router keeps track of that connection. YouTube responds, and the router sends the information to computer A. Computer B connects to Amazon, and when Amazon responds, the router sends that information to computer B and so on. However, if somebody sends a signal to your router without any of the computers first connecting, your router has no idea where to send that information, so it drops the connection.

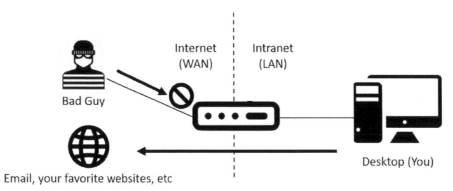

There are people all over the world scanning the internet and trying to find weak targets. If you just connect your computer right to your modem, those bad guys will find it and relentlessly poke and prod it for any and every weakness. However, you read this book and know you need a router, so this is not an issue. Most of you reading this have more than one computer or device to connect to the internet, so you need a router anyway.

This accidental feature of a NAT router can be considered the first and most simple version of a firewall. A *firewall* can be any device or software that determines what and how devices can communicate with each other.

Why do hackers try to get you to download email attachments with malware? Because then you make the connection out to the internet and bring the malware into your home. Why do hackers try to get you to click links to malicious websites? Because you initiate the connection out to them and then they can download malware to your computer. When we talk about peer-to-peer networks in the next chapter on "Bypassing the Firewall," it is because these networks create gaping holes in your firewall for people to load malware onto your computer. For bad guys to attack your network at any scale, they must figure out how to get around the firewall.

One note of caution here. Apple Mac computers have an "internet sharing" feature where you can connect one computer right to your modem and then connect other computers to it. Do not use this arrangement because it takes away the external firewall feature from the first computer. Macs do have a host-based firewall that should be turned on (I explain this in the "Your Computer" chapter) but this should be a secondary security layer, not the first.

What to Look for in a Router?

NAT provides the basics, but older routers could still fall prey to some simple attacks that can confuse the router and either cause it to fail or to be taken over. Then you have a real issue. First, if you have a router older than five years, replace it. Especially if your ISP gave it to you.

If you have some technical abilities, then I suggest not even considering a consumer-grade router and looking at business-grade versions. In the last few years, several companies have started creating business-grade routers at consumer-grade pricing. This will give you the ability to create your own firewall rules and overall have more security and control. I will talk more about these in the Advanced section of the book.

If the business-grade router will not work for you, then the consumer-grade one should do a bit better than rely solely on NATing. It should have a purpose-built firewall.

Specifically, that should be a firewall with the *no inbound connection rule*. The problem here is that consumer-grade routers rarely talk about firewall capabilities on their packaging. Therefore, when you are standing in Best Buy it is impossible to know for sure. You will have to figure out what router you want to get and then go to their website and find the owner's manual for that router. This can be a bit trying. I found a Netgear router manual and searched for "firewall." I found the exact rule I am talking about here:

Feature		Default behavior
Firewall	Inbound (communications coming in from the Internet)	Disabled (bars all unsolicited requests)
	Outbound (communications going out to the Internet)	Enabled (all)

Linksys was more difficult because I could only find "guides" as opposed to decent manuals. However, in each Linksys guide, I found a mention of the firewall and a barely visible picture that mentions an "SPI firewall," where SPI stands for *stateful packet inspection*. That is what you are looking for.

If your router does not explicitly say it has a firewall, then you might be able to tell indirectly if the router has features for defeating said firewall. What I mean by that is there are times when you want to allow a connection initiated from the internet, so the router has ways to allow it despite the firewall. A feature called *port forwarding* allows you to manually allow outside services to connect to your LAN. Another feature is called Universal Plug and Play (UPnP), where devices on your LAN can talk to your router and tell it to open ports. These two features indicate that you have a firewall.

Nerd Alert! Firewalls

Firewalls have gone through many "generations," and the *stateful packet inspection* (SPI) is an early generation. *Stateful* meaning that the router can keep track of communication and know which way the traffic is always going. The idea of not letting outsiders initiate contact has been around for quite a while. Given the power of this concept, it is almost criminal that this is not universally implemented.

A later-generation firewall is called *deep packet inspection* or DPI. It goes a step further and reads every packet (so it looks at all the websites you go to, all your emails, and all your attachments) and looks for malware or other known attacks. Originally the biggest issue with these was that all that inspection required some heavy-duty processing power and could have slowed your connection. However, today DPI is almost worthless because most internet traffic is HTTPS encrypted and the router has no way to decrypt that information. If you have a DPI firewall, do not worry, it will still do the stateful inspection part.

Router Settings

As mentioned, if you have a router over five years old, I recommend getting a new one. The router is the key to your home network, and if it has a vulnerability, then the bad guys can own you. There are a few more reasons to get rid of older routers.

Many router manufacturers ship every router with the same username and password, often something like "admin" and "password," respectively. This website even makes it easy to look up the default credentials: http://www.routerpasswords.com/. Since most people have no idea about this, it has been and continues to be a great way for hackers to take control of your home network and see everything on it or use it to attack others. Today, most manufacturers at least assign different passwords to each device and put it on a sticker on the device and/or in your manual. Regardless, change the password when you first get a router, or do it now for your existing one. Many routers also let you change the username, and I recommend you do that too.

Your manual should have the instructions for logging into your router. If you do not have the instructions anymore, you can usually Google the model number of your router and manual and find it online. In general, the way to access your router is to go to your computer and open a browser. In the URL (address) line at the top, type 192.168.1.1 or 192.168.0.1. If this does not work and you have a PC, then search for "cmd," and when a black-and-white window appears, type in "ipconfig." The "Default Gateway" IP address is what you are looking for to put in your browser. This should get you to the administration page where you can figure out how to change the password. I highly recommend using your password manager to generate and store the password.

Another issue with older routers is that the firmware (software that is specific to controlling the hardware itself) is not always automatically updated. So when security vulnerabilities come along, most people do not have the patches installed either. (See the section on keeping software updated in the "Your Computer" chapter.) Once logged into your router to change your password, also look to set it to auto-update your firmware. This may prove difficult. Some may only allow manual updates, so you must do it yourself and remember to check on it periodically (or get a new router that auto-updates).

🚫 MAY BREAK THINGS: Some devices on your network may need services on the internet to be able to reach them. Examples are game systems like Microsoft X-Box and Sony PlayStation. This can be fixed with port-forwarding, but you must know how to do that.

Turn Universal Plug and Play (UPnP) off if you can. As I mentioned before, this is a way for devices on your LAN to tell your router to allow connections from the internet, thus defeating your firewall in a sense. If you are connecting smart home devices (which we will cover later) to your LAN, they may well be opening holes in your firewall without you knowing it.

🚫 **MAY BREAK THINGS:** If you mess this up, nothing on your network will be able to connect to the internet.

The last thing to set while in the router is the DNS. DNS stands for Domain Name Servers. You know you want to get to Apple's website, so you enter apple.com. However, your computer has no idea what that means because it only understands IP addresses. Your computer must go to the internet and look up the IP address for apple.com through your router. Your router will automatically use your ISP's DNS servers, which tend to be a little slower and are completely unfiltered, and are used by your ISP to track all your browsing. Your ISP can track you anyway, but it is the principle of the thing. In your router network settings, find the part that refers to DNS, and it will be defaulted to automatically using the ISP settings. You might have to switch it to manual to turn that off and then enter the new DNS IP. I recommend 1.1.1.1, which is offered by a company called Cloudflare that swears they are not tracking you.[2]

Switch

The switch is simply a way to enable more wired devices to connect to the router. There is not anything interesting from a security standpoint for a consumer-grade switch. Most routers have a switch included to allow more connections directly to that box. But you can add more external switches as needed, including adding switches to switches as deep as you need to go. The only limitation is that each switch port can only support a cable that is up to 100 m (328 ft) long before you must add another switch or final device.

Business-grade switches are sometimes also called *managed switches* and offer an excellent security feature called *virtual local area networks* or VLANs. I will talk about these in depth in the Advanced section.

Wi-Fi

Often your laptops, smartphones, tablets, home speakers, Chromecast, Apple TV, and/or other IoT devices are connected wirelessly. The wireless connection is called Wi-Fi.

In the network diagram, I show a Wi-Fi access point, meaning all that box does is provide a radio for the wireless network. In a way, the wireless access point is just like the wireless version of a switch. However, in the consumer world, it is rare that the box is not at least a Wi-Fi access point/router combination, so I put all the settings related to wireless in this section. But if you do have a separate router and access point, then these settings are in the router.

Encryption

The first thing you must do on your wireless network is set up encryption. If your wireless connection is not encrypted, then anybody can use your internet connection. But even worse, anybody can see your traffic and possibly get access to your computers and devices. There are a few Wi-Fi-specific encryption methods. WEP (Wired Equivalent Privacy) was the first version of encryption for Wi-Fi. It is obsolete now and easily cracked with free tools you can get on the internet. WPA (Wi-Fi Protected Access) was the next version, and while better than WEP, it too has issues that would allow an advanced attacker to get access to your communications. WPA2 came out in 2004 and is still secure, so this is what you should use. However, it can never be that easy. Your router might have WPA2-Personal or WPA2-Enterprise options. In this case, select WPA2-Personal because the other one is for corporate or government networks and requires additional infrastructure to work. Another name for WPA2-Personal is WPA2-PSK, where the PSK means *preshared key*. In yet other routers, you might have a choice between WPA2-PSK (AES), WPA2-PSK (TKIP), or WPA2-PSK (AES/TKIP). The only acceptable choice is WPA2-PSK (AES) because TKIP (Temporal Key Integrity Protocol) is an old encryption method. The AES/TKIP method tries AES (Advanced Encryption Standard) first, but if the device trying to connect can only support TKIP, it falls back to TKIP. This is no better than TKIP alone, so if a device is that old, you do not want it on your network. Once you figure out how to set WPA2, you will have to set a network name (a.k.a. SSID [service set identifier]) and password. Whenever you connect a device in the future, you will have to select this SSID and enter this password. Again, I recommend using a password manager to generate and store this password.

The WPA3 standard came out in 2018 and will be even more secure, but chances are your devices do not have it yet. When they do, go with this option.

WPS

🚫 **MAY BREAK THINGS:** This may disable the ability to simply pair up a device to your Wi-Fi by pressing the button on your router.

There is yet another setting that is critical to turn off. Wi-Fi Protected Setup (WPS) was a feature the Wi-Fi industry created to make it easier to set up your wireless network. WPS provides three different methods for connecting to your wireless network[1] without using the WPA2 password I told you to set up in the previous section.

The first WPS method involves a button on your router marked with this symbol:

. If you push this button while a device is trying to connect, then the device is allowed on the network. Obviously, this requires somebody to have physical access to your router, so maybe it is not horrible, but it still is not great. If somebody gets on your network this way, there is no way to boot them off except to get a new router.

There is a second method where you have to log in to the router and type in a PIN from the device trying to connect. This method is not a security issue but is utterly stupid as an alternate method because if you can log into the router, you can just get the WPA2 key and connect the device that way.

The third way is the one with the critical flaw. The router has an eight-digit PIN printed on it, and anybody who has that PIN can connect to the network. The protocol is flawed in two ways. First, the last digit is a checksum, meaning there are really seven digits. Then for some reason (they designed it this way!), the attacker only must guess the first four digits, at which time the router sends a signal that they were properly guessed. Then the attacker only needs to guess the last three digits. Guessing a four- and then three-digit number separately is significantly easier than a single seven-digit number. So much easier that a decent computer can do it in seconds.

If your router has WPS (and it will be on by default), then turn it off. If you cannot turn it off, then get a new router.

Wi-Fi on the Road

It can be a pleasant change of pace to get away to your local Starbucks or your hotel and get some work done using their free public Wi-Fi. The problem is that anybody can intercept everything you are doing. Even if you are just surfing the internet and not concerned about anything you are sending or receiving being intercepted, public Wi-Fi is a bad idea. Hackers can access information on your computer and maybe even upload malware.

There are two major solutions: a VPN and using a cellular connection. VPN stands for *virtual private network*, and it is software that creates a secure connection from your computer to a service somewhere, that in turn connects to the internet. When you use any internet connection, wired or wireless, all your data is encrypted from your computer to the service. The other option, a cellular connection, is when you use your smartphone to provide the internet connection and avoid public Wi-Fi entirely.

If your employer provides VPN and you are working, then use it. This is exactly why they provide it for you. Your computer will create an encrypted connection to your company network. Then from your company network, you have a connection to the internet. From a technical perspective, this is the same as being at the office and going on the internet. As a bonus, all the company firewalls and secure web gateways will be in place, making it safer than your home network if your company

IT team is any good. However, remember that since your company set up the VPN, they can see everything you do. Keep all your VPN usage strictly for work.

As for personal usage, there are other third-party VPN services out there, but you must trust them. I have no idea how you can know which VPNs to trust.[3] The VPN providers can track where you are and which sites you visit. They can also install spyware on your computer along with their software. This goes for free ones especially, but there is no way to know whether the paid ones are doing the same things or not, regardless of their marketing. Most VPN services are outside the US and claim this is an advantage because they are outside US law enforcement jurisdiction. Well, this might be good if you are avoiding the FBI (though why would they risk making the FBI mad to protect you and the $30 a year you are paying them?), but it cuts both ways in your protection too. There is nobody to sue or press charges against if things go badly.

Yes, yes, if you Google something along the lines of, "How to be safe on public Wi-Fi," you will get a million articles on why a VPN works. I also know that they are all written by the VPN providers themselves. There is more detail on this in the Advanced section of the book, but my advice is to avoid using third-party VPN providers.

Using your smartphone is called *tethering* and is a great way to get your computer on the internet securely, because you are avoiding public Wi-Fi altogether. Instead, you are using the phone's LTE connection direct to the cellular tower.

Back in the early '90s cell phones were all analog. When they connected to the cell tower, a bad guy could simply hook up an antenna and pick your connection information right out of the air. They would then use this information to "clone" your phone and then make calls on your tab. Phone companies realized that this would be a disaster for cell phone adoption, so when they migrated to digital, they made sure to add encryption when the phones connected to the towers. This method of cloning phones died with analog along with all the ways a hacker can intercept your wireless communications (at least in the phone-to-tower connection).

The downfalls are that you must pay for the data and your smartphone battery may die. Pay for your freaking data or pay by being hacked. As for the battery, use a USB cable direct to your computer instead of setting up your own Wi-Fi network. The cable is more secure than any Wi-Fi network could ever be, and your phone will charge off the much larger computer battery. If you do not want to use your smartphone for some reason, a similar option is to use a separate device to create your connection, like Verizon's Inseego Jetpack or AT&T's Netgear Nighthawk that also connect to the cellular system.

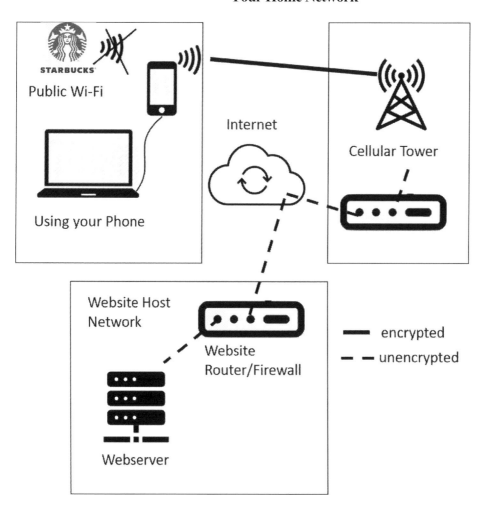

Public Wi-Fi

Using your Phone

Internet

Cellular Tower

Website Host
Network

Website
Router/Firewall

Webserver

—— encrypted

— — unencrypted

To start, plug the same cable you use to charge your phone into a USB port on your computer:

iPhone to PC or MAC:

> In the iPhone, go to **Settings > Cellular > Personal Hotspot**. (If this says, "Set up personal hotspot," then you must call your phone company to enable this.) Toggle **Off** "Allow others to join."

> With either a Mac or PC, you might have to have the latest version of iTunes installed. When you plug the USB cable into the computer, the iPhone will ask if you "Trust this device." Tap **Trust**. The computer should auto-sense the network connection and work.

> Note: As I write this, iTunes is being replaced by Apple Music, so I am not sure where

that functionality will move to as of this publication.

Google Android to PC:

> **Settings > Network & Internet > Hotspot & Tethering > USB Tethering.** If prompted, then "**Trust this device**."

> The PC should auto-sense the network connection and work.

Samsung Android to PC:

> **Settings > Connections > Mobile Hotspot and Tethering > USB Tethering**. If prompted, then "**Trust this device**."

> The PC should auto-sense the network connection and work.

Android to Mac:

> If you want to connect an Android phone to a Mac, you must use the Wi-Fi or Bluetooth method. In other words, create your own wireless hotspot and have your computer connect to it like you do your home network. USB, unfortunately, is not natively supported.

All Those Devices (IoT)

The last thing in the diagram in the beginning of this chapter to consider is all those devices that connect to the internet either through the wired or wireless connections: Chromecast, your smart TV, security/baby cameras, Apple TV, Roku, your refrigerator, your Nest thermostat, wireless door locks, and on and on. The connected home is fantastic but opens a whole new set of security issues. These devices are often called the *internet of things* or IoT. *Internet of things* generally refers to anything that is not a computer or phone, but they are technically IoT devices also. Your router is an IoT device.

A lot of these devices are cheap, have a lot of vulnerabilities, cannot be remotely patched, and come with default usernames/password combinations. This includes ISP-provided routers.

Protect from the Internet

In 2016 the internet saw one of the most powerful attacks it had ever seen. Malware called the Mirai botnet had captured thousands of closed-circuit TV cameras and routers. The Mirai botnet then told all those cameras and routers to send all their videos and messages to targets that the bad guys wanted to take down. So much information flooded those servers that they were overwhelmed and taken offline.

There are two things to note. First, none of those cameras were behind firewalls. I know this because the botnet scans the internet for vulnerable devices. If they were behind a firewall, then the botnet would not have seen them. Those cameras were connected right to the internet with no router, or if there was a router, then port forwarding was enabled. The second is that the cameras were set to their default usernames and passwords because when the botnet discovered them, it tried a list of only sixty manufacturer default username/password combinations.

As for the routers that were attacked, they are the firewall, so they cannot be protected in that sense. When the botnet hit them, all it had to do was run through its list of sixty username/password combinations. Many of these were the free, old, crappy routers given to them by their ISP.

Here are the lessons:

1. Use newer routers that can be remotely patched and come from reputable companies.
2. Set those routers and all IoT devices to auto-update if possible.
3. Put the IoT devices behind that router (firewall).
4. For all devices, but especially the router, change the username and password before you even connect them to the internet.

Protect from Within

🚫 **MAY BREAK THINGS:** It is hard to get this right and not break things. It might be a different issue for every device you have.

The above protects you from being attacked from the internet. There is an even bigger concern here. You are putting them on your side of the router, the LAN. If they come preinstalled with malware, then they can bypass your firewall and either attack your computers from the inside or invite outsiders into your LAN. The only ways to protect against this are to only buy from reputable manufacturers (admittedly subjective) and something called *network isolation*.

What the heck is network isolation? Just as the router isolates your LAN from the internet, you can isolate different parts of your LAN. The only option with most home routers to enable this is the guest network. Guest networks were created so you can provide your perverted brother-in-law with a connection when he comes over for the holidays and not worry about his computer infecting your system with all kinds of malware. This is also a good idea for your IoT devices.

However, this has two issues. The first is this does not help with wired IoT devices.

Alexa can get by on wireless, but I want my Smart TV on a wired connection to ensure the most reliability. The other issue is that if you want to control your devices with your phone, they must be on the same network. Alexa, for example, requires setup through the Alexa app on a phone. If your phone is on the main network and the Alexa is on the guest network, then they will not connect. Same with Chromecast. If you want to cast video from your computer (or phone) to your TV, then they must be on the same network. You might be able to sign into the guest network with your phone, set up whatever needs to be done, then remove your phone from the guest network. However, some guest networks will not even let the devices talk to each other when both are on the guest network. This will vary by manufacturer.

Still, this is potentially a good way to isolate the cheaper, less-known, wireless IoT devices to the internet and protect your main network from them. Only put your computers and cell phones on the main network (wired or wireless).

Setting up the guest network varies by manufacturer, but you need to connect to your router and turn it on if it is not on by default.

This is a little confusing, so I will make it worse. A router with a guest network generally only provides the guest part on the wireless side in the form of a different SSID (network name), usually named something like "guest." The main wireless network has an SSID like Netgear, D-Link, Linksys, etc., which you can change, by the way. But the point is the main wireless network is connected to the wired one. Hopefully, the next picture helps.

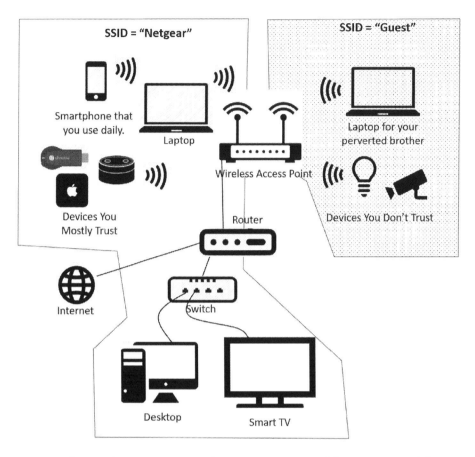

Using the wireless guest network to separate trusted from untrusted devices. Unshaded is the primary network and shaded is the guest network.

Smart TVs

If you have paid any attention to the price of TVs the last few years, you know that their prices have been dropping precipitously. The first reason for that is straightforward. Intense competition is forcing manufacturers to innovate features and reduce prices. The other reason is that once you buy, they collect data on you and make money selling targeted ads based on what you are watching, so it is worth selling that TV to you for a bit less to make up the money later.

Automatic content recognition (ACR) is a technology in smart TVs that takes screenshots or samples pixels to monitor to detect what you are watching. It does not matter if you are watching broadcast (over the air), cable, streaming services, or even DVDs. They can tell what you are watching and when you are watching it. The TV manufacturers collect this data and sell it and/or use it to put ads right on your TV. Additionally, TVs with remotes that listen to your voice without pushing a button are always on and monitoring you. Some TVs even have cameras built in for video calls, but you might not know when the camera is on and who is on the other side. It is only possible to opt out of some of this data collection, and it depends entirely on the manufacturer. Consumer Reports has this article explaining a lot of this, but it will be changing constantly: https://www.consumerreports.org/privacy/how-to-turn-off-smart-tv-snooping-features/. I find this crazy invasive but do not expect people to go through and try to figure all of it out. I just want people to be aware of this potential invasion of privacy and give them the tools to fight it if they also find it disturbing.

Smart Speakers

Alexa from Amazon is an amazing device. Simply ask and you will get an answer or music, or pizza delivered. Google Home and Apple HomePod quickly followed. Just be aware that the speaker is always on and listening to everything going on in your house. It records each time you tell your kids to go to freaking bed and every fight with your wife. It also captures every time your mom calls to lay down a guilt trip (at least your end of the conversation), every complaint about work, what you are listening to on TV; it is an open microphone in your house. And it is not just a machine that only turns on when you say "Alexa." There are people flat out listening all the time.[4] Amazon says this is to better train the machines, but does it really matter?

Again, I am not saying you must get rid of these devices. I am just letting you know.

Fitness Trackers

Originally, the only thing these things did was track your steps and heartbeat, so maybe not such a big deal. They quickly added location tracking, however, so now you have another thing that can be used to stalk you if the data gets into the wrong hands.

Now Amazon "Halo" is getting into the action, and it is always listening just like the smart speakers. It is trying to determine from your voice what emotions you are going through.[5] Others are tracking your blood sugar levels and body fat percentage. This is all information that could be used to diagnose health issues. This could also be used later for blackmail or to deny insurance or increase your health insurance rates.

Smart Cameras

Amazon owns Ring cameras, and it has recently been discovered that they use artificial intelligence (AI) and the camera feeds to help police use your Ring camera to look for suspects. Admittedly, it is cool, but it is also a massive violation of privacy since who knows what Amazon and the cops are doing with your feeds. Not only that, but AI is notoriously bad at identifying people of color. Again, I am not saying do not buy or use these, but be aware.

Amazon Sidewalk

If Google and Facebook are the terrors of internet privacy, then Amazon is the terror of IoT. The latest announcement from them is something called Amazon Sidewalk. This uses two technologies, Bluetooth low-energy (BLE, not to be confused with low-energy Jeb Bush, which would be LEJB) and long-range WAN (LoRa). This allows your Amazon devices to all communicate into something called a *mesh network*. The idea is to allow Amazon devices such as Alexa and Ring cameras to connect far beyond your household (i.e., much further than traditional Wi-Fi). Not only that, but this mesh network can also connect entire neighborhoods. For example, if you lose your dog and it has an Amazon dog tag on it, then you could use this network to find your dog. Just like all things Amazon does, this is brilliant and terrifying at the same time. Not only can Amazon now track every movement of Fido, but they can also probably track everything you, your kids, and everybody else do. Like if you are home or not.

As a bonus, Sidewalk is already enabled in your device! Yep, nobody asked you if this was cool. Jeff Bezos just decided for you. However, he was kind enough to let you turn it off.

> For Alexa, make sure you have the latest version of the Alexa app on your phone. Go to **Settings > Account Settings > Amazon Sidewalk** and toggle **Off**.

I am sure it is similar in your Ring application.

More IoT later

My concern in this chapter is the IoT devices with malware trying to attack your computers. Given the data that the IoT devices contain, it might go the other way in the future. Computer malware may be trying to get access to your Alexa feed. In the Advanced section of this book, we will revisit the LAN and talk about virtual LANs (VLANs). A business-class router, set of switches, and access points can allow you to mix and match any number of isolated LANs across wired and wireless access. This allows you to ensure that devices on separate VLANs cannot access each other.

Another cool device we will discuss is a Pi-hole, which will filter ad networks. It will also let you monitor what websites all your computers and devices are trying to communicate with and cut them off if you want.

References:

[1] https://www.routersecurity.org/wps.php

[2] https://www.cloudflare.com/learning/dns/what-is-1.1.1.1/

[3] https://lifehacker.com/researchers-issue-security-warnings-about-several-popul-1791617644

[4] https://www.bloomberg.com/news/articles/2019-04-10/is-anyone-listening-to-you-on-alexa-a-global-team-reviews-audio

[5] https://www.nytimes.com/2020/11/27/opinion/amazon-halo-surveillance.html

Advanced

Everything covered so far is highly recommended. If you are aware of the threats and did everything in this book so far, congratulations, you are better off than most of the public.

This next section is a bit more advanced and for some extra layers of security. The thing to keep in mind is that it is impossible to drive your risk to zero. There is always some new technical vulnerability or, given that we are all human, simply a time when we will let our guards down. Not to mention the fact that we must rely on others (software and hardware makers, family, stores, banks, government). Perhaps you could move to Montana and dig twenty-foot underground concrete bunkers with no connections to the outside and figure out your own food and ammo supply. The question is always how much risk you can tolerate versus how much effort you can put into being secure. This is a question everybody must answer on their own.

Not only that, but security professionals do not agree on all of this. I am sure that many would have criticisms of what I provide in this book. A great example is that I assume iPhone users will create and use an Apple ID and Android users will do the same with a Google account. It is possible to set up your phones and not be connected to their manufacturer overlords. But that opens an entirely new realm of trying to find alternatives for email, contacts, maps, and app stores. It would be completely overwhelming for most of us.

The key questions for security decisions are: (1) What am I trying to protect? and (2) Who am I trying to protect it from? I have mentioned a few times that if you are running from the NSA, good luck to you, and by the way, this book is not going to help much. If you completely distrust Apple, Google, and Microsoft, then in a similar sense, you are kind of screwed. On the one hand, I advise that you turn off all tracking that they do for advertising, but on the other hand say it is okay to do your cloud backups there. These are trade-offs. You get little or no value for the risk of your data being lost when they track you for advertising purposes. But you do get value out of using them to sync email and contacts or hold your backups. Further, they explicitly share that advertising data with advertisers (by definition), but I would also venture to guess that they keep people's backups more secure than 99.9% of us regular users. They also claim employees are not supposed to be reading your emails, contacts, and backups.

I do have far more issue with Google than Apple and Microsoft. They do read your email. They read your email and then serve up ads based on it right in Gmail itself. It has been reported that even when you turn off location tracking, Google does it anyway. Google's entire business model is to give away the software and then harvest your data for sale. And they make billions off it. So, yes, in the Technical section I show how to opt out of their tracking and speak against using the Chrome browser, but that does not mean they do not have other methods to track you. On the other hand, I tell you to use them for your Android phone backup. They claim that this data is encrypted on your phone and then sent to the Google cloud (Android 9 and later), so they are not supposed to have access to it. I can only go by what they claim. And, yes, in the Advanced section I recommend using a Chromebook for your most secure accounts.

Next on the issues list is Facebook, who, by the way, own Instagram and WhatsApp. Just like Google, they make virtually all their money on advertisements. And just like Google, they are almost impossible to avoid. Even if you do not have a Facebook account yourself (Who are you?), your friends are putting your picture in their feeds and tagging them with your name. Facebook is equal or second only to Google in terms of the ability to track you across the internet. I outlined in the Basic section some of the safeguards you should put in place with your Facebook account, but all I have to say about them in the Advanced section is right here: Delete your account. Delete your wife's account, and do not let your kids have one. I know nobody is going to listen to me, including my own family, because most people feel the benefits they get are worth the risk. That is a fair assessment.

The last thing I will say here is that I do not go into great detail on how to set things up in this section. I provide general outlines and leave the rest up to you.

19

ADVANCED BACKUP
How To Do It Right

In the Technical section, I advised that computers be backed up on local hard drives connected to the computer and that phone and tablets either not be used for storing critical data at all or backed up using the built-in cloud backup provided by Apple or Google. In both cases, I went for the easier route. This is more than most people ever consider and works well enough. However, here we set up a real backup system.

The theory for backing up data is that there should be three copies: the original, one local backup, and one offsite backup. The original is obviously the version stored on your computer or phone or tablet. The local one is a large network-attached storage (NAS) device. The cloud one can be any cloud-based backup including Google Drive, Microsoft OneDrive, Apple iCloud, Box, Dropbox, or one of many smaller ones.

There are several advantages to this system. The first is that it is by far the most robust. The cloud aspect means protection from a disaster that happens at your home, like a fire, flood, or theft. The cloud is not perfect, however, so the NAS protects against a disaster at your cloud provider or your internet connection. All data is captured and distributed in near real time. So once you write a document or take a picture from any device, then it can be uploaded almost instantly. All your information is accessible from any device, so if you take a picture with your phone, your wife can look at it on the family computer. It also makes moving from an old computer to the new one easier, because you don't need to manually copy all the files over. Finally, there is quite a bit of additional protection from ransomware.

Sound good? Here is what you need. You have to pick a cloud provider, but I went with Microsoft OneDrive. The Microsoft 365 family plan gives six people access to all the Office apps (Word, Excel, etc.) and 1 terabyte (TB) each of data. You can use it as your email provider, too, if you wish. It is $99.99 a year. You will also need a NAS device. There are several on the market, but Synology and QNAP are popular choices. They both have software that allows you to connect to the cloud provider and synchronize any changes. This is your local backup.

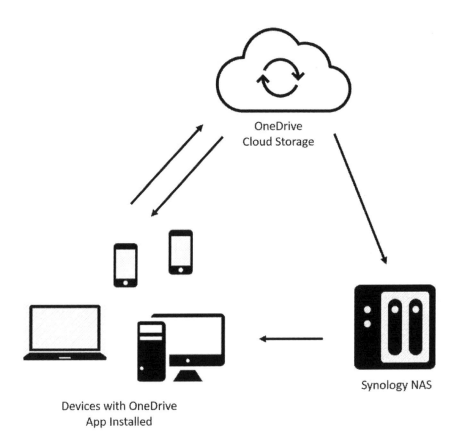

OneDrive
Cloud Storage

Synology NAS

Devices with OneDrive
App Installed

When you install the OneDrive app on all the devices, it automatically uploads any documents or pictures to the cloud. Then you connect the NAS to the OneDrive cloud account, and it senses any changes and synchronizes with them. Now all your devices are backed up and can all access all your files also—either from the cloud or your NAS.

Despite it being called *network attached*, do not set up the NAS as a network drive on any of your computers. Instead, access it through your browser with the web interface it offers. The reason is that ransomware can see network-attached drives and then go encrypt the entire drive. This means any NAS (or USB-attached drive) will get encrypted too. By connecting to the cloud instead, this is not possible. Another tip is to set the NAS up only to activate (turn on) and sync periodically, say a couple times a week. This saves power and is an additional buffer against ransomware because if you see your computer has been hit, you can disconnect your NAS.

Some might argue that this is not full computer backup because it does not have the computer images and applications included. This is not something I have ever worried about. I can reinstall the OS and any applications. However, if this is something you worry about, then Backblaze is a common cloud backup system whose application provides full computer backups in the cloud.

20

RANSOMWARE DEFENSES

I would like to point out all the layers of defense this book provides against ransomware.

1. Most ransomware comes through email, but after reading this book, you know not to click links or download untrusted enclosures.
2. You have antivirus turned on and kept updated. It can stop some percentage of ransomware.
3. You use a standard account instead of an administrative account, and this blocks some ransomware from working.
4. You have *controlled folder access* turned on on your PC and do not allow apps on your Mac to access files unless you explicitly provide permission. This should stop any ransomware at this point, but we have more layers.
5. If the NAS is not set up as a network drive on your computer, then ransomware does not see it and cannot encrypt it.
6. Even if ransomware does somehow get past all of this and starts encrypting files, it cannot do a full encryption of your OneDrive cloud like it can a network drive. The latest copy of your files in OneDrive will be encrypted, but all you must do is check the version history and turn back to the unencrypted version. Some ransomware tries to encrypt the files multiple times to get around this, but they can only do this so many times, and you should be able to turn back to an unencrypted version.
7. The NAS should not be set up to instantly synchronize with OneDrive. Rather it should only do it on a delayed schedule, say twice a week. Then if you see the ransomware attack, you might have bought time to unplug your NAS and save the data.

21

SEPARATE EMAIL AND COMPUTER FOR CRITICAL ACCOUNTS

There are so many ways that you or somebody else on your main computer could be reading an email or surfing the web and unknowingly download malware. Many times, there is no way you would know it. All the things I have recommended certainly limit the risks, but if you are banking or trading online to any extent and want that extra layer of security, here it is.

Get a separate computer that is only to be used by you (and maybe your spouse) and only for the most valuable online accounts. In theory, this could be a PC. If so, then on this computer it is especially critical that you follow the guidelines I lay out in this book. A Mac might be great for this, but who can afford at least $1,000 for a single-purpose machine? If you have Linux know-how, that is ideal because you can also use the Brave browser and an email provider like Proton. You might even be able to harden a Raspberry Pi for this purpose and have a $50 computer. If you go this route, you can still use the concepts in the rest of this chapter. However, for most people, I recommend getting a Chromebook for both cost savings and security.

Yes, a Chromebook by Google, where you must use the Chrome browser and a Gmail account. All this after I rail on using Chrome in this book. Google will be able to see what financial institutions you are connecting to and even your IP address, so they can correlate it to anything else you do with Google products. However, if this is the only instance of Chrome you use, then what they can cross-reference is limited.

When I started writing this book, I could get an Acer Chromebook 14 from Walmart for $149. However, due to the pandemic causing a shortage of laptops, especially in schools where Chromebooks are extremely popular, it is more like $285. Hopefully by the time you read this, they will be $149 again.

Now, this is a very low-powered computer, mind you, but from a security perspective, it is ideal. The entire idea of a Chromebook is that it is not meant to run programs itself. Rather it is built around the Chrome browser so you can go to websites and have all the heavy computing done by the website you go to. In this case, the speed of your internet connection is more important than the power of your computer. The great thing about this from a security perspective is that a Chromebook will not allow other programs (i.e., malware) to install or run.

Unfortunately, there are malicious Google Play apps and Chrome extensions, but you must download them on purpose, and not be infected by accidentally clicking a link or downloading an attachment. For this Chromebook, do not ever install anything other than the password manager extension. In the Nerd Alert, the last security feature is important to note. If you think you did mess up and download something, you can reinstall the OS with the push of a button. You will only have to reinstall your password manager.

Nerd Alert! Chromebook Security

I copied this Chromebook security overview directly from a Google support page in case you wanted more detail.[1]

Chromebook Security

Chromebooks use the principle of "defense in depth" to provide multiple layers of protection, so if any one layer is bypassed, others are still in effect. Even though it is still important to take precautions to protect your data, Chromebooks let you breathe just a little bit easier. Your Chromebook has the following security features built in:

Automatic Updates

The most effective way to protect against malware is to ensure all software is up-to-date and has the latest security fixes. This can be difficult to manage on traditional operating systems with many software components from many vendors, all with different update mechanisms and user interfaces. Chromebooks manage updates automatically, so Chromebooks are always running the latest and most secure version.

Sandboxing

On a Chromebook, each web page and application run in a restricted environment called a "sandbox." If the Chromebook is directed to an infected page, it cannot affect the other tabs or apps on the computer, or anything else on the machine. The threat is contained.

Verified Boot

Even if malware manages to escape the sandbox, the Chromebook is still protected. Every time the Chromebook starts up, it does a self-check called "Verified Boot." If it detects that the system has been tampered with or corrupted in any way, typically it will repair itself without any effort, taking the Chromebook back to an operating system that is as good as new.

Data Encryption

When using web apps on a Chromebook, all important data is stored safely in the cloud. Certain kinds of files, like downloads, cookies, and browser cache files, may still be present on the computer. The Chromebook encrypts this data using tamper-resistant hardware, making it difficult for anyone to access those files.

Recovery Mode

If anything goes wrong with a Chromebook, you can simply push a button or use a quick keyboard combination to enter recovery mode and restore the operating system to a known good version.

If you get a Chromebook, there are a few things to do to lock it down. When you sign in for the very first time, you will need a Gmail account. Get a brand-new Gmail account from Google (Chromebooks require that you have a Gmail account, but you can get as many Gmail accounts as you want for free) separate from your regular email. When coming up with the name, do not use any identifying information like any part of your name or birthday or anything. Maybe your favorite character from a book or history.

I then use that new Gmail account to sign up for a different password manager account. It could be another Bitwarden account or even a different provider that has a free version for one device (like Dashlane). Again, this is for isolation purposes, so your daily email is not used in any way on this machine.

In Chrome, turn off the password fill and third-party cookies.

Restrict the Chromebook so only you can sign on with this dedicated account:

> Sign into Chromebook with the owner (administrator) account. In the bottom right, select the **time**, and a window pops up. Select the settings icon ⚙ **>People > Manage Other People.** Make sure "Enable guest browsing" and "Show usernames and photos on

the sign-in screen" are toggled **Off**. Toggle On "Restrict sign-in to the following users:".
Then add or delete users here. Ideally only enter your dedicated Gmail account here,
but you could add your spouse's if they have one.

In theory, if your spouse has separate financial accounts and has their own Gmail
account solely for the use of those financial accounts, then you could add them here
and share the Chromebook, but each of you should log in using your respective
accounts. It is up to you two to figure out if you will share login information with
each other or not.

On the Chrome browser itself, very carefully type in the website address that you
want to visit, and then when it goes there and you are sure that it is the correct
website, find the login page. Without filling in your credentials, bookmark the page.
From this point forward, never type the website URL in manually again. Always use
the bookmark to avoid things like www.chase.cm (instead of ".com"), where you
might get phished.

Finally, this computer is isolated to its own VLAN. It is the only one allowed on this
VLAN, and I even enforce that with a MAC address lockdown. I will cover all this in
the next chapter.

You should only use this computer where money can be stolen directly.
Recommended accounts that are only accessed through this separate Chromebook:

    Bank
    Credit Union
    Brokerage
    Retirement 401(k), 403(b), 457, IRA, Roth IRA, etc.
    College savings plans like 529s or Coverdale
    Social Security account
    IRS account
    Any accounts connected directly to any of the above accounts,

Also, for the above accounts, don't use your daily email for contact and notifications
(usually a profile setting), rather, use this new Gmail account instead. Only check
that email from this Chromebook. This is another defense from credential stuffing
which I talked about in the very first chapter and any keylogging malware that
might get on your primary computer.

Accounts that are important, but you can run from your main computer and email:

    Utilities (phone, gas, electric, water, etc.)

Credit Bureau accounts
Credit cards
Retailers with credit cards on file
Government agencies that you pay with credit card (DMV is the most common one for me)

The caveat to all the above accounts is that you use your credit card to pay (or auto-pay) and not a debit card linked to an important bank account (as discussed in the chapter on payments).

References:

[1] https://support.google.com/chromebook/answer/3438631?hl=en

22

YOUR LAN REVISITED

Get a Business Router and Switches

In the chapter on networking, I gave as much advice as I could assuming most people got their router and Wi-Fi from their ISP or Best Buy. The combination of high costs and required technical ability puts commercial-grade networking equipment out of reach for most of us. In the last couple of years, both barriers, but especially price, have come tumbling down. Commercial-grade routers, switches, and Wi-Fi access points are now on par with to two times as much as consumer-grade versions but are far more powerful and secure. On the technical side, most business-grade versions will simply work when they are plugged in, just as the consumer versions. So the additional technical ability required is just to take advantage of the more powerful features.

Having said that, selecting and then setting up the equipment is not for the faint of heart and far beyond the scope of this book. If you have some technical ability and enjoy a little research, then this could be a fun project. However, my goal here is to discuss some concepts, and if you feel the need for this level of security, then you can try yourself or hire somebody to implement it.

VLANs

The first and most powerful feature of a business-class network is the ability to create virtual LANs, a.k.a. VLANs. Your router isolates your LAN from the internet, but you can also break the LAN into logically isolated smaller networks that are isolated from each other. This way, if you buy a cheap, smart washing machine with malware on it, it cannot access your computer on a different VLAN.

Not only does the router have to support VLANs, but so do the switches (a.k.a. "managed switches") in your network because you need the ability to assign VLANs clear down to the ethernet port of each switch.

VLANs also work with business-grade Wi-Fi access points that can support multiple wireless networks. After setting up multiple SSIDs, you can assign VLANs to each different SSID, and the wireless networks will be isolated. Additionally, you could assign a VLAN to an SSID and physical switch port and devices, allowing the same VLAN to communicate even though one is wirelessly connected and the other is wired.

Just setting up VLANs does not isolate them; you must add firewall rules to do that. This is where the technical knowledge comes in.

I put my computers, NAS, and printer on my primary LAN and then smart TV, Alexa, and other smart devices on a separate VLAN. Not only that, but I have a different VLAN for my phones to keep them separated. Finally, I have a super-locked-down VLAN that I only allow one computer on, and it is the one I use to access my banking and other financial accounts as mentioned in the last chapter.

Below is the design that works for me. Notice that VLANs can span wireless and wired connections, so the combinations are countless. You could even go crazy and isolate every device on its own VLAN.

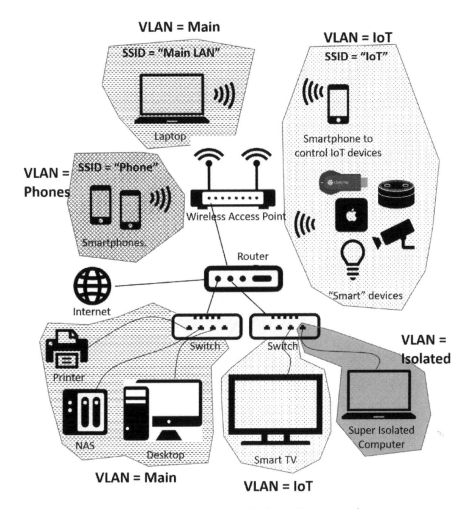

VLAN = Main

SSID = "Main LAN"

Laptop

VLAN = IoT

SSID = "IoT"

Smartphone to control IoT devices

VLAN = Phones

SSID = "Phone"

Smartphones

Wireless Access Point

Internet

Router

"Smart" devices

Switch

Switch

VLAN = Isolated

Printer

NAS

Desktop

Smart TV

Super Isolated Computer

VLAN = Main

VLAN = IoT

Multiple VLAN Network

This is all great from a security perspective but will break things, and it takes some know-how to fix them. The biggest thing is that you cannot control your IoT devices with your smartphones or computers if they are on different VLANs unless you can set up something called mDNS. Yet more technical challenges. You can connect out to the internet and back, but that does not work for things like setting up Alexa and Chrome-casting from your computer to your TV. I have a separate, cheap smartphone that is not connected to the cellular network for controlling the IoT devices.

MAC Whitelist and 802.1x Authentication

MAC stands for *medium access control*. Clearly, even knowing what the acronym stands for is of little use, but a MAC address (hexadecimal number) is assigned to every device intended to connect to a network. The first part of the MAC address is a unique identifier for the manufacturer, and the rest is kind of like a serial number. In theory, every MAC address is unique. When your device then asks your router (DHCP server, actually) for an IP address, the router then assigns an IP address attached to that MAC address.

When setting up your network, you can add a layer of security by creating a whitelist based on the devices' MAC addresses. In the case of Wi-Fi, a hacker would have to break your super-tough password, and then they would still get rejected because the MAC address of their computer is not on the whitelist. The router will then refuse to assign an IP address to their machine and will not allow them on the network. As for the wired part of your network, if a hacker can physically get to a switch port, they can just plug their computer in. This might not sound like a threat, but remember that you do have people over that you might not be able to trust—your babysitter, housekeeper, Comcast technician, and perverted brother-in-law. If you have a MAC address whitelist, then you can prevent people from just plugging in.

Of course, when you want to add a new computer or device to a network, you will have to update the whitelist. In my VLAN picture above, I do not show a guest network, but you can also set that up without a whitelist and let your perverted brother-in-law surf away.

It is possible for computers to present any MAC address (at least until it is restarted), so if a hacker can monitor your network somehow, then they could potentially see another computer's MAC address and spoof it. However, the attacker has the chicken-and-egg issue of not being able to get on the network to see the MAC addresses without having a legit MAC address in the first place. The only way this is possible is if the attacker can get a signal analyzer on a wire in your network and listen to the actual electrical signals going by. Probably not something to worry about in a home network.

A MAC address whitelist, assuming your router supports it, is relatively easy because all you must do is add the addresses to a list, and the router does the rest. However, if you really want to go secure, then you can set up 802.1x authentication (do not confuse this with 802.11x Wi-Fi), so an additional level of authentication is required for a machine to connect to your LAN. This is more difficult because you must set up a RADIUS (Remote Authentication Dial-In User Service) authentication server and set up your devices to use it. Many IoT devices will not be able to do this at all, but in any case, you would only do this on most secure LANs.

HTTPS Encryption

When you go to a website using "https://" and get that lock in your browser, it indicates that the connection is encrypted. It shows that the website you are visiting is indeed the one you typed into your browser. We talked about it in the Technical section. This type of connection and encryption is also called TLS or *transport layer security.*

We are revisiting this because I want to discuss some aspects of that encryption before we talk about VPNs. TLS is end-to-end encryption, meaning the entire connection, from your computer clear to the webserver, is encrypted. Here is a diagram:

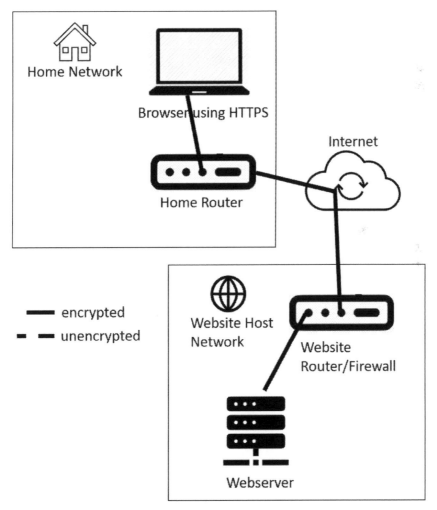

HTTPS End-to-End Encryption

The solid lines indicate that the connection is encrypted and as you can see, goes from your computer in your home to the webserver (and back). In the next section, we will talk about a VPN encrypting your traffic. In all the pictures, if you connect to a website that supports https (most do today), then you will have two layers of encryption in place in some parts, but only https is end to end.

VPN

If you search the internet for "best security practices," a VPN will surely come up. A VPN, or *virtual private network*, is an encrypted connection to another network through the internet. Unlike a TLS (Transport Layer Security) connection, a VPN connection goes from your computer to a VPN termination (a firewall or server) and not necessarily clear to the destination. There are a few different reasons to use a VPN.

VPN for Work

Many of us use our company VPN for work all the time. For work, the idea is to securely connect to the corporate network so we have access to work applications, files, and other resources. Obviously, this stuff cannot be made freely available over the internet.

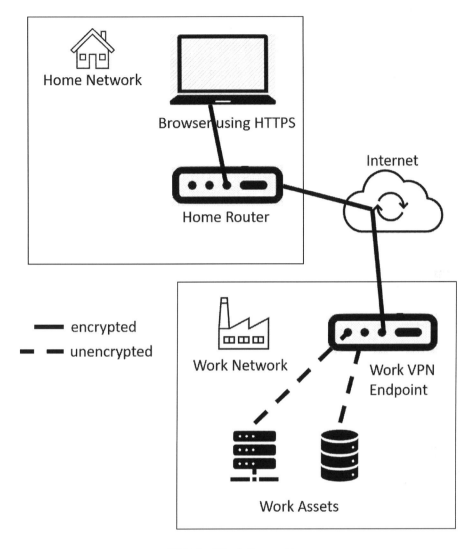

VPN to Work Encryption

For work, a VPN makes perfect sense, and you can trust it (err, well you must) because it is run by your employer.

If you happen to be connected to your work VPN and then browse the internet, you will have an encrypted connection to work and an unencrypted connection out to whatever website you are looking at (not shown in the diagram). As far as the website is concerned, you are connecting directly from work, and it cannot tell what your original home IP address is.

VPN to Hide

The idea behind a VPN at home is to connect to a distant server with an encrypted connection and then from there, search the internet. The idea is that it is much more difficult for you to be tracked. Many websites you go to will try to track your IP address and then correlate that to other data for marketing purposes. Some websites will even use your IP address to determine what services you are allowed. For example, Netflix has different programming in other countries (or no service at all in some places), so if you can connect to a VPN server in another country, you can fool Netflix into providing the programming of that country.

The biggest boost to VPN usage was the fact that the big ISPs paid enough politicians off that they can do whatever they want. That includes tracking our internet usage and selling it to advertisers. Your ISP must be able to know where you want to connect because that is what they do. However, they get paid through our subscriptions, so it is somewhat dubious that they can also sell off our data. If you use a VPN, the ISP can see that you are connected to it but cannot see any of the data going across the link. Not only that, but your ISP can also probably even see your VPN connect to the website that you are browsing. However, if there are hundreds or thousands of people connecting to the same VPN, then your ISP will not be able to tell who is connected to what site individually.

Since setting up a VPN requires the right equipment and know-how, an entire industry sprung up where people set up the VPN for you. It seems like a great idea because for a few dollars a month, you can avoid being tracked, watch Netflix programming from around the world, and securely use public Wi-Fi.

The problem most people do not seem to understand is that now the VPN provider can see every website you visit. They may be the ones selling your data to advertisers (and whoever might want to blackmail you). Because of this, they all market that they never track your logs (records). They even set up in foreign countries so they can avoid having to tell the FBI (or pick your US federal agency) your browsing history, if this is a concern for you. Here is the rub: how do you know you can trust a company in a foreign country specifically selected because they can avoid US law enforcement? The answer is you cannot, and this entire industry is nonsense.[1]

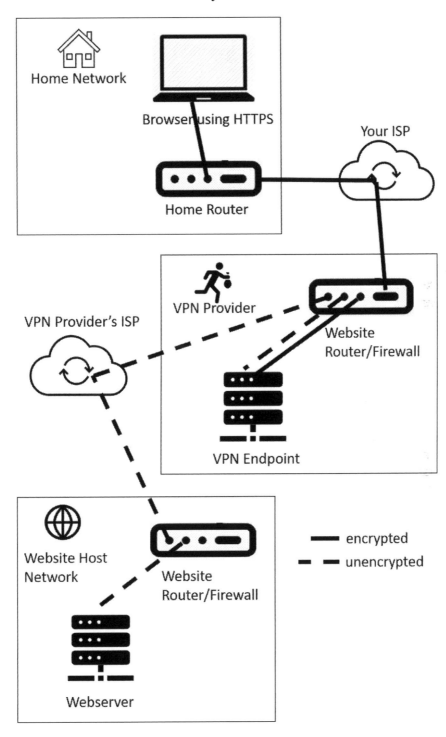

Hiding with a VPN

For Netflix (Amazon Prime, Disney+, any of them) programming, they have figured this out and actively track and block VPN IP addresses. It is also illegal, for what it is worth. Using a VPN for this reason is out.

For blocking your ISP, I hate them as much as the next guy, but trust them more than some outfit setup in Panama. However, a better solution for that is TOR. I will come back to that in the next section.

Using a VPN for Public Wi-Fi

You could build your own VPN. If you have a business-grade router at home, then you can use it as the VPN termination. This takes more technical know-how than the average person possesses, but this is how you should do a VPN if using public Wi-Fi.

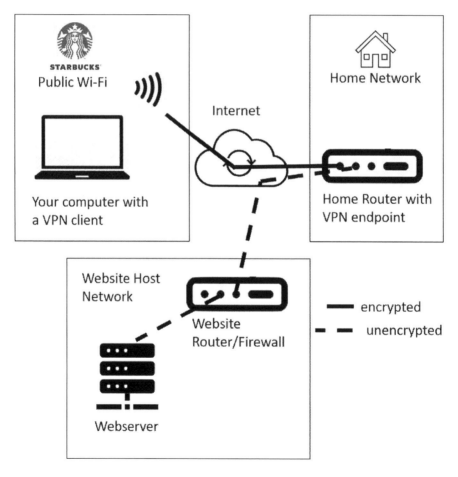

VPN to Home, Then Internet

Another alternative is setting up a Raspberry Pi in your home as a VPN termination. There are many projects on the internet on how to do this. I have never done it, so I wonder if this little computer can keep up with things like video streaming. But again, free public Wi-Fi usually does not have a lot of bandwidth to begin with.

However you set up a VPN, you connect to the free Wi-Fi hotspot, then connect a VPN to your home network. This leg is now protected from all the prying eyes at the hotspot.

This is cool, but check out the HTTPS connection a few pictures back. If you only go to HTTPS websites (the vast majority these days), you already have end-to-end encryption from your browser to the website itself. The VPN is just adding another layer from your computer to the VPN termination. My point here is the VPN is not doing much.

I still prefer the phone method (as mentioned in the Technical section) for a couple reasons. The first reason is you must initially connect to the free Wi-Fi before connecting to the VPN, and for that little bit of time, you are not secure. The moment your computer sees that, it will automatically try to connect your email and messenger and whatever else you have running. The bad guys have a small window of time to get the IP address assigned to your computer and fingerprint it, especially if they set up a captive portal (a website that you must use to sign in before you are allowed on the internet), and otherwise mess with you or divert your communications.

The other reason the phone method is better is because even if you manage to get the VPN running, there is no firewall between you and the bad guys now. So they can attack your computer directly. They can scan it and hack at it the entire time you are connected to the public Wi-Fi. I know my phone has a firewall (at least the NAT part) because when I am on the cellular system and check my IP address on my phone, it is a private IP address (i.e., it starts with 192, 10, or 127). Yet if I go to the website What Is My IP? it will show a public IP address.

TOR for Anonymity

TOR is short for *the onion router*. It was a system developed by the US Navy to protect military communications. The whole reference to the onion is the idea that your communications are "wrapped" in multiple layers of encryption. Then each layer is "unwrapped" as your connection traverses the internet, until the last hop when you finally reach your destination.

The nodes of TOR are supported today by individuals that are into this stuff and allow others to use it for free. The way TOR works, these people setting up the nodes can only see the nodes they are attached to, but not the beginning and final endpoints. The data passing through is all encrypted, so you don't have to explicitly trust them. TOR is also how you access the dark web if you happen to want to check that out. However, if your purpose is simply to cover up your browsing from your ISP and whatever website you go to, then TOR is the answer, not a VPN run by somebody else. The biggest drawback to TOR is that it is much slower because of all the additional encryption and hops all over the internet.

You can check TOR out here: https://www.torproject.org/, or if you prefer, the Brave browser comes with TOR built in.

Pi-hole

The Raspberry Pi is a tiny computer you can buy for about $50. It has all kinds of fun uses for computer hobbyists. But a cool thing you can do with one is download a program called Pi-hole and set it up as your router's primary DNS. It keeps a huge inventory of advertising and tracking websites. If any computer on your network requests one of these addresses, then it returns a bogus IP address. The website or app or device is not able to download the ads. Beyond the built-in list of advertising addresses, you can add to the blacklist if you find other sites you do not like, such as IoT devices calling out to the internet for unknown reasons. Here is the website for setting up Pi-hole https://pi-hole.net/.

If you set up VLANs with firewall rules to isolate them as discussed previously, then you must poke holes in the firewall to allow devices on the VLANs to use the Pi-hole. The Pi-hole requires a static IP, so it is nice to also set that in your router DHCP (Dynamic Host Configuration Protocol) so there is not a conflict. In the Technical section of this book, I recommend the router DNS be set to 1.1.1.1 instead of the ISP-provided one. You also set the Pi-hole to that DNS because it needs a DNS lookup of its own for any sites not on its blacklist. You can also use your firewall to block all port 53 outbound requests because computers and some devices can be set to ignore what the router says to use for DNS and use their own.

The Pi-hole even turned out to be a bit of a network monitor for me. I had a security camera connected to my LAN and would have had no idea that it called out to a website every ten minutes had I not seen it listed in the Pi-hole history. Pi-hole was not blocking it because that is not the purpose of the Pi-hole, but when I saw that, I was able to go into the camera's settings and figure out how to turn it off. No reason to waste bandwidth on that.

References:

[1]https://thenextweb.com/contributors/2018/05/28/be-cautious-free-vpns-are-selling-your-data-to-3rd-parties/

23

PRIVACY
It Just Never Ends

Internet Erasure

At some point, you have probably googled yourself or somebody else. People google people they have started dating, and employers google potential employees. So of course, stalkers and criminals can google you.

There is a whole industry out there of stalker websites like MyLife, Radaris, Spokeo, Whitepages, Been Verified, Intelius, and more. They scrape people's information (copy information off websites with computers) from public sites (think county treasurers, assessors, state motor vehicle departments), social media, and other websites. If you Google a person's name and town, many of these stalker websites will show up in your search. They claim to know people's age, address, family members, criminal history, work history, and more.

Here is a GitHub link that provides an updated list of many of these sites and ways to opt out: https://github.com/yaelwrites/Big-Ass-Data-Broker-Opt-Out-List. If you embark on this opt-out journey, it is quite tedious, and you probably need a spreadsheet and calendar to track your progress. Then you will have do it over every year because even if they delete you upon request, they will re-scrape your information from someplace again.

DeleteMe is a company that works to delete you from many of the websites. It costs several hundred dollars a year and you can sign up here: https://joindeleteme.com/privacy-protection-plans/. The DeleteMe service also checks to see that your entries are really removed and stay off during your subscription. Other services like DeleteMe include Kanary (www.thekanary.com), PrivacyDuck (www.privacyduck.com), OneRep (onerep.com), and Reputation Defender (www.reputationdefender.com) (all listed in the GitHub link).

Unfortunately, some of the shadier sites will not respond to removal requests from third parties or at all. One of those shady sites is Blockshopper.[1,2] Blockshopper can be used to find who is listed as the owner of a residential property. It is also often used for stalking because you can search by name or address. Blockshopper claims that since they are scraping this information off public websites (local clerk of courts) that they are not violating anybody's privacy. However, if you can prove that you have a restraining order on somebody or are in law enforcement, then they might delete your information.

Way Beyond the Major Credit Bureaus

We discussed freezing your credit at the major credit bureaus, but there is a big steaming pile of minor ones out there. The Consumer Financial Protection Bureau page maintains a list of them here: https://files.consumerfinance.gov/f/documents/cfpb_consumer-reporting-companies-list.pdf.

You can check out this list and see which ones will allow you to opt out. All of them are required to let you see what information they have on you. If you want to go down this path, then I would say opt out of all the ones you can and get reports for all the ones you cannot. Check the reports every year to see if somebody did anything bad. Maybe one day a service will come along to opt out of all of these for you, but I am not aware of any as of this writing.

Bug Your State and Federal Congress(wo)man

If you find this chapter or other parts of this book alarming (I do), then write or call your state and federal lawmakers. The stalker websites need to be eliminated. California passed a law called the California Consumer Privacy Act (CCPA), and I fail to see how any of those sites are fully complying, though I am not a lawyer. Even if they are in violation, it only applies to residents of California.

The credit bureaus do provide valuable services, but it is far too easy for bad actors to use them for identity theft. At a minimum, all the minor ones should also be forced to implement freezes or opt out entirely. Better still, there should be a single clearinghouse website where consumers can go and turn them on only as needed. The default should be that they are all frozen until a person proves their identity. Then the person should be able to turn selected services on or off when needed or after a specified time, automatically freeze them again.

Your LAN Revisited

References:

[1] https://www.consumeraffairs.com/online/blockshopper.html

[2] https://blog.sfgate.com/abraham/2010/03/17/blockshopper-enabling-stalkers-with-home-owner-information-website/

Made in the USA
Columbia, SC
05 October 2021

46655661R00157